The ADHD Handbook for Schools
Effective Strategies for Identifying and Teaching Students with Attention-Deficit/Hyperactivity Disorder

Harvey C. Parker, Ph.D.

Specialty Press, Inc.
Plantation, Florida

Specialty Press, Inc.
300 Northwest 70th Avenue, Suite 102
Plantation, Florida 33317
(954) 792-8100 • (800) 233-9273

Printed in the United States of America

ISBN 1-886941-61-0

Table of Contents

Chapter 1
Introduction:
Children's Mental Health
Services and the School's Vital Role

The Centers for Disease Control and Prevention published a report in June 2005 detailing the results of a national survey on the prevalence of emotional and behavioral difficulties in children in the United States. The findings indicated that a growing number of children suffer from difficulties with emotions, concentration, behavior, and getting along with others. Up to one in ten children suffer from a serious emotional disturbance. Shockingly, seventy percent of children with a diagnosable disorder do not receive mental health services.

In the *National Action Agenda for Children's Mental Health*, former United States Surgeon General, Dr. David Satcher, warned that the suffering experienced by children and adolescents with mental health needs and their families has created a health crisis in the United States. Growing numbers of children are suffering needlessly because their emotional, behavioral, and developmental needs are not being met. Dr. Satcher called for action, noting that it is time that we, as a nation, took seriously the task of preventing mental health problems and treating mental illnesses in youth.

The need for such action is particularly great for children in minorities for they are less likely to have access to mental health services, and the care they do receive is often of lesser quality.

The poor also often do not have access to mental health services. Impoverished children are affected by mental health disorders at a significantly higher rate and at a much more intense level than children in affluent populations. This is often due to their living situation and their inability to access affordable services.

To improve services for children with mental health problems and their families, Dr. Satcher stated that we need to take three steps:

1. improve early recognition and appropriate identification of mental disorders in children within all systems serving children;

2. improve access to services by removing barriers faced by families with mental health needs, with a specific aim to reduce disparities in access to care; and

3. close the gap between research and practice, ensuring evidence-based treatments for children.

1

How are Children's Mental Health Services Accessed?

The George Washington University's Center for Health and Health Care in School's discussed the current challenges and future directions in providing mental health services to children in the United States. Sarah Olbrich emphasized the important role played by schools. Olbrich noted that mental health services are provided in the United States in four ways:

1. through specialty mental health practitioners such as psychologists, psychiatric nurses, psychiatrists, and psychiatric social workers;
2. through general medical/primary care practitioners such as family physicians, nurse practitioners, internists, and pediatricians;
3. through human services such as social welfare, criminal justice, educational, religious, and charitable services; and
4. through voluntary support networks such as self-help groups and organizations.

Many children in need of care are not receiving it. Barriers to access of available services include lack of health insurance, an overloaded mental health system, misdiagnosis, and parent's concern about stigma and their own mental health issues.

The majority of federal money for children's mental health is spent on services for youth with serious mental health disorders, the group that represents the smallest proportion of children receiving mental health services. The result of this funding focus is that children may only have access to a provider for services after they have entered systems such as special education or the juvenile justice system. Only three percent of funding went to early identification and intervention efforts.

The School's Vital Role

The National Association of School Psychologists cautions that failure to address children's mental health needs is linked to poor academic performance, behavior problems, school violence, dropping out, substance abuse, special education referral, suicide, and criminal activity.

Schools play a vital role in protecting the mental health of children. Along with parents, schools teach children positive behavior, social competence, and emotional well-being in addition to academics. Teachers can build a child's self-confidence. They can create a sense of belonging and connectedness for the child. They can encourage children to explore their talents and abilities leading to a sense of accomplishment and pride.

Schools can play a vital role in providing access to services that would otherwise be denied to many children. Of the fifteen million children and adolescents who receive mental health services annually, nine percent receive care from the health care sector, mainly from specialty mental health specialists, and seventeen percent receive care from the human services sector, mostly in the school system.

School psychologists, school counselors, school social workers, and school nurses provide mental health services to children in schools and help parents, teachers, and other school staff address the mental health needs of students.

According to Olbrich, for many children in the United States, schools function as the most frequent provider of mental health services. Such services in schools may include evaluation, individual and group counseling, crisis intervention, and referral. These services are provided in many different ways. Some schools have stand-alone services. Others hold programs throughout the community for specific mental health issues. Some schools have school-based health centers.

Besides creating a supportive environment that fosters mentally healthy traits, schools implement programs targeted at specific issues or skills for development (e.g., bullying prevention, conflict resolution, social skills training, parent training, substance abuse prevention). Schools also provide interventions for individual students with mental health needs through counseling, classroom accommodations, and special education services.

School psychologists provide consultation services with teachers and families. They do assessments that can lead to diagnosis and eligibility for special education and related services under the Individuals with Disabilities in Education Act (IDEA).

Schools also contract with organizations and agencies within the community to provide mental health services. Such community-based programs may be able to provide a more comprehensive range of services than a school psychologist or counselor could.

Schools have been criticized, however, because often children with mental health needs are not identified early, services are often delayed, and children with emotional disturbance are often excluded from programs. Dr. Steven Forness has pointed out that children with mental health needs are usually identified by the schools only after their emotional or behavioral problems cannot be managed by their regular classroom teacher. Dr. Forness believes that schools could be doing a better job of identifying children, and at identifying them sooner. It can often take five, six, seven or more years before a child with signs of emotional disturbance or learning and behavior disorders receives services in school. Forness recommended that:

- school professionals, especially classroom teachers, be better trained to recognize early symptoms of emotional and behavioral disorders;
- school definitions of mental health disorders (emotional disturbance, in particular) should be modified as they are too restrictive; and
- there should be more proactive programs in school to identify mental health disorders in children.

Mental health concerns can develop as early as infancy and, like other aspects of child development, they must be addressed. The earlier we do so the better.

Common Mental Health Conditions

According to the Center for Mental Health Services, the most common mental health disorder in children are anxiety, conduct, depression, learning, attention, eating, and substance abuse. Approximate rates of occurrence are listed in the following table.

Disorder	# of children affected
Anxiety	8 to 10 out of 100
Conduct Problems	7 out of 100
Depression	6 out of 100
Learning	5 out of 100
Attention	5 out of 100
Eating	1 out of 150
Substance Abuse	Not known

Anxiety disorders include phobias, panic disorder, obsessive compulsive disorder, post-traumatic stress disorder, and generalized anxiety disorder. Anxious children have difficulty learning. Worry and stress affect concentration, planning, and the ability to handle test taking, meeting deadlines, and socialization.

Children and adolescents with conduct disorders have difficulty controlling behavior. They act impulsively in defiant and destructive ways. Youngsters with conduct disorder often commit serious offenses as they become adolescents. Such offenses may include lying, theft, aggression, truancy, fire-setting, and vandalism.

Depression can occur at any age and children who are depressed often feel sad and worthless. They lose their motivation to achieve in school and may avoid play activities. Their self-esteem suffers and they lose confidence in their ability to succeed. Appetite and sleep can be affected and other physical complaints are more frequent in depressed children.

Learning disorders make it difficult for children to perform academically. Learning disorders can show up as problems with oral and written language, reading, understanding mathematical facts and concepts, coordination, attention, or self-control.

Attention disorders make it difficult for children to focus and many children with attention disorders also have problems with hyperactivity and impulsivity. They often have significant problems remaining still, taking turns, keeping organized, and completing assignments and tasks.

Eating disorders can affect a child or adolescent's body-image and create an intense fear of gaining weight. Eating disorders can be life threatening. Children and adolescents with anorexia nervosa may not be able to maintain a healthy body weight. Those with bulimia nervosa feel compelled to binge and then rid their bodies of food by vomiting, abusing laxatives, taking enemas, or over exercising. Eating disorders affect many more girls than boys.

Bipolar disorder can be extremely debilitating for children and adolescents and their families. Bipolar disorder causes exaggerated mood swings that range from excitement or mania to depression. Affected children or adolescents may talk excessively, need very little sleep, and often act in grandiose ways without exercising sufficient judgement over their behavior. Irritability accompanied by extreme temper outbursts and periods of low mood are common signs of bipolar disorder in children.

Autism is less common than the other mental disorders listed and occurs in about ten to twelve of every ten thousand children. These children have problems interacting and communicating with others. Autism has an early onset, appear-

ing before age three. It causes children to act inappropriately, often repeating behaviors for long periods. Some will bang their head, rock, or spin objects. Symptoms of autism range from mild to severe. Those in the severe range may lack language and will show a very limited awareness of others.

Schizophrenia affects about five of every one thousand children. Young people with schizophrenia have periods where they may hallucinate, withdraw from others, and lose contact with reality. Their thinking becomes inappropriate and they suffer from a thought disorder that can include delusional ideas.

Substance use is very prevalent among adolescents and may involve cigarettes, alcohol, marijuana, cocaine, hallucinogens, stimulants, and inhalants. Tobacco and alcohol are the most frequently abused drugs in the United States. Fifty percent of all deaths from age fifteen to twenty-four involve alcohol or drugs. Warning signs of substance abuse in adolescents include a decline in school performance, new friends, delinquent behavior, and a worsening of family relationships.

These common mental health disorders and other, less common ones, will be more fully discussed in chapter fifteen. Strategies schools and teachers can use to help students with these disorders will also be provided.

Purpose of this Book

This brief introduction regarding the children's mental health crisis in the United States and barriers to access for mental health services helps us realize the diversity and complexity of the mental health needs faced by children. Professionals across many disciplines and parents must work hard to address these challenges. Primary care physicians, mental health specialists, social agencies, and schools are at the forefront of delivering mental health services.

The primary purpose of this book is to promote awareness and understanding of Attention-

Deficit/Hyperactivity Disorder (ADHD), one of the most common of the mental health disorders listed earlier. ADHD affects a great many children in the United States and, in fact, it has been shown to have similar rates of prevalence in all countries throughout the world where it has been studied.

In September 2005, the Centers for Disease Control and Prevention released the results of a national survey that documents that 4.4 million, or 7.8 percent, of four to seventeen year old children have a parent-reported history of ADHD diagnosis and 2.5 million of that number (56.3%) were taking medication for it at the time of the survey. The findings also showed that some racial and ethnic groups and the uninsured with a history of AD/HD diagnosis were less likely than others to be currently taking medication for it. In addition, there were significant variations from one state to another in terms of rate of diagnosis and treatment. This variation in rates of reported diagnosis and treatment underscores the need to educate professionals in the health care community about ADHD. Everyone, regardless of location, ethnicity, or race should have access to medical professionals who understand the disorder and respond to it using evidence-based treatment.

The CDC report added that ADHD poses substantial costs both to families and society. The disorder has been associated with strained familial and peer relationships, suboptimal educational achievement, and increased risk for unintentional injuries. Health-care costs associated with ADHD are conservatively estimated at $3.3 billion annually.

Medical and mental health professionals have diagnosed and treated children with ADHD for more than fifty years. Educators became more aware of the disorder in the past two decades and schools have programs and services for children with ADHD. Such programs and services will help identify children at risk for ADHD and im-

prove outcomes for those diagnosed.

Our knowledge of this condition is expanding rapidly. ADHD has always been one of the most well-studied psychiatric disorders of childhood and adolescence and there have been many books written on the subject. Only a few, however, are devoted specifically to the problems that children with ADHD face in school and the services and programs that schools may implement to help them.

The remainder of this book focuses on the characteristics of ADHD, ways to identify and assess children with ADHD, treatments for ADHD, and strategies that school personnel can use to improve the learning and performance of children with ADHD.

Summary

Access to appropriate mental health services in the United States is limited for many children, especially those who are poor and in minorities. Most mental health services are provided through primary care physicians, mental health specialists, social service agencies, and support and advocacy groups. Schools play a vital role in identifying children in need of mental health services and in providing access to such services.

Unfortunately, the demand for assessment and treatment is great and children at risk for mental health disorders are often not identified early. Disorders such as anxiety, conduct problems, depression, learning difficulties, attention disorders, and substance abuse are fairly common.

The primary purpose of this book is to inform educators about ADHD, a condition that affects nearly eight percent of children. Educators can play a vital role in improving outcomes for students affected by ADHD. Future chapters discuss characteristics, causes, and treatments for children affected by ADHD and provides practical strategies for educators to implement in schools.

Chapter 2
Characteristics of Children with Attention-Deficit/Hyperactivity Disorder

ADHD is a fairly common psychiatric disorder that is diagnosed and treated in children of all ages and in adults. ADHD receives a great deal of attention in the media because of the controversy surrounding treatment, particularly the practice of giving stimulants to children. Teachers are usually quite familiar with children who have ADHD and know from first-hand experience the types of challenges these children face in the classroom.

The primary characteristics found in children with ADHD, namely, inattention, impulsivity, and hyperactivity, are exhibited by all children to some degree. What distinguishes children with ADHD from others is that these characteristics are prevalent to a far greater degree and in a wider range of situations and circumstances than would be true of children without this disorder.

ADHD symptoms can have a serious impact on the social, emotional, and academic performance of children. Paying attention in class, following rules, being able to exert self-control and think about consequences before acting, interacting appropriately in games and sports, and developing meaningful relationships with others can be a challenge for some students with ADHD.

Schools and teachers have limited resources to provide extra time and help. Accommodations are sometimes made in regular education settings and when needed, the school may be able to provide more assistance in special education programs.

This chapter will familiarize you with the characteristics of children with ADHD, the prevalence of this condition, and the challenges these children face being at risk for developing other emotional, behavioral, and learning problems.

Problems with Attention Span

A deficit in attention span may not be as visible as hyperactivity or impulsivity, but it is usually the symptom of ADHD that causes the most problems in school. In the classroom, children who are inattentive are often unable to stay focused long enough to finish assignments. They have trouble following their teacher's directions and they often drift off and lose their place. Distracted by their surroundings or by their own thoughts, children who are highly inattentive often begin more things than they finish. Problems with organization can result in missed assignments and confusion.

Although frequently inattentive, the child with ADHD is not incapable of attending to things that appeal to his interests. He usually has a ready supply of attention while performing highly enjoyable activities, such as playing video games or watching television. Novel or unusual situations can capture an ADHD child's attention for lengthy periods of time as can special projects or hobbies. In addition, during one-on-one situations, when the child is being closely observed, attention span may seem quite normal.

Problems with Impulsivity

Many children with ADHD have problems with impulse control. This refers to the child's inability to regulate emotions and behavior. The child acts quickly, without giving sufficient forethought to the consequences of his behavior.

Impulsivity can cause the student to skip over reading the directions for an assignment and to frequently make careless errors. Impulsive behavior disturbs the classroom environment. The impulsive student loses books, drops pens and pencils, calls out, and leaves homework and classwork everywhere, except where it is supposed to be. He does these things not maliciously, but without thinking.

Social impulsivity leads to loss of friendships with no understanding as to why. Children with ADHD who are hyperactive and impulsive have a knack for getting on other peoples' nerves. Other children find their behavior annoying because they never seem to realize when enough is enough.

Problems with Hyperactivity

Not all children with ADHD are hyperactive. A good many, in fact, show normal activity levels or may even be underactive. However, you can't miss the ones who are hyperactive. "Faster than a speeding bullet," one mother said about her hyperactive four-year-old who literally didn't stay still for one minute all day long. Preschool children with ADHD are always touching something, darting about, rarely satisfied, hardly ever sticking with one thing for very long, and needing supervision. Fortunately, hyperactivity is often at its worst in young children. As children get older they tend to slow down.

In elementary school, the child's activity level changes from running to restless. Fidgeting, squirming, shuffling feet, drumming fingers, playing with something all the time, talking, making noises, tipping the chair back, getting up, and walking around the room are typical descriptions by teachers of the hyperactive children in their class. Hyperactive girls may express their energy in less physical ways, primarily through excessive talking.

As the ADHD child goes through adolescence, obvious characteristics of hyperactivity become more subtle. A wagging foot, tapping pencil, or talkativeness may be signs of the teenager's restlessness. The important thing to remember is that not all children with ADHD are hyperactive.

Problems with Executive Functions

Inattention, hyperactivity, and impulsivity do not fully explain the difficulties that children and adults with ADHD have. Understanding executive functions provides a broader view.

What guides our behavior? How do we manage impulses? What systems do we have available to us to keep us on track and maintain goal-directed behavior? The set of processes that people use to problem-solve and respond in purposeful and goal-directed ways are referred to as executive functions. Executive functions enable us to initiate behavior, inhibit competing actions or stimuli, select relevant task goals, plan and organize a means to solve complex problems, shift problem solving strategies flexibly when necessary, monitor and evaluate behavior, and utilize working memory to actively store information for use in problem solving. The frontal regions of the brain are presumed to control executive functioning.

From infancy on we see maturation of attentional control, problem solving ability, self-regulation of emotion and behavior, and the development of goal-directed behavior and self-monitoring. Eighteen-month-old children show the ability to control their actions and inhibit behavior to obtain a goal well beyond what they were able to do as infants. With every passing year the brain matures and our executive function processes grow stronger reaching maximum development in adulthood.

Certain conditions, however, can interfere with the normal development of executive functions. For example, trauma to the frontal lobe (head injury), infections, lead poisoning or exposure to other toxic substances, and insufficiency of neurotransmitter chemicals can slow down or impair executive functioning and lead to symptoms of ADHD. Chapter three will discuss the causes of ADHD and executive function impairments in greater detail.

ADHD Name Changes

Over the past fifty years, children with symptoms of ADHD were popular subjects for study. The name given to the disorder changed through the years to keep up with the growing body of knowledge learned from this extensive research. Previous names for this condition included: minimal brain dysfunction, hyperkinetic reaction of childhood, attention deficit disorder (with hyperactivity; without hyperactivity; and residual type), and, most recently, attention-deficit/hyperactivity disorder.

Currently, the *Diagnostic and Statistical Manual of Mental Disorders: Fourth Edition-TR* (DSM-IV-TR), published by the American Psychiatric Association, specifies criteria that need to be met to be diagnosed as having ADHD. These criteria are listed on the following page.

There are three subtypes of the disorder: combined type; predominantly hyperactive-impulsive type; and predominantly inattentive type.

- *Predominantly Inattentive Type* for someone with serious inattention problems, but not much problem with hyperactive or impulsive symptoms;
- *Combined Type* for someone with serious inattention problems and serious problems with hyperactivity and impulsivity; and,
- *Predominantly Hyperactive-Impulsive Type* for someone with serious problems with hyperactivity and impulsivity, but not much problem with inattention.

To be diagnosed with either type of ADHD, symptoms must have been present before age seven, impairment from these symptoms must be present in two or more settings (i.e., at school, work, and at home), and symptoms must not be the result of another medical or psychiatric disorder. There is a category called ADHD Not Otherwise Specified for those with prominent symptoms of inattention or hyperactivity-impulsivity that do not meet the criteria for ADHD.

Researchers have found that there is a higher proportion of boys to girls who are hyperactive and impulsive and that these symptoms are exhibited earlier and lead to negative behavior problems. Children who are hyperactive and impulsive show difficulty getting along with peers and they may actually be disliked by other children who find their behavior to be annoying.

Individuals with the predominantly inattentive type of ADHD have problems with attention span, but not hyperactivity or impulsivity. To be diagnosed with this type, symptoms of inattention must have been present before age seven, impairment from these symptoms must be present in two or more settings (i.e., at school, work, and at home) and must not be the result of another medical or psychiatric disorder.

Diagnostic and Statistical Manual of Mental Disorders Fourth Edition-Text Revision
Attention-Deficit/Hyperactivity Disorder

A. Either (1) or (2):

(1) six (or more) of the following symptoms of **inattention** have persisted for at least 6 months to a degree that is maladaptive and inconsistent with developmental level:

Inattention

(a) often fails to give close attention to details or makes careless mistakes in schoolwork, work, or other activities

(b) often has difficulty sustaining attention in tasks or play activities

(c) often does not seem to listen when spoken to directly

(d) often does not follow through on instructions and fails to finish schoolwork, chores, or duties in the workplace (not due to oppositional behavior or failure to understand instructions)

(e) often has difficulty organizing tasks and activities

(f) often avoids, dislikes, or is reluctant to engage in tasks that require sustained mental effort (such as schoolwork or homework)

(g) often loses things necessary for tasks or activities (e.g., toys, school assignments, pencils, books, or tools)

(h) is often easily distracted by extraneous stimuli

(i) is often forgetful in daily activities

(2) six (or more) of the following symptoms of **hyperactivity-impulsivity** have persisted for at least 6 months to a degree that is maladaptive and inconsistent with developmental level:

Hyperactivity

(a) often fidgets with hands or feet or squirms in seat

(b) often leaves seat in classroom or in other situations in which remaining seated is expected

(c) often runs about or climbs excessively in situations in which it is inappropriate (in adolescents or adults, may be limited to subjective feelings of restlessness)

(d) often has difficulty playing or engaging in leisure activities quietly

(e) is often "on the go" or often acts as if "driven by a motor"

(f) often talks excessively

Impulsivity

(g) often blurts out answers before questions have been completed

(h) often has difficulty awaiting turn

(i) often interrupts or intrudes on others (e.g., butts into conversations or games)

B. Some hyperactive-impulsive or inattentive symptoms that caused impairment were present before age 7 years.

C. Some impairment from the symptoms is present in two or more settings (e.g. at school [or work] and at home).

D. There must be clear evidence of clinically significant impairment in social, academic, or occupational functioning.

E. The symptoms do not occur exclusively during the course of a Pervasive Developmental Disorder, Schizophrenia, or other psychotic disorder and are not better accounted for by another mental disorder (e.g. Mood Disorder, Anxiety Disorder, Dissociative Disorder, or a Personality Disorder). (pp. 83-85)

Code based on type:

314.01 Attention-Deficit/Hyperactivity Disorder, Combined Type: if both Criteria A1 and A2 are met for the past 6 months

314.00 Attention-Deficit/Hyperactivity Disorder, Predominantly Inattentive Type: if Criterion A1 is met but Criterion A2 is not met for the past 6 months.

314.01 Attention-Deficit/Hyperactivity Disorder, Predominantly Hyperactive-Impulsive Type: if Criterion A2 is met but Criterion A1 is not met for the past 6 months.

Children with the inattentive type of ADHD have slow tempo in completing tasks and they often become over-focused on their thought processes. Teachers tend to describe them as daydreamy, confused, lethargic, and sluggish. They are an important group of children for teachers to know about since studies indicate that they are at high risk for academic failure. Children with predominantly inattentive type of ADHD have a higher rate of learning problems than those with the hyperactive-impulsive type and may be at higher risk for developing emotional difficulties related to depression, anxiety, and low self-esteem.

ADHD is the technically correct term for either of the three types indicated above, However, the term ADD has been used to describe those children in the predominantly inattentive group.

Please refer to the following page for an ADHD Symptom Checklist. You can reproduce this checklist and use it to evaluate whether a student has symptoms of ADHD.

Prevalence of ADHD

Prevalence of ADHD within the United States school-aged population has generally been estimated to be between five percent and seven percent. As noted in chapter one, in September 2005, The Center for Disease Control released the results of a national survey that documents that 4.4 million, or 7.8 percent, of four to seventeen year old children have a parent-reported history of ADHD. Differences between boys and girls have been found, with boys being anywhere from four to nine times more likely than girls to have ADHD.

Girls Versus Boys with ADHD

The vast majority of research done in the area of ADHD has been done on boys with very few girls included. In 1999, psychiatrist Joseph Biederman and his colleagues at Massachusetts General Hospital studied a large group of girls be-
tween ages six and eighteen with and without ADHD and compared the two groups. Girls in the ADHD group were more likely to have problems with conduct, mood, anxiety, and substance use than those in the non-ADHD group. Although the girls with ADHD did exhibit disruptive behavior disorders, the frequency was about half as compared to boys with ADHD. However, the rate of mood and anxiety disorders in the ADHD girls group was about equal to that found in boys with ADHD. There was an indication that problems with substance use were more common among girls with ADHD than had been previously found to be true for boys. For example, girls with ADHD were about four times as likely to be smokers. In comparing cognitive skills and academic performance of girls with ADHD and those without ADHD, the ADHD girls were about 2.5 times more likely to be diagnosed with a learning disability, more than sixteen times more likely to have repeated a grade in school, and almost ten times as likely to have been placed in a special class at school.

Psychologist Stephen Hinshaw and his colleagues studied girls with ADHD who were attending a summer treatment program at the University of California, Berkeley and found that compared to a matched control group of non-ADHD girls, they were very impaired academically and socially. Another psychologist, Kathleen Nadeau, has written extensively about ADHD in girls as has Ellen Littman and developmental pediatrician, Patricia Quinn. Their book, *Understanding Girls with ADHD,* is an excellent resource.

The lesson to be learned from these studies is that ADHD is a serious problem in girls just as it is in boys. Clinicians should be aware of ADHD symptoms in girls and should provide treatment just as aggressively as they do when boys have ADHD. Parents need to take ADHD symptoms in girls seriously as well and should seek help early.

ADHD Symptom Checklist

Student_____ Date_____ Rater_____

Below is a checklist containing the eighteen symptoms of ADHD. Items 1-9 describe characteristics of inattention. Items 10-15 describe characteristics of hyperactivity. Items 16-18 describe characteristics of impulsivity. In the space before each statement, put the number that best describes the child's behavior (0=never or rarely; 1 = sometimes; 2 = often; 3 = very often).

Inattention Symptoms
____   1. Fails to give close attention to details or makes careless mistakes in schoolwork, work, or other activities.
____   2. Has difficulty sustaining attention in tasks or play activities.
____   3. Does not seem to listen when spoken to directly.
____   4. Does not follow through on instructions and fails to finish schoolwork, chores, or duties in the workplace (not due to oppositional behavior or failure to understand instructions).
____   5. Has difficulty organizing tasks and activities.
____   6. Avoids, dislikes, or is reluctant to engage in tasks that require sustained mental effort (such as schoolwork or homework).
____   7. Loses things necessary for tasks or activities (e.g., toys, school assignments, pencils, books, or tools).
____   8. Is easily distracted by extraneous stimuli.
____   9. Is often forgetful in daily activities.

Hyperactive-Impulsive Symptoms
____   10. Fidgets with hands or feet or squirms in seat.
____   11. Leaves seat in classroom or in other situations in which remaining seated is expected.
____   12. Runs about or climbs excessively in situations in which it is inappropriate (in adolescents or adults, may be limited to subjective feelings of restlessness).
____   13. Has difficulty playing or engaging in leisure activities quietly.
____   14. Is "on the go" or often acts as if "driven by a motor."
____   15. Talks excessively.
____   16. Blurts out answers before questions have been completed.
____   17. Has difficulty awaiting his or her turn.
____   18. Interrupts or intrudes on others (e.g., butts into conversations or games).

Count the number of items in each group (inattention items 1-9 and hyperactivity-impulsivity items 10-18) you marked "2" or "3." If six or more items are marked "2" or "3" in each group this could indicate serious problems in the groups marked.

Co-Existing Disorders

Unfortunately, children who have ADHD also have a greater likelihood of having other problems, the most notable being problems with learning, behavior, and social or emotional development.

ADHD and Learning Disorders

In terms of learning, children with ADHD have a greater likelihood than other children of having a learning disability. Children with learning disabilities commonly show their greatest weaknesses in the basic psychological processes involved in understanding or in using spoken or written language. For learning disabled students, such weaknesses may result in reading, writing, spelling, or arithmetic skill deficits.

There has been considerable confusion, and some controversy, regarding the relationship between learning disabilities and ADHD. Some have said that these two conditions are one in the same, with ADHD merely being a form of learning disability. Others argue that they are separate and distinct disorders, but with a fairly high degree of co-existence. In the past, it was generally accepted that the incidence of learning problems and underachievement within the population of children with ADHD was quite high, with estimates ranging as high as ninety-two percent. In practical application this greatly overestimates the number of children with ADHD that would qualify for help in school with a co-existing learning disability diagnosis. Most state departments of education have specific criteria that need to be met in order for a student to be classified as learning disabled. Often, this criteria includes heavy emphasis on academic functioning and requires the student to manifest a discrepancy between potential (often measured by IQ) and achievement (often measured by an individually administered achievement test). Studies found that when such an ability/achievement discrepancy formula was used to classify students as learning disabled, a much smaller percentage of elementary-aged children with ADHD would be classified as learning disabled. When appropriate diagnostic criteria for a learning disability and ADHD are applied, the prevalence of a co-morbid learning disability is probably in the range of ten to twenty-five percent in children with ADHD. However, since there is a significant overlap between ADHD and learning disabilities, school personnel identifying students with ADHD should also be alert for signs of co-existing learning disabilities.

ADHD and Behavior and Emotional Disorders

Children with ADHD have other behavioral and emotional disorders at a much higher rate than non-ADHD children. Between forty and sixty percent of children with ADHD will show signs of oppositional defiant disorder (ODD) and half of those children, in turn, will develop a conduct disorder (CD).

The child with ODD is characterized by a pattern of negative, defiant behavior and irritable mood and is often described as difficult, although without the more serious aggressive components of behavior typically found in children with conduct disorder. The CD child or adolescent exhibits behavior which more dramatically transgresses social and legal norms. CD behavior is more profoundly aggressive and frequently can manifest itself in stealing, running away, lying, fire-setting, school truancy, destruction of property, or physical cruelty.

Parents of children with ADHD with ODD complain about the strong-willed, stubborn, and argumentative aspects of their child's behavior as much or more than they do about the inattentive, impulsive, and hyperactive components. It is also quite common for teachers to find the ADHD/ODD child's defiance more disagreeable than his short attention span and hyperactivity. A large part of the treatment planning for the

ADHD/ODD child invariably addresses the oppositional aspects of the disorder. Indeed, such treatment planning is extremely important, for if oppositional defiant disorder develops into conduct disorder, the prognosis for a good outcome is much less favorable. It is estimated that such children are four times more likely to be retained in school and eight times more likely to drop out of high school before graduation. They have a greater likelihood of developing adult anti-social personality, substance abuse disorder, and other psychiatric and social problems.

Children with ADHD also have higher rates of emotional disturbance. They are at risk for low self-esteem, anxiety, depression, and socialization problems. Due to lack of success in school, within the family, or in social relationships, children with ADHD can become extremely demoralized leading to apathy, irritability, and withdrawal. Although the development of such problems can easily occur in hyperactive as well as non-hyperactive, inattentive children, they are more likely to occur within the non-hyperactive subgroup both because of their tendency to internalize rather than externalize stress and their seemingly more passive, sensitive nature.

Treatment of their emotional distress obviously requires considerable understanding on the part of parents and teachers in order to provide them with the support necessary to foster a more positive attitude towards themself and others.

It is important to note that although ADHD can lead to greater anxiety and depression, so too can anxiety and depression lead to diminished motivation and interfere with cognitive processes involved in the regulation of attention, concentration, and mood. Children and adolescents suffering from anxiety or depression may show behavioral signs that closely resemble ADHD symptoms. Sometimes this is a sudden, temporary reaction to an environmental situation involving family, school, or peer problems. In other cases, the emotional disorder is more chronic and pervasive, the origin of which may lie in the family or biological history of the individual. It is certainly not difficult to understand how children with problems on their mind would have difficulty paying attention in school and may become restless and impatient. Therefore, the symptoms alone cannot tell us the entire story. Understanding the whole child including family, home environment, social relationships, and previous background is essential before intervention is attempted.

Summary

ADHD is a neurobiologically-based disorder that has three core symptoms: inattention, hyperactivity, and impulsivity. Children affected by ADHD have difficulty inhibiting or regulating their behavior. Executive functions having to do with focusing, planning, organizing, problem solving, and memory are also deficient in those with ADHD. This can lead to significant impairment in academic performance and social functioning at home, in school, and in community settings.

Although the name has changed for ADHD over the years, the symptoms that characterize the disorder have not. The DSM-IV-TR is the manual used by clinicians to define characteristics of ADHD and it contains the criteria used to make a diagnosis.

There are three types of ADHD: predominantly inattentive type; hyperactive-impulsive type; and combined type. ADHD affects between five and seven percent of children in the United States with girls less often affected than boys. ADHD is often complicated by other learning, behavior, or emotional problems.

Chapter 3
Causes of ADHD and
Contributing Factors

British pediatrician, George Still, is credited with writing one of the first scientific articles in a medical journal describing children who have characteristics that we have come to know as ADHD. It has been more than 100 years since Still's article, and during this time, there have been many theories proposed to explain the causes of ADHD.

There is general consensus among clinicians and scientists that ADHD is a heterogenous disorder that can be caused by a range of biological, psychological, and social conditions that act individually or together. This chapter will review some of the research that explains these different causes of ADHD and factors that contribute to having this condition.

ADHD—A Neurological Disorder

Scientific journals and textbooks contain numerous articles and studies that assume that ADHD is largely, or entirely, due to abnormal brain functioning. ADHD is frequently referred to as a neurological disorder, however, it would be wise to keep in mind that there are other (non-neurological) factors that can affect the expres-

sion of ADHD behavior. These can include environmental and social influences.

As discussed in the last chapter, certain areas of the brain control our ability to pay attention, plan, organize, inhibit impulses and movement, and remember. These functions are vital to effective self-management and problem solving. As I described in the last chapter, they are often referred to as "executive functions." The frontal regions of the brain are presumed to control these executive functions. The frontal regions are highly interconnected with the limbic (motivational) system, the reticular activating (arousal) system, the posterior association cortex (perceptual/cognitive processes and knowledge base), and the motor (action) regions. In people with ADHD, development of executive functions lags behind and often never fully develops to the extent found in those who do not have ADHD.

Head injuries sustained as a result of automobile accidents, falls, or other head trauma can result in impairments in executive functioning. When such injuries affect the frontal region of the brain, the result can be disturbances in attention, hyperactivity, and self-control. Animal studies have also helped us identify the frontal region of the brain as being involved in ADHD-like symptoms. Chimpanzees, for example, were trained to perform certain psychological tests. Scientists then disabled the frontal region of their brains through surgery or other means and repeated the tests and observed their behavior. When the frontal region of the brain was altered, the chimpanzees showed behavior patterns that were quite similar to children with ADHD. They became more hyperactive, impulsive, and less able to pay attention for long periods of time. They could not inhibit their behavior and had social problems with other animals. When other areas of the brain were altered, these patterns of ADHD-like behavior did not appear. However, less than ten percent of children with ADHD can be shown to have suffered brain injuries. This has led scientists to conjecture that something else may be affecting the development of this part of the brain.

Many scientists have implicated neurotransmitters (chemicals in the brain that enable nerve cells to transmit information to other nerve cells) as a cause of ADHD. The brain is a complex information network made up of billions of nerve cells called neurons which transmit information to each other in much the same way as signals are transmitted electronically in a telecommunications network. However, messages within the brain are transferred by electrical conduction within a nerve cell and by chemical conduction between nerve cells. Once a message is carried along the axon (cell body) of a sending nerve cell, it has to cross a small space called a synapse to reach a receiving cell. At the tip of the axon are tiny sacs that contain neurotransmitter chemicals which are automatically released by the sending nerve cell. These neurotransmitter chemicals excite the receiving nerve cell, causing that cell to fire and thus once again propel the message along the axon to receptors in the next nerve cell. Once the message is received

the neurotransmitter chemical is deactivated or taken up from the synapse and stored in sacs so as not to cause repeated firing of the receiving cell.

Dopamine, norepinephrine, and serotonin are examples of neurotransmitter chemicals that play an important part in brain activity. They make up the dopaminergic, noradrenergic, and serotonergic chemical systems. These systems regulate our senses, thinking, perception, mood, attention, and behavior. The malfunction of any of these neurotransmitter systems can have a wide ranging impact on how a child behaves and learns.

Support for the idea that brain chemistry is responsible for ADHD comes from a number of sources. Certain drugs (stimulants and non-stimulants such as atomoxetine), known to affect neurotransmitters such as those listed above, can temporarily improve the ability of children with ADHD to regulate behavior and attention. These drugs increase the amount of these neurotransmitters in the brain. At least two genes that regulate dopamine have been identified as being associated with ADHD. One of these genes is involved in removing dopamine from the synapse between neurons and the other affects the sensitivity of neurons to the dopamine itself.

Studies using electroencephalography (EEG) while children with ADHD were sitting at rest and also while they were performing certain mental tasks, have found that there was lower brain activity in the frontal region. Other studies found that there was less blood flow in the frontal region, particularly in the caudate nucleus, an important structure in the pathway between the most frontal portion of the brain and the structures in the middle of the brain known as the limbic system. These areas are important in inhibiting behavior and sustaining attention. Dr. Alan Zametkin, using positron emission tomography (PET), found that adults with ADHD had less brain activity, particularly in the frontal lobe.

This study was repeated with twenty adolescents with ADHD, and Zametkin again found reduced activity in the frontal region, more on the left side than the right. Other studies have found that when children were given drugs that lower brain activity, such as phenobarbital and dilantin, problems with inattention and hyperactivity increase.

In the past ten to fifteen years, magnetic resonance imaging (MRI) studies have found differences in the brain structure of people with ADHD. Dr. George Hynd and his colleagues at the University of Georgia (1991) found that the caudate nucleus of children with ADHD was somewhat larger on the right side than on the left. They also found, in other studies, that the corpus callosum, a large band of nerve fibers that connects the right and left sides of the brain, was somewhat smaller in children with ADHD than in children without ADHD. Additional studies done by Xavier Castellanos and Jay Giedd (1997) and Pauline Filipek (1997), and their colleagues, found further evidence of smaller brain regions (structures in the basal ganglia and certain regions on the right side of the cerebellum) in children with ADHD.

The Role of Genetics

There appears to be a strong role that genetics plays in the development of ADHD. Studies involving families with ADHD children, twins who have ADHD, and adopted children with ADHD, as well as molecular genetics studies offer strong evidence of the important role that genetics plays.

ADHD tends to run in families. Blood relatives of individuals with ADHD have a greater risk for ADHD. Drs. Stephen Faraone, Joseph Biederman and their colleagues (1991) have studied the familiality of ADHD and have found that siblings of children with ADHD have a two- to three-fold greater risk of ADHD than siblings of normal controls.

Investigators often study twins to sort out the degree of genetic influence on a trait or disorder. Twins can be monozygotic (MZ), identical twins who have all of their genes in common; or dizygotic (DZ), non-identical or fraternal twins who, on average, share half of their genes. If we accept that MZ and DZ twins share their environment to the same extent, then any greater similarity in MZ than DZ twins should reflect genetic effects. Dr. Florence Levy and her colleagues (1997) in Australia found a much higher concordance of ADHD for MZ than DZ twins. That finding is consistent with high heritability of ADHD.

Investigators also study children with ADHD who were adopted away from their biological parents. These studies provide another way to understand the influence of genes and the environment. In such studies, the adopted-away offspring of affected parents are studied and compared with control adoptees. It turns out that biological parents of individuals with ADHD are more likely to exhibit ADHD or related disorders than are adoptive parents.

The strong evidence of genetic effects, the effect of stimulant medication on children with ADHD, and the concentration of neurons rich in dopamine and norepinephrine in the neural areas involved in executive function led to investigation of the role of candidate genes involved in the noradrenergic and dopaminergic systems By studying molecular genetics, Drs. Edwin Cook and Mark Stein (1995) as well as Dr. Gerald LaHoste and his team (1996) found that ADHD has been associated with the dopamine transporter gene (DAT1) and the dopamine D4 receptor gene. Presumably, mutations in the respective genes may give rise to ADHD.

Maternal Infection, Alcohol, or Substance Use During Pregnancy

The thalidomide tragedy, with its subsequent devastating effects in causing limb deformities, is the most dramatic example of how substances ingested by the mother during pregnancy may have adverse effects on the fetus. Infection, alcohol, and recreational drug use during pregnancy have all been investigated as increasing the risk for ADHD in a developing fetus.

The evidence on the role of maternal infections is greatest in the case of influenza as a contributory predisposing factor to schizophrenia. When influenza occurs during the second trimester, it is associated with an approximate doubling of the risk of schizophrenia. Maternal rubella has well-established devastating effects on fetal development, leading to mental retardation, blindness and deafness. Heavy consumption of alcohol in the first trimester is known to be associated with physical consequences on fetal development (fetal-alcohol syndrome) and has important psychological consequences, particularly in relation to patterns of inattention/over activity.

Researchers have found an association between mothers who smoked tobacco products or used alcohol during their pregnancy and the development of behavior and learning problems in their children. Nicotine and alcohol can be toxic to developing brain tissue and may have sustained effects on the behavior of the children exposed to these substances at early ages.

Traumatic Brain Injury

Annually, more than 500,000 children are hospitalized due to traumatic brain injury (TBI). This results in 3,000 to 4,000 deaths. An additional 15,000 of these children will require prolonged hospitalization, often with a poor outcome. The majority of head injuries, however, are of a mild nature with outpatient management or a simple overnight stay in the hospital being all the treatment needed.

Open-head injuries typically involve localized brain damage. Closed-head injuries, often the result of traffic accidents or falls, are more common, and typically involve widespread damage.

Child abuse, unfortunately, is another fairly common cause of head injury. Psychiatric disorders develop in about half of the survivors of head injuries. Severe closed-head injury can result in a distinctive syndrome of social disinhibition. These disinhibited children are outspoken, forgetful, over-talkative, impulsive, or careless about their own cleanliness and appearance.

Keith Yeats and his colleagues (2005) conducted a study of the long-term affects on attention in children with TBI. The investigators relied on data collected as part of a prospective longitudinal study of children injured between the ages of six and twelve, including children with moderate to severe TBI and a comparison group of children with orthopedic injuries (OI) not involving the head. Parents completed standardized ratings of attention problems soon after the child's injury and again during a long-term follow-up assessment that occurred on average four years post-injury. The children were also administered neuropsychological tests at the long-term follow-up assessment that measured attention and executive functions.

As expected, children with severe TBI displayed deficits in both cognitive and behavioral aspects of attention compared with those with OI not involving the head. In addition, they were substantially more likely than children in the OI group to display clinically significant attention problems. Approximately twenty percent of the severe TBI group displayed symptoms consistent with a diagnosis of combined type ADHD where as only four percent of the OI group did so. These findings confirm previous research showing both cognitive deficits in attention and executive functions and increased behavioral symptoms of attention problems and ADHD after childhood TBI.

Environmental Contaminants

The most studied neurotoxicant is lead. It has been clearly established that exposure of fetuses and children to amounts of lead produces deficits in cognitive functioning. Dr. Herbert Needleman, a child and adolescent psychiatrist, is an expert in this area, and he and other researchers have discovered that lead exposure can cause problems with attention, language function, and social adjustment. Doctors have known of lead's toxic effects since the turn of the century. In 1904, the first article about childhood lead poisoning from paint appeared in an Australian medical journal. France and Austria banned the interior use of lead paint in 1909, but a United State's ban on residential use didn't come until 1978. At that time, studies showed that eighty-eight percent of children in the United States had elevated lead levels.

Dr. Needleman (1998) suggests that the elimination of lead poisoning would reduce cognitive and attention deficits in children. The greatest impact would occur among the economically and socially disadvantaged populations of children. Between 1976 and 1994, the mean blood lead concentration in children in the United States was reduced by almost eighty percent, in direct proportion to the amount of lead produced. While it does not seem likely that lead poisoning accounts for more than a very small portion of children with ADHD, an association between elevated blood lead levels and hyperactivity has been demonstrated in a number of studies.

Food Allergies

There are a number of controversial areas in medicine. ADHD, and it's relation to food allergy, is certainly one of them. One of the main proponents of the food allergy/ADHD connection is Dr. Doris Rapp, a pediatric allergist. Dr. Rapp observed that many children in her practice had significant physical and behavioral changes when exposed to certain foods. They may have red ear lobes, dark circles under their eyes, or glazed eyes after eating certain foods. These children could have tremendous swings in behavior and display hyperactivity.

Prior to Dr. Rapp, another allergist, Dr. Benjamin Feingold, was quite outspoken in his belief that food allergies play an important role in causing children to be hyperactive. Feingold's 1975 publication, *Why Your Child is Hyperactive*, advised parents to put their hyperactive children on an elimination diet wherein foods containing artificial flavorings, dyes, and natural salycilates would be avoided.

While there is some evidence for an effect of diet upon the behavior of certain predisposed individuals, researchers have found that the effect is rather small. In these studies, children with ADHD are given suspect foods one at a time and their behavior is observed and compared to placebo conditions. Generally, the foods involved vary from child to child and include "natural" foods such as eggs, wheat flour, and citrus fruit as well as "artificial" ones such as food dyes. The action appears to be on irritable and non-compliant behavior rather than specifically on ADHD. One can conclude only that parents who have noticed that diet affects their children's behavior are, probably, sometimes right. Prescription of the diet is not yet justified, however, families who wish to explore the possibility further should be supported.

Other Medical Conditions

Other medical conditions can cause symptoms that look like ADHD, but which really are not. Hyperthyroidism, a disorder resulting in overproduction of a hormone produced by an overactive thyroid gland, can result in accelerated heart rate and hyperactive behavior. Treatment with medication to reduce the production of thyroid hormone will improve this condition. There are some types of seizure disorders that result in episodic periods of inattention characterized by prolonged staring, brief loss of conscious awareness, eye blinking, and sometimes, tremor. While such occurrences can happen several times a day, the seizure disorder should not be mistaken for ADHD. In such cases where a seizure disorder is suspected, the child should receive a thorough neurological examination.

There are other psychiatric disorders, such as anxiety disorders, depression, or bipolar disorders, that can occur in children or adolescents. These disorders may result in ADHD-like characteristics but should not be confused for ADHD.

Mental retardation, autistic disorder, and Gilles de la Tourette syndrome are additional neuropsychiatric disorders that could produce symptoms of inattention, distractibility, and impulsivity and could be confused with ADHD.

Medication Side Effects

Certain medications may cause ADHD-like behavior. Phenobarbital and dilantin, anti-convulsants used to treat children with seizure disorders, may give rise to inattention and hyperactivity. Children taking theophylline for asthma treatment may exhibit signs of ADHD-like behavior due to the medication's side effects. These effects are short-lived and disappear when the medication wears off.

Familial Factors

A range of psychosocial factors are associated with ADHD, including maternal stress during pregnancy and poor quality or disrupted early caregiving as may be seen in children in institutions or foster care.

Studies investigating parenting style and methods of discipline in families of hyperactive and normal children do not indicate that parents, by virtue of their parent-child interactions, cause their children to develop ADHD. However, most people would agree that children who live in families which lack structure, routine, discipline, and order may have a greater likelihood of developing disruptive behavior disorders which can result in symptoms of inattention, impulsivity, and hyperactivity. Children from homes with chaotic family interactions will often demonstrate poor organizational skills, difficulty with self-regulation, failure to accept responsibility for their actions, and so on. Behavior of this sort, resulting from difficulties in family functioning should not be confused with ADHD.

Summary

ADHD is universally considered a neurological disorder among experts. However, it can have multiple causes. Most children with ADHD have probably inherited the disorder. A small number of children with ADHD were probably victims of head injury, infection, or illness that affected brain functioning. Neurological research is ongoing and promises to yield more definitive answers in the future. Research into dietary causes of ADHD have failed to be convincing as to any definitive role that food allergies play for other than a small percentage of children with ADHD-like symptoms. Other medical conditions and psychosocial factors can contribute to problems of children with ADHD or can cause problems that look like ADHD, but which are manifestations of other disorders.

Chapter 4
ADHD Across the Lifespan

More often than not, symptoms of ADHD will first appear in childhood and will persist into adulthood. Obviously, the manifestation of ADHD symptoms differs across the lifespan. ADHD affects young children far differently than it does adults and the impact of symptoms, resulting impairment, and methods of treatment vary by age and level of development. This section looks at ADHD at different stages of development: early childhood, middle childhood, adolescence, and adulthood.

Early Childhood

ADHD can often be identified in children between the ages of three and five, especially if hyperactivity and impulsivity are present. Many young children with ADHD do not follow a normal course of development and, in fact, early warning signs such as those below may portend future problems in social and emotional development.

- noncompliance with instructions
- trouble socializing with other young children
- shifts from one activity to another rarely showing sustained interest in anything
- clumsiness
- higher number of injuries due to accidents
- destroys toys or breaks things
- not easily calmed
- displays hyperactive behavior; fidgety and restless
- trouble settling down for naps or quiet time
- a lot of energy; in high gear all the time, very active and restless
- trouble with paying attention to a lesson or activity
- weak fine motor coordination; trouble controlling crayon or pencil when drawing or writing
- aggressive behavior when frustrated
- frequent mood changes; irritability
- difficulty sharing and taking turns
- impulsive, cannot wait for things
- calls out
- needs close supervision
- slower to develop and use language
- difficulty with articulation
- trouble understanding directions or explanations
- difficulty rhyming

- lack of interest in storytelling
- trouble memorizing the alphabet or days of the week

Early warning signs of problems in cognitive skills, language development, temperament, behavior, or social-emotional development should be taken seriously in young children. Young children with learning, attention, and socialization problems can be identified and the earlier interventions are instituted the easier it is to overcome these problems. The U.S. Department of Education recognizes the importance of early intervention and federal law requires schools to provide early identification and intervention services.

It is certainly possible to identify slow learners and potential dyslexic children at the age of five or six—in time to provide them with greater reading support. Preschool and kindergarten teachers should be aware of children who have trouble with phonological awareness—the insight that words are composed of sounds. Children who have weak phonological awareness at an early age may be at higher risk for developing future problems in reading. These children may have trouble naming letters and digits and may not be able to discriminate speech sounds or hear rhymes. They may be slower in naming pictures or colors or with development of fine motor skills.

Teachers can advise parents of young children who are experiencing signs of early reading difficulty to work on building language skills through songs, nursery rhymes, reading to the child, and games. The National Center for Learning Disabilities (NCLD) suggests parents of preschoolers make sure their child has the following resource materials: at least one alphabet book (e.g., Dr. Seuss's *ABC* book; magnetized alphabet letters to play with; crayons and pencils readily available for writing with; paper readily available for writing and drawing; a table or surface readily available for writing on; rhyme

books (e.g., Joseph Slates' *Miss Bindergarten Gets Ready for Kindergarten*); several picture books; beginning reading and alphabet games (on a computer, e.g., *Reader Rabbit*); other materials and games to learn about the alphabet. Preschool and kindergarten teachers could recommend that parents read a picture book with their child regularly, recite nursery rhymes, have conversations with their child, take the child to the bookstore or library, and set a good example for the child by reading books, magazines, or newspapers themselves. Preschool teachers should have supplies of similar materials available in the classroom to use with the child.

In addition to literacy skills, it is important for preschoolers to acquire numerical awareness. They should become familiar with what numbers mean and should be able to demonstrate that they can identify digits and understand concepts of size (e.g., bigger and smaller). Early numerical awareness may assist children in acquiring mathematical skills such as addition and subtraction in kindergarten.

In addition to acquiring skills related to learning to read and understanding numbers, preschool provides a place for youngsters to develop skills related to attention control, behavioral inhibition, and socialization. It is customary for normal preschool-aged children to be overactive and impulsive from time to time. Their attention is captured by things that interest them, but usually for short periods. They shift quickly from one activity to another. We expect preschoolers to be somewhat uninhibited and impulsive and generally we don't get too upset when they get frustrated and have occasional temper tantrums or crying spells. Hopefully, we anticipate their frustration, plan for their short attention span and vary their activities enough to sustain their interest. As they mature through the preschool stage they begin to learn to attend for longer periods of time, to inhibit their behavior, and to socialize with other children. However, preschoolers with

ADHD significantly lag behind in the development of attention, inhibition, and socialization.

ADHD in Early Childhood in School

Symptoms of ADHD, especially symptoms of hyperactivity and impulsivity, arise early in childhood with a mean age of onset being between three and four years. However, clinicians are cautious about diagnosing ADHD in young children because there is concern that the diagnosis may be applied inappropriately without enough consideration for the normal variations seen in the development and temperament of youngsters. This has led researchers to investigate whether symptoms of inattention, hyperactivity, and impulsivity diminish or persist as young children grow up and whether such symptoms significantly impair the young child's ability to function normally.

Dr. Susan Campbell studied three-year-olds with a pattern of hyperactive, impulsive, and related disruptive behavior. Nearly one-half continued to experience behavioral problems by school age, and nearly one-third received a diagnosis of ADHD. Dr. John Lavigne, and others at the Children's Memorial Hospital in Chicago, found that in more than fifty percent of cases, preschool children's disruptive behavior persisted for up to four years from the time they were first identified as having a behavior problem.

How seriously do these behavior problems impact young children? In 2001, George DuPaul and his colleagues at Lehigh University found that preschoolers with ADHD demonstrated early social and academic deficits. At home, they were twice as likely to be non-compliant to commands and their parents were three times more likely to exhibit negative behavior toward them. In the classroom, the ADHD preschoolers were much more likely to have negative social interactions, especially during unstructured, free-play activities. They also had weaker academic skills as compared to a non-ADHD comparison group.

In their book, *ADHD in the Schools,* George DuPaul and Gary Stoner point out that there is a paucity of studies examining the efficacy of behavioral treatments for preschool children with ADHD. They indicate, however, that it appears that classroom interventions based on behavioral principles are effective in reducing disruptive behaviors in preschool settings.

It would seem that ADHD symptoms in early childhood should be addressed by healthcare professionals, parents, and educators. Preschool classrooms that have the following characteristics work best for youngsters with ADHD:

- teachers trained in understanding the needs of young children with ADHD
- small class size
- assistance of a teacher's aide
- assistance of an expert in classroom behavior management
- use of multiple behavioral interventions such as a reinforcement program, social skills group, daily report card program, etc.

Sandra Rief, in the second edition of her best-selling book, *How to Reach and Teach Children with ADD/ADHD*, found that successful early childhood educators:

- provided a loving and nurturing classroom setting
- celebrated and respected every child's uniqueness
- provided hugs, smiles, and praise/positive attention generously
- established close contact and communication with parents
- had clear, specific, and firm expectations
- provided structure, consistency, and follow-through
- instituted procedures and routines that provided structure to the classroom environment
- exhibited flexibility, kindness and under-

standing of the needs of students and clearly loved children

- provided lots of music, movement, and hands-on activities
- gave students the opportunity to make choices
- encouraged children to explore and make discoveries on their own
- incorporated multi-disciplinary techniques and developmentally appropriate activities and materials that were fun and engaging
- implemented behavior management approaches and supports
- considered each student's learning style, temperament, and strengths and limitations
- clearly labeled the environment in pictures (that made it easy for children to access materials and clean up independently)
- built language-rich, literacy-rich environments and curriculum containing many rhymes/verse, literature, stories, songs, reading/writing.

Children with ADHD or other special needs lucky enough to be taught by teachers who provide these classroom environments will have a better chance of experiencing success and accomplishment.

ADHD in Early Childhood at Home

Parents of preschoolers with characteristics of ADHD find that they are non-compliant, hyperactive, demanding, and mischievous at home. These behaviors present considerable challenges to parents and often parental stress is at a peak during these preschool years. Efforts to manage the ADHD preschooler's behavior may produce higher levels of non-compliance from the child and both parent and child become frustrated in the face of efforts to discipline. Poor self-con-

trol results in frequent temper tantrums by the child and greater amounts of directing, demanding, and conflict between mother and child. This can significantly affect the self-esteem of both the parent and the child and can have a deleterious impact on the ability of the mother and child to bond normally. Mothers often show signs of depression and disengage from their children because parenting is often unsatisfying. Fathers often withdraw as well because of the unpleasant atmosphere in the home. It is hard for parents to find relief. Babysitters are frequently hard to find. Friends and relatives may offer more criticism than help. Parents often feel alone and inadequate, further increasing their stress, depression, and lack of confidence in parenting skills.

Parents of young children tend to delay presenting their children for assessment and clinicians may be reluctant to make an early diagnosis. Therefore, effective treatment of the young child's ADHD symptoms may be delayed until the child gets older. Similar to findings that early educational intervention may help preschoolers overcome potential learning problems, early therapeutic interventions for preschoolers with ADHD may prevent the development of more severe disruptive behavior later in childhood and adolescence. The school is often at the forefront in helping a parent become aware of the difficulties a child has and it provides assistance and direction to the parent who is seeking help.

Parents can greatly benefit from training in ADHD and child behavior management. Most traditional approaches to parent training in behavior management teach the following skills: increasing parental attention and positive reinforcement to the child for engaging in socially appropriate and compliant behavior; reducing any positive reinforcement (such as parental attention) being provided to the child for engaging in disruptive or defiant behavior; and applying punishment when the child exhibits inappropriate or non-compliant behavior. In most programs, positive reinforcement may involve parental attention, snacks, toys, privileges, or tokens that can be exchanged for privileges and toys. Punishment usually takes the form of time-out, but it can also include loss of privileges or tokens. In addition, parents are provided with guidelines to clearly give instructions and in the use of home token economy programs and daily report cards for use in school.

Parents and teachers of preschool-aged children should work together to motivate the child to follow class rules, pay attention, and socialize appropriately. Parents may augment the social experience at school by involving the child in closely supervised after-school or weekend play dates. The teacher and parent may work on specific social skills (i.e., taking turns, asking to share, walking away when frustrated) that can be reinforced at home and in school.

Stimulant medications are routinely used to treat ADHD in school-age children and increasingly in preschool children. Preschoolers with ADHD are being treated with stimulants for extended periods of time although there has been very little research on the effects of stimulants in young children. Findings from the limited research indicate that many ADHD preschoolers respond to stimulants, showing improvement in core ADHD symptoms.

A recently published study (Chacko, et al., 2005) examined the effectiveness of stimulant medication in five and six year olds with ADHD. They concluded that stimulant medication is an effective treatment for young children diagnosed with ADHD and that low doses generally provided maximum benefit. Results from a comprehensive NIMH-funded, multi-center study of preschoolers age 3 to 5.5 years, The Preschool ADHD Treatment Study (PATS), will be available soon.

Middle Childhood

During the middle childhood stage of development there are increased expectations placed on the child for self-control, cooperation, compliance, and self-management both in the classroom and at home. Children are exposed to greater amounts of information and must, therefore, pay greater attention to their environment. Attention must become more controlled and sustained and a child must learn to independently plan how to spend his time and attention (Teeter, 1998).

By the age of six years, children with ADHD are noticeably different from their normal peers in their ability to pay attention and inhibit behavior. Generally, by the time they are nine or ten years of age many will be identified as having ADHD and will begin treatment. If the problems of ADHD are not adequately addressed between the ages of six and twelve years, more serious secondary problems may develop. As discussed in the previous chapters, some children will develop oppositional defiant disorder or conduct disorder. Many will suffer low self-esteem due to their inability to achieve the same levels of success as their peers. Still others will develop mood disorders and depression.

Assessments for ADHD are most often performed during middle childhood. Fortunately, the symptoms of ADHD are more clear-cut during middle childhood and differences between normal and abnormal behaviors are more easily discernible than was true in early childhood. ADHD symptoms have a greater impact on academic and social functioning at this point and impair performance. Because the disruptive behavior of the ADHD child with combined or hyperactive-impulsive type adds stress to their family and their classroom, parents and teachers become alarmed. The child with the inattentive type of ADHD may go unnoticed for a while longer, but nevertheless may struggle with school work, have trouble staying focused and organized, and may not be able to keep up academically or socially.

Since much of the research on treating ADHD has been done with children in the middle childhood years, we know a lot about how to help this group of children. Clinicians target the following goals when working with this age ADHD child, their families, and their teachers.

1. Training parents to become better educated about ADHD. Parents are often supplied with resource material to read or watch. They are encouraged to contact support organizations such as Children and Adults with Attention-Deficit/ Hyperactivity Disorder (CHADD), the Attention Deficit Disorder Association (ADDA), or the Learning Disabilities Association of America (LDAA).

2. Training parents and the child to improve communication and problem-solving abilities within the family and decrease familial stress and conflict that often arises in families affected by ADHD.

3. Parent training to improve child compliance and to encourage the child to take on more responsibility and exert greater self-control.

4. Identification of ways to improve the child's sense of accomplishment and increase self-esteem by finding opportunities for the child to succeed.

5. Consultation with school personnel to ensure the proper learning environment for the child in school. Educate teachers about ADHD, set up behavioral programs in the classroom. Alert teachers to potential accommodations that may help the child learn and perform in school. Identify any needs the child may have for special education or related services. Determine additional academic support services that may be needed (i.e., tutoring).

6. Determination of any other deficits related to learning such as speech and language deficits, hearing or vision deficits, motor incoordination, or social-emotional deficits that will need to be ad-

dressed through further assessment and treatment.

7. Social skills training to help the child improve social relationships by acquiring skills related to making friends, anger control, assertiveness, etc.

8. Use of medication to improve attention, self-control, and other executive functions. The physician may try different medications to see which are most effective. Strength of dosing and time of dosing will be modified based on the child's individual response to the medications.

Classroom interventions for children with ADHD in the middle childhood years usually focus on: strengthening academic skills to overcome deficits in reading, written language, and mathematics; implementing classroom accommodations to enable students with ADHD to perform better in school; and using contingency management programs to improve on-task behavior and social compliance. These interventions will be discussed more fully in chapter twelve.

Adolescence

As many as eighty percent of children diagnosed with ADHD in middle childhood will continue to have symptoms of overactivity, inattention and impulsivity through adolescence. Longitudinal studies following groups of children with ADHD into their adolescent years consistently find that teens with ADHD have higher rates of disruptive and non-disruptive problems including anxiety, depression, oppositional behavior, and school failure. Rate of substance abuse is also higher, but this is only found in those teens who have conduct disorder (more severe defiance associated with running away, truancy, lying, stealing, etc).

School problems can intensify in middle and high school. Greater demands are placed on students in secondary schools. They have more teachers to cope with, more work to be responsible for, more activities to organize, and they tend to be less closely supervised by teachers. The ADHD adolescent starts middle school with several teachers each of whom probably has one hundred or more students to teach. It is easy to get lost in this large group.

Raising an adolescent with ADHD is challenging to parents and other family members. There is likely to be more conflict between the ADHD teenager and parents. When the adolescent with ADHD has additional problems related to substance abuse, delinquency, or learning difficulties or when there is other stress or adversity in the family, conflict increases.

Family counseling is often initiated to address parent-adolescent conflict and dysfunctional ways of communicating that may have developed over several years within the family. Parents may benefit from instruction in behavior management with adolescents and use of problem-solving communication strategies. Arthur Robin and Sharon Foster developed a program called Problem-Solving Communication for Families and Teens (PSCT) to teach families communication skills. Clinicians trained in PSCT use assessment, problem-solving training, communication strategies, and cognitive restructuring modalities to improve family interactions and problem-solving patterns.

Study strategies training can help adolescents with ADHD improve skills in time management, organization, reading comprehension, note-taking, memory, test-taking, and self-advocacy. *Study Strategies Made Easy,* written by Leslie Davis, Sandi Sirotowitz and myself is used in schools throughout the country to help teens acquire skills important in learning how to learn. Refer to chapter thirteen for more information on study strategies along with sample worksheets and exercises for students in elementary and secondary school.

Social skills training has been used to help adolescents with ADHD. Training programs such as *Skillstreaming the Adolescent* by Arnold Goldstein and Ellen McGinnis shows how to teach fifty prosocial skills such as expressing feelings, apologizing, setting a goal, starting a conversation, and responding to failure. Skill areas are divided into six groups: beginning social skills, advanced social skills, dealing with feelings, alternatives to aggression, dealing with stress, and planning skills. There is an instructor's manual, student manual, program forms, skills cards, and a video to use as teaching aids. This and other social skills training programs are described in more detail in chapter fourteen.

Medication research focusing on adolescents who have ADHD is scant compared to research done on pre-adolescent children. However, the efficacy and safety of ADHD medications appears to be similar across age groups. Stimulant medications can significantly improve social behavior, on-task behavior, and academic performance. Non-stimulants such as atomoxetine (Strattera) and tricyclic anti-depressants, and noradrenergic medications (Wellbutrin) have been used successfully with adolescents with ADHD.

Compliance with medication can be more difficult. Teenagers often choose on their own to discontinue medication because they perceive it as being unnecessary or unhelpful, despite contrary views held by their doctors, parents, or teachers. Other reasons adolescents stop medication are that they are unhappy with side-effects, the medication makes them feel less like themselves, or they dislike the effects on their appetite. Teens should be given an opportunity to express their concerns. Providing information about how these medications work, their main effects and side-effects, and the benefits that can result can sometimes improve compliance. These issues regarding medication for

ADHD will be discussed fully in chapter eleven.

Some parents are concerned that use of ADHD medication during adolescence may lead to later substance abuse. In fact, studies have found that adolescents medicated with stimulants do not show any increased vulnerability to addiction. Tim Wilens and his colleagues at Massachusetts General Hospital have found that taking stimulant medications may lower the risk for future substance abuse in adolescents with ADHD.

Adulthood

Within the past twenty years, the persistence of ADHD into adulthood has been increasingly recognized. Unfortunately, compared to studies of children, there are relatively few studies of adults with ADHD. Many of these studies have focused on issues related to the identification of the disorder, the presence of other psychiatric disorders in adults with ADHD, and the use of medication treatments.

- The prevalence of adults with ADHD is still uncertain. Figures vary depending on what criteria is used and who is reporting symptoms.

- There is a lack of consensus on the specific diagnostic criteria that should be used for adults with ADHD. The procedures that have been developed for evaluating ADHD in adults include self-reports of both current and past symptoms as well as collaborative reports of the same symptoms from parents and/or spouses obtained by checklists, interviews and review of past records (i.e., school report cards and transcripts, medical records). The wording of the ADHD criteria in the DSM-IV-TR is appropriate for children but not for adults. Existing protocols have been modified by changing the wording of symptoms and the number of symptoms required for cutoffs (Murphy & Barkley, 1996).

- Differentiating ADHD from other mental disorders in adults can be difficult. Many of the symptoms of adult ADHD are also found in anxiety disorders, depression, and bipolar disorder.

Dr. Sam Goldstein explains that the picture of ADHD in adulthood can be very variable. He divides adults with histories of ADHD into three categories:

1. those who seem to function fairly normally as adults although they have had childhood ADHD

2. those who continue to have significant problems with ADHD as well as life difficulty involving work, interpersonal relations, self-esteem, anxiety, and emotional lability; and

3. those who develop serious psychiatric and anti-social problems and are quite dysfunctional.

The sections that follow contain outcome information about academic and occupational functioning, social skills, and family functioning in adults with ADHD.

Academic and Occupational Attainment

Adults with ADHD have more difficulty achieving in school and in their employment. They are less likely to go on to higher education and are more likely to be employed in skilled labor positions and to change jobs more often. Adults with ADHD may do better in occupations that are fast-paced, exciting, and which don't reuqire a great deal of attention to detail, paperwork, and organizational skills. This does not mean that adults with ADHD cannot succeed in jobs that do require attention to detail repetitiveness, orgnaization, etc. Many are successful in finding ways to manage these tasks despite their problems with attention and concentration.

Social Skills

A few studies have looked at how adults with ADHD function in social interactions. Symptoms such as inattention and impulsivity are likely to contribute to social difficulties. Adults with ADHD are often described as having difficulty with the give and take of conversation. They may ramble on, unaware of cues given off by the person they are talking with that they should alter the style of their communication. Drs. Gabrielle Weiss and Lilly Hechtman (1993) found that young adults in the ADHD group they studied were significantly worse at social skills in job interviews and other situations that required assertiveness and oral communication. Dr. Michele Novotni, in her book, *What Does Everybody Else Know That I Don't?*, gives many illustrations of how ADHD symptoms can impact adult social interaction and offers strategies for improvement.

Family Functioning

Due to the high heritability of ADHD, adults with ADHD who become parents are more likely to have children who also have ADHD. As a result, these parents have a double challenge. They must manage their own ADHD symptoms and they must help their child manage theirs. ADHD can interfere with a parent's patience and ability to use effective parenting strategies. Children with ADHD have a greater need for a parent with a clear and consistent parenting style, established routines, and structure in the home. Parents may have to implement different behavioral treatment programs requiring consistent delivery of rewards and consequences. They may have to be good time managers to keep their child on track so they have time for schoolwork, household responsibilities, and recreation. Often treatment of ADHD symptoms in a parent leads to improvements in parenting skills. Unfortunately, ADHD may have a negative impact on marital stability as higher rates of separation and divorce have

been found in adults with ADHD. *Moms with ADD: A Self-Help Manual* by Christine Adamec and *Voices from Fatherhood: Fathers, Sons and ADHD* by Patrick Kilcarr and Patricia Quinn offer many tips for parents, particularly if they suffer from ADHD as an adult.

Summary

ADHD can be a life-long disorder for up to many of those diagnosed in childhood. The onset of symptoms can start in early childhood and can have a serious impact on the social and emotional functioning of youngsters. Learning in school can also be affected. Teachers working with preschoolers who have ADHD can provide accommodations in the classroom along with close supervision of the student to improve social adjustment and learning.

Most children with ADHD are diagnosed in middle childhood. Problems in elementary school with behavior, learning, and socialization often lead to evaluation and treatment. Medical interventions can be quite successful both in early and middle childhood. Symptoms will often persist into adolescence. Hyperactivity may diminish, but problems with organization, attention, and self-control may provide challenges for the ADHD teen who has to manage a growing number of responsibilities.

ADHD often persists into adulthood where it can impact social relationships and occupational performance. Many diagnosed adults will benefit from medical interventions, coaching, counseling, and organizational strategies designed to improve their ability to manage their daily responsibilities.

Chapter 5
Assessing ADHD in
Children and Adolescents

Problems with attention and behavior management are two of the most common reasons for referral of children for evaluation. The purpose of this chapter is to describe existing guidelines for assessment of ADHD, the role played by community and school-based professionals in performing an assessment, and the types of procedures and specific instruments used during an assessment.

As discussed earlier, ADHD has been defined in a number of ways over the past several decades, but there is an emerging consensus that it is characterized by the display of developmentally inappropriate frequencies of inattention, and/or hyperactivity and impulsivity. This leads to impairment in functioning wherein the child with ADHD has difficulty demonstrating self-control and maintaining consistent work performance over time.

Community-based and school-based professionals use the DSM-IV-TR criteria to determine whether a child qualifies for a diagnosis of ADHD. Symptoms of inattention, hyperactivity, and impulsivity must have been initially exhibited in early childhood (i.e., prior to age seven)

and must be chronically displayed across two or more settings (i.e., school, home, community, workplace). A child must be reported to exhibit at least six of the nine inattention symptoms and/or at least six of the nine hyperactivity-impulsive symptoms. These symptoms must not be the result of other factors such as poor academic instruction or classroom management practices, sensorimotor impairments, language impairments, mental retardation, or emotional disturbance. Furthermore, there must be evidence that the child's functioning is impaired by these symptoms.

The primary characteristics of ADHD are not difficult to spot in a classroom. However, not all children who exhibit signs of inattention, impulsivity, or hyperactivity have ADHD. These symptoms may not always be due to a "disorder" but may reflect medical, emotional, environmental, or other factors.

Children who are frustrated by difficult schoolwork may display inattention. Students who are preoccupied by problems at home, with friends, or elsewhere may have trouble staying focused and concentrating. Nervousness can produce restless, fidgeting behavior. Unmotivated students often do not complete assignments or pay attention. Certain medical conditions or other psychiatric disorders and learning disorders can result in inattention. Many of these problems are commonly found in children and should not be confused with ADHD.

Difficulty with school assignments can cause inattention.

Joseph had trouble in school ever since he transferred from Norcross Elementary across town to his new school. Fifth grade was fifth grade his mother had told him, so he shouldn't have to worry about being able to do the work. However, Joseph was having more trouble now than he ever had before. He used to be the first one in his class to raise his hand and now he hardly ever knows the right answers. This new class seems to be further ahead of his last one. The other students seem brighter. He's getting discouraged and finds himself daydreaming a great deal. All this change is causing him to feel overwhelmed and he can't seem to keep his mind on his work.

Being worried or depressed can cause inattention.

Susan's parents were recently separated. Since then her life hasn't been the same. Her father found an apartment and moved out. Her mother got a new job with better pay, but longer hours. Susan's grandmother moved in with them to help out. Susan misses her father and worries about him being alone. She frequently hears her mother telling others that they have financial problems, and she knows her mother doesn't like working so hard. Susan wishes things were back the way they were before her parents split up, but she is afraid that won't happen. With all these problems on her mind, Susan is having difficulty concentrating in school.

Some medications can cause inattention and hyperactivity.

Jeff has suffered from asthma since he was a preschooler. It got so bad sometimes that breathing became very difficult. Things got better after his doctor diagnosed his condition and gave him medication which improved his respiration. However, whenever he takes the asthma medication he gets "hyper" and gets in trouble in school.

Students who are learning English as a second language may have trouble paying attention.

English is a second language for Ana. She just moved to this country from South America and her family always spoke Spanish. She's having a hard time catching on in seventh grade and most of the time she doesn't understand the teacher or the other students. Being bored, her mind wanders, and she often cannot force herself to pay attention to things she doesn't understand.

Lack of motivation to succeed in school can cause inattention and acting out.

Every year Robert's teachers say the same thing, that he is just not working up to his ability. He doesn't seem to care. Robert sits in class and talks to others, fools around, and disrupts the class. He doesn't pay attention or complete assignments. Homework is never done, and when it is completed it usually contains numerous mistakes. Robert's teachers send notes home almost every other day, but they never hear from his parents. It seems that his parents don't care whether Robert does well in school.

Guidelines for Assessment of ADHD

In 2000, the American Academy of Pediatrics (AAP) published guidelines for physicians to follow in doing an assessment of ADHD. Among its recommendations were:

- the primary care physician should initiate an evaluation of children between ages six and twelve who present with inattention, hyperactivity, or impulsivity;

- the diagnosis of ADHD requires that a child meet the DSM-IV criteria;
- the assessment requires evidence directly obtained from parents or caregivers regarding the core symptoms of ADHD in various settings, the age of onset of symptoms, duration of symptoms, and the degree of functional impairment;
- the assessment of ADHD requires evidence directly obtained from the classroom teacher (or other school professional);
- the assessment should include evaluation for associated conditions; and
- other diagnostic tests are not routinely indicated to establish a diagnosis of ADHD, but may be used for the assessment of co-existing conditions (e.g., learning disabilities, mental retardation).

The AAP recommended that specific questionnaires and rating scales that have been developed to assess the behavioral characteristics of ADHD be used in the assessment process. These scales can accurately distinguish between children with and without ADHD, however, they must be interpreted in the context of the overall evaluation of the child.

Furthermore, the AAP recognized that the child's classroom teacher typically has more information about the child's behavior than other professionals at the school, and should, whenever possible, be contacted to provide information about the child. This information can be obtained through narrative reports (oral or written), questionnaires, or rating scales and any reports should focus on the presence of the core symptoms of ADHD.

For children who are educated in their homes

by parents, evidence of the presence of core symptoms in settings other than the home should be obtained. When a child spends considerable time in other structured settings (i.e., after-school care), additional information should be sought from professionals in those settings.

Since other psychological and developmental disorders are frequently found to co-exist in children who are evaluated for ADHD, the evaluator should consider the possible presence of such co-existing conditions. This may include conditions such as parent-child interaction problems, motor disabilities, speech and language disorders, oppositional disorder, conduct disorder, learning problems, anxiety disorder, depression, etc. The child may be referred to specialists in these areas for more comprehensive assessment.

The National Association of School Psychologists (NASP) also cautions that a diagnosis of ADHD should be done with care and with the understanding that attention problems may reflect normal development or other psychological conditions. NASP advises that attention problems can co-exist with other significant disorders or be symptomatic of very different problems. NASP recommends that assessments should be conducted prior to diagnosis and treatment, and that such assessments should include direct input from school and home.

Members of the Assessment Team

Physicians, clinical psychologists, school psychologists, clinical social workers, speech-language pathologists, learning specialists, audiologists, occupational therapists, and educators may each play an important role on the assessment team. School districts often employ these health care specialists and they are usually part of the assessment team when children are referred for evaluation to determine if they have a disability that requires accommodations, special education, or related services.

The Physician

The child's pediatrician or family physician is often one of the first professionals parents talk to when they suspect their child is having a problem. The physician, usually familiar with the child's medical history and already having some knowledge of the family through previous treatment contact, is in a good position to help the parent. However, depending on what the doctor says, the assessment process may begin or end with this first request for help.

Physicians have sometimes been criticized either for not taking parents seriously enough when they believed their child had a significant attention or behavior problem or, at the other extreme, for being too quick to prescribe medication to treat the problem without first having a comprehensive assessment done.

Many physicians, even pediatricians, have not had a great deal of training in child psychology or education during medical school, internship, or residency programs. On one hand, the doctor may overlook a potential problem and just give well-meaning advice to the parent when indeed much more is needed to help the child and the family adjust. On the other hand, the doctor may prematurely offer medication for the child as a means of handling the problem without doing a full assessment. In such circumstances the parent who gives the child medicine does so without a full understanding of the child's problem and without being aware of other treatments the child may need. This often results in misconceptions about ADHD and compliance to medication usage in such cases is usually only short-term.

Physicians, like other professionals, have become more knowledgeable about ADHD and are more careful about obtaining a comprehensive assessment prior to treatment. Primary care physicians, psychiatrists, and neurologists will start by taking a medical and social history. The history may alert the doctor to health, family, emo-

tional, or environmental problems that could account for the development of ADHD symptoms.

Routine physical examinations of children with ADHD are often normal, nevertheless, they are necessary to rule out the possibility of there being another medical illness, that could cause symptoms. Vision or hearing deficits should be ruled out. Tests such as chromosome studies, magnetic resonance imaging (MRI), or computerized axial tomograms (CAT scans) are not to be used routinely for evaluation of ADHD. There is a small but growing body of research that is demonstrating that ADHD can be accurately assessed using quantitative EEG (QEEG) data. This classification technique is based on the observation of distinct, measurable changes that ADHD patients exhibit in their brain wave activity relative to normal subjects. QEEEG will be discussed in more detail later in this chapter.

Child and adolescents psychiatrists and neurologists, specialists trained in the assessment and treatment of ADHD and other neurological and psychiatric disorders, play an important part in identifying this condition as well as other related conditions such as learning disabilities, Tourette's syndrome, pervasive developmental disorder, obsessive compulsive disorder, anxiety disorder, depression, or bipolar disorder. Children and adolescents who have co-existing conditions and those who do not respond well to standard medication therapies may benefit from consulting a specialist.

Since ADHD is considered by the U.S. Department of Education to be a health impairment, some states may require that children suspected of having ADHD who are being evaluated for special education receive a medical evaluation, even though federal policy does not require a medical diagnosis (Schrag, 1992 Personal communication). This will require a strengthening of school-community professional partnerships. Teachers and physicians, previously unaccustomed to talking with one another directly about student performance, will need better communication if accurate data is to be obtained for purposes of medical diagnosis and follow-up care.

The Clinical or School Psychologist

The clinical or school psychologist administers and interprets psychological and educational tests of cognition, perception, and language development (such as intelligence, attention span, visual-motor skills, memory, impulsivity), as well as tests of achievement and social/emotional adjustment. Results of such tests provide important clues as to whether a student's difficulties are related to ADHD and/or other problems with learning, behavior, or emotional adjustment.

Psychologists and other mental health professionals often integrate data collected from parents and teachers who complete behavior rating scales about the child. Most of the rating scales used to assess ADHD provide standardized scores on a number of factors, usually related to attention span, self-control, learning ability, hyperactivity, aggression, social behavior and anxiety.

Remember, there is no test for ADHD. Even though psychological and educational testing can provide a clear picture of the child's strengths and weaknesses, satisfactory performance on these tests does not rule out ADHD.

School-based Child Study Team

Public schools are required by federal law to evaluate students suspected of having a disability. The Individuals with Disabilities in Education Act (IDEA 2004) requires schools to follow specific procedures and standards to perform such evaluations.

Frequently, the evaluation process is either initiated by the teacher or the parent. A child study team, made up of school personnel such as the guidance counselor, a learning specialist,

the principal or his designee, one or more of the student's teachers, or others at the school, will meet to discuss the student.

As a first step in the assessment process, the child study team will collect information about the student from his parents and teachers. If this information indicates that the student is showing signs of a disability, further assessment may be done by the school psychologist and other school professionals.

Assessments should always include information about the student's current and past classroom performance, academic skill strengths and weaknesses, attention span, and other social, emotional, and behavioral characteristics. Such information can be gathered through teacher interviews, review of cumulative records, analysis of test scores, and direct observation of the student in class.

Assessment data enables the school to determine the needs of the student. The student may be eligible for special education and related services or for a 504 Plan that provides accommodations in the regular classroom.

Assessment Procedures

A multi-method approach is involved in the assessment of ADHD. Information about the child is collected through the following methods: physical examination and laboratory studies; interviews with parents, teachers, and the child; behavior rating scales completed by parents, teachers, and the child; psychometric tests administered in a psychoeducational assessment; and a review of previous educational and medical records. What follows is a description of these procedures.

The Clinical Interview With the Parent

Clinical interviews are the most frequently used assessment procedure by health care professionals. Clinical interviews are best viewed as components of a multi-method approach to assessment of children's functioning. When done well the clinical interview with the child's parent or guardian offers a rich source of information about the child.

Usually done by a health care professional, school psychologist, social worker or other member of the school's child study team, the clinical interview with the parent is intended primarily to document important aspects of the child's medical, developmental, family, social, and academic history.

Clinical interviews have advantages and disadvantages. The opportunity to establish rapport with parents and other care-givers is an important advantage that interviews offer over other assessment procedures. Another advantage is that interviewers can explore details of children's problems and circumstance of their life from different perspectives. A disadvantage of the clinical interview is that they are vulnerable to low reliability and misinformation. For example, children, parents, and teachers may not report certain types of behavior, such as attention problems, social difficulties, or learning deficits unless the interviewer specifically asks about these areas of functioning. To avoid missing important information about the child, practitioners are encouraged to combine interviews with other assessment procedures such as those that will be described throughout this chapter.

Semi-structured and structured interviews are often better to use than less formal interview procedures as the interviewer can ask standard questions that cover important points. Without such structure, interviewers may spend too much time on some areas and not enough time on others. Examples of structured interviews will be provided later in this chapter. Structured interviews provide information to make a wide range of DSM-IV-TR diagnoses and have components for assessing psychosocial impairment resulting from psychiatric symptoms and disorders.

Parents bring more than just information about the child to the interviewer. They also bring with them a mixture of emotions about themselves, their child, and the school. For some parents, the interview will be their first attempt at getting help for the child and it will be the first time they've ever talked to anyone outside the family about their child's problems. Other parents will be used to discussing these issues, having sought help for their child in the past. In either case, the parents are likely to have been deeply affected by their child's problems. The interviewer will need to be sensitive, understanding, and non-judgmental.

Russell Barkley and Kevin Murphy have published a stuctured diagnostic interview that is quite comprehensive and which can be used by clinicians to collect information from parents. This can be found in *Attention Deficit Hyperactivity Disorder: A Clinical Workbook.*

The Child and Adolescent Developmental History Form is available on myADHD.com. This form asks about the child or adolescent's history and includes sections on family composition, current concerns, developmental and medical information, family information, school information, child management techniques used in the home, and the child's strengths and accomplishments.

Document the Presenting Problems

One portion of the interview should focus on whether the child exhibits behavioral, emotional, social, or cognitive symptoms that would be indicative of a mental disorder. Often the interviewer will have parents complete checklists of DSM-IV-TR symptoms (or ask parents about the presence of these symptoms), their onset, severity and frequency, and how they impact on the child's ability to function normally.

Document the Developmental and Medical History

Another portion of the clinical interview should review the early birth, developmental, and medical history of the child. Questions should be asked about previous illnesses, accidents, and hospitalizations that the child may have had. Does the child take any medications that could result in ADHD-like symptoms? Was he evaluated and treated before? If so, by whom, and what was that professional's conclusions and recommendations?

Document Information About the Family

The interviewer should take a detailed history of the family make-up. The marital history of the parents and their educational and occupational backgrounds, ages of the child's siblings and relevant information about their medical history and social adjustment, the atmosphere in the home, and how family members get along are all important. Determine what stressors, if any, exist in the family and how the family adjusts to such pressures. Frequently, life with an ADHD child can be quite stressful, resulting in marital disharmony, depression, and tension in the home.

It is important to document how the family has coped with the child's difficulties up to now. To this end, it is helpful to understand parental discipline styles, behavioral interventions currently utilized by the parents, consistency of parental interaction with the child, and the quality and quantity of time spent with the child.

It is also important to determine if either biological parent has had a history of ADHD, learning problems, or any psychiatric illness. Frequently problems with inattention, reading, handwriting, etc. may be found in other biological relatives, but were not diagnosed as ADHD or a learning disability.

Document Information About the Child in School

The interview should document the parents' perceptions as to the child's previous academic performance in school. Going through the child's school history, grade by grade, and asking about school performance, learning problems, and socialization each year may reveal a pattern of chronic inattention, impulsivity, and overactivity.

The interviewer should determine what standardized tests have been administered and whether previous psychoeducational assessments have been performed.

Trial interventions that were used in the past should be documented and teaching styles that seemed to benefit the child should be noted.

Document Information About the Social Development of the Child

Questioning parents about the child's friends often reveals problems the child may have in social development. The interviewer should obtain a sense of how the child interacts with others. Are there any problems with showing empathy, being considerate, managing impulses, dealing with frustration, taking turns, being shy, and so on?

The Teacher Interview

ADHD assessments should include teacher interviews regarding the student's classroom performance. Teachers are an important source of information about the child. They are the one's who often initiate referrals for a school-based assessment. They interact with the child on a daily basis and observe the child's academic performance, social behavior, and emotional reactions. In part, the purpose of the teacher interview is to:

- learn about current concerns the teacher has about the child;
- identify and prioritize specific prob-

lems that can be targeted for intervention efforts;

• understand the child's strengths that can bolster interventions;

• identify trial interventions that have failed or succeeded; and

• assess the practicality of proposed interventions.

Given the demands of the school day, teachers have limited time for interviews. For children in preschool or elementary school the interview should be conducted with the child's primary teacher. In secondary school their may be several teachers that could be interviewed. It is not uncommon to do such interviews as a group where each teacher could provide input about the child.

The advantages and disadvantages regarding clinical interviews with parents applies to teacher interviews also. It is best to combine the teacher interview with other assessment procedures such as behavior rating scales for teachers to complete and review of past educational records. This will increase the chances of getting complete information about the child in school.

There are several interview formats developed for teachers. For example, Edward Shapiro's *Teacher Interview Form for Academic Problems* focuses on reading, mathematics, and writing. This is in contrast to the behavioral interview which focuses on the specification and delineation of target behaviors, the identification and analysis of environmental conditions surrounding target behaviors, and the use of this information to formulate, implement and evaluate interventions. The goal is to obtain a functional behavioral assessment (FBA). The FBA is then used to develop a behavioral intervention plan (BIP). Interviewing teachers is usually the first step in creating such a plan.

In a behavior interview, information is obtained regarding the student's skill strengths and weaknesses and other social, emotional, or behavioral characteristics. The student's adjustment in class should relate to aspects of the instructional environment, namely: the curriculum in which the student is working; teacher's expectations for the class and for the individual student; methods of instruction employed by the teacher; incentives for work completion; methods of teacher feedback to students; and comparative performance of other students in the class.

Behavioral interviews with the child's teacher have advantages over other assessment procedures such as rating scales, cognitive testing, and direct observation.

First, the behavioral interview offers flexibility as to the type and amount of data one could receive regarding the student. The interviewer has the flexibility to explore areas of interest as they come up. This could provide additional understanding of the child's problems. This flexibility is not available in other assessment methods.

Second, the interview process is not only an opportunity to collect information about the child, but also serves as a starting point for the interviewer to assess the teacher's receptivity to intervention strategies and to evaluate any misconceptions or unrealistic expectations that the teacher may have concerning the child.

During the interview process, the teacher and interviewer seek to organize information about the child, and as they do so the problem situation tends to get clarified. In some cases, it may become apparent that the child is having attentional problems because he is being asked to do work which is at his frustration level, or perhaps the child is being influenced by other factors in the classroom.

The Child Interview

An interview with the child is an indispensable part of the assessment process. Depending upon the child's age and intellectual development, one or more interviews will be held with the child for the following purposes:

- to establish rapport;
- to understand how the child views his problem;
- to identify which of the child's problems would be appropriate targets for intervention;
- to understand the child's strengths and resources that can be used to support prospective interventions;
- to assess the level of cooperation of the child; and
- to observe the child's behavior, affect, and social interaction.

Observations made during the interview sessions about the child's behavior, level of activity, attentiveness, or compliance with the interviewer's requests should not be taken as true of the child in other settings. Most ADHD children behave well during such interviews and can exhibit excellent attention and self-control. Rarely do they act out or display hyperactivity or impulsive behavior at these times. Normal behavior in a one-on-one setting does not decrease the likelihood of the child having ADHD.

The child may be asked to provide factual information about family members, school, and friendships. Light questioning of this sort provides more structure to the interview, gives direction to the child, and encourages the child to get into a conversational mode.

As the interview proceeds, more open-ended questions may be asked in an effort to obtain the child's impressions and feelings. Typically, questioning of this type would involve discussion of family, school, and social interactions. During this time, the interviewer can gently probe deeper into problem areas which the parents may have brought up earlier. The purpose of this line of questioning would be to ascertain whether there is agreement between parent and child as to specific problems and to determine the child's per-

ception as to the cause or severity of such problems.

It is important to help the child feel comfortable during the interview process. The interviewer needs to take great care not to be accusatory, judgmental, or unhappy with the child's reports, but should instead be concerned, interested, and helpful. As the child relaxes, questioning can proceed in the area of affective disclosure. Asking the child to talk about things he worries about, feels sad about, or situations that make him upset or angry, helps the interviewer gain information about emotional factors which could contribute to the child's adjustment and behavior.

Before ending the interview, the child should be reassured that the information he provided will be helpful in understanding him better. If further evaluation is going to be done, the child should be given a brief description of what he can expect the next time he comes to the office. The interview should end on a positive note with the child feeling that his participation in the assessment process is important and that the end result of all this effort will be to provide help to him and his family.

Behavior Rating Scales

Many rating scales have been developed over the past forty years to assess general behavioral and emotional functioning in children and adolescents. Most of these rating scales have parallel versions for parents and teachers. Some rating scales have versions for children and adolescent to self-report. The advantage of rating scales with parallel parent, teacher and self-report versions is that the scores across the different informants can be compared.

Earlier scales developed in the 1960's and 1970's, were normed on small samples and lacked rigorous standardization. Newer scales provided more superior measures because they utilized a broader pool of items, employed newer rating formats, and were developed on larger samples of subjects, therefore resulting in better standardization.

Many of the behavior rating scales used to assess ADHD focus very heavily on a number of factors, usually related to attention span, self-control, learning ability, hyperactivity, aggression, social behavior, anxiety, etc.

There are several advantages to using rating scales.

1. They are easy to administer and inexpensive. Time for administration is usually modest. They can be sent by mail or electronically or can be answered over a telephone.
2. They provide a standard set of behaviors to be evaluated thereby reducing variability in the information that is obtained about the child and ensuring that specific target behaviors will be assessed.
3. They offer a means by which to evaluate the frequency and severity of specific behaviors and provide age and sex-graded norms to determine whether reported behaviors are appropriate or deviant in relation to normal peers.
4. Rater bias and subjectivity of responding is reduced by using a standardized presentation of questions.
5. They can be routinely administered in health settings and schools and many rating scales have good data on reliability and validity.

Rating scales also have a number of disadvantages.

1. Information that may be relevant to the subject, but that is not covered by the items of the scale will be missed. With rating scales alone, it is not possible to explore the informant's responses and subjective experiences, nor is it possible to observe behavior directly.
2. Rating scales can be subject to rater bias based upon characteristics of the rater. For example, mothers who are depressed tend to rate their children as having greater behavior problems than do non-depressed mothers.
3. Slight changes in the wording of instructions, or the wording of the items themselves, may have a significant effect on the informant's response.
4. Data obtained from ratings rely totally on the rater's familiarity with the child and, to some extent, upon the rater's familiarity with normative behavior of other children of the same sex and age. Elementary school teachers, who spend several hours a day with a student, for example, may be more familiar with the student's behavior than a middle or high school teacher whose contact with the student is limited to one period per day. Therefore, in secondary education settings it is essential to receive ratings from several teachers so as to accurately assess behavior throughout the day.
5. Rating scales are also subject to rater bias based upon other characteristics of the child (e.g., likeable children may be rated less negatively on scales of hyperactivity and inattention than aggressive/stubborn children).

Despite these shortcomings, behavior rating scales can offer important information that is helpful in the assessment process. Some of the more popular rating scales developed to assess child behavior are described below.

The ADD-H Comprehensive Teacher Rating Scale (ACTeRS)

The ADD-H: Comprehensive Teacher Rating Scale (ACTeRS) by Rina K. Ullmann, Esther K. Sleator, and Robert L. Sprague was developed for identifying and monitoring the behavior of children from kindergarten to fifth grade who manifest deficits in attention span or demonstrate unusually active or restless behavior in the classroom.

The ACTeRS scale contain twenty-four items relevant to classroom behavior. The items are rated on a five-point scale and yield four factors: Attention, Hyperactivity, Social Skills, and Oppositional Behavior.

The ACTeRS Parent Form employs the same sets of behavior to measure the same four factors as the Teacher Form: Attention, Hyperactivity, Social Skills, and Oppositional Behavior. The Parent Form enhances the Teacher Form items with additional descriptive information to help parents make accurate, informed observations about their children. In addition to the original four scales, the Parent Form includes a fifth scale in which parents provide details about early childhood behavior.

The ADHD Rating Scale

The ADHD Rating Scale, developed by George DuPaul, lists the eighteen DSM-IV characteristics of ADHD. Respondents are asked to rate the severity of these characteristics. The scale can be completed by parents and teachers with separate norms available for each set of respondents.

BASC-2: Behavior Assessment System for Children, Second Edition

The BASC-2 is a comprehensive set of rating scales developed by Cecil Reynolds and Randy Kamphous. These scales measure areas for both IDEA and DSM-IV classifications. The BASC-2 has scales for children's self-report, parents, and teachers.

The BASC-2 Teacher Rating Scales (TRS) measure adaptive and problem behaviors in the preschool or school setting. Teachers, or other qualified observers, can complete forms at three age levels: preschool (ages two to five), child (ages six to eleven), and adolescent (ages twelve to twenty-one) in about ten to twenty minutes. The forms describe specific behaviors that are rated on a four-point scale of frequency, ranging from "Never" to "Almost Always." The TRS contains 100-139 items.

The Parent Rating Scales (PRS) measure both adaptive and problem behaviors in the community and home setting. Parents or caregivers can complete forms at three age levels: preschool (ages two to five), child (ages six to eleven), and adolescent (ages twelve to twenty-one) in about ten to twenty minutes. The PRS contains 134-160 items and uses a four-choice response format. This form requires approximately a third-grade reading level for completion and offers a Spanish version.

The Self-Report of Personality (SRP) provides insight into a child's or adult's thoughts and feelings. Each form: child (ages eight to eleven), adolescent (ages twelve twenty-one), college (ages eighteen to twenty-five) includes validity scales for helping judge the quality of completed forms. The SRP takes about 30 minutes to complete.

The Behavior Rating Inventory of Executive Function (BRIEF)

The BRIEF was developed by Gerard A. Gioia, Peter K. Isquith, Steven C. Guy, and Laren Kenworthy. This is a questionnaire for parents and teachers of school-aged children that enables professionals to assess executive function behaviors in the home and school environments. It is designed for a broad range of children, ages five to eighteen years, including those with learning disabilities and attentional disorders, traumatic brain injuries, lead exposure, pervasive developmental disorders, depression, and other developmental, neurological, psychiatric, and medical conditions. The Parent and Teacher Forms of the BRIEF each contain eighty-six items within eight theoretically and empirically derived clinical scales that measure different aspects of executive functioning: Inhibit, Shift, Emotional Control, Initiate, Working Memory, Plan/Organize, Organization of Materials, and Monitor.

Brown Attention-Deficit Disorder Scales

These scales, developed by Thomas E. Brown, include forms for children, adolescents and adults. The Brown ADD Scales assess impairments of executive function. The children's edition features six clusters frequently associated with ADHD: Organizing, Prioritizing, and Activating to Work; Focusing, Sustaining and Shifting Attention to Tasks; Regulating Alertness, Sustaining Effort and Processing Speed; Managing Frustration and Modulating Emotions; Utilizing Working Memory and Accessing Recall; and Monitoring and Self-Regulating Action. The children and adolescent scales have separate forms for parents, teachers, and self-report.

The Child Behavior Checklist (CBCL-Teacher)

The CBCL was developed by Thomas M. Achenbach. The Teacher Report Form (TRF) of The Child Behavior Checklist is designed to obtain teachers' reports of children's academic performance, adaptive functioning, and behavioral/emotional problems. Teachers rate the child's academic performance in each subject. Space is also provided for reporting cognitive and achievement test scores for the child, if available. For adaptive functioning, teachers use a seven-point scale to compare the child to typical pupils for how hard the student is working, how appropriately the student is behaving, how much the student is learning, and how happy the student is.

The TRF has 118 problem items, of which 93 have counterparts on the CBCL/6-18. The CBCL/6-18 obtains reports from parents, other close relatives, and/or guardians regarding children's competencies and behavioral/emotional problems. The remaining items concern school behaviors that parents would not observe, such as difficulty following directions, disturbs other pupils, and disrupts class discipline. Teachers rate the child for how true each item is now or was within the past two months.

The TRF scoring profile provides raw scores, T scores, and percentiles for Academic Performance, Total Adaptive Functioning, the eight cross-informant syndrome scales and six DSM-oriented scales that are also scored from the CBCL/6-18 and YSR, Internalizing, Externalizing, and Total Problems. Syndromes were based on principal components analyses of 4,437 referred students and were normed on 2,319 non-referred students.

Although not specifically developed to evaluate ADHD, the CBCL has been widely used for this reason and is a favored scale due to its comprehensiveness. A major strength of the CBCL-TRF is its usefulness for assessing affective disorders such as anxiety and depression in addition to factors related to behavioral disorders. In addition, the Inattentive and Nervous-Overactive scales have been found to identify children who meet criteria for ADHD.

The CBCL/6-18 obtains reports from parents, other close relatives, and/or guardians regarding children's competencies and behavioral/emotional problems. Parents provide information for twenty competence items covering their child's activities, social relations, and school performance. The CBCL/6-18 has 118 items that describe specific behavioral and emotional problems, plus two open-ended items for reporting additional problems. Parents rate their child for how true each item is now or within the past six months..

The CBCL/6-18 scoring profile provides raw scores, *T* scores, and percentiles for three competence scales (Activities, Social, and School), Total Competence, eight cross-informant syndromes, and Internalizing, Externalizing, and Total Problems. The cross-informant syndromes scored from the CBCL/6-18, TRF, and YSR are: Aggressive Behavior; Anxious/Depressed; Attention Problems; Rule-Breaking Behavior; Social Problems; Somatic Complaints; Thought Problems; and Withdrawn/Depressed. The six DSM-oriented scales are: Affective Problems; Anxiety Problems; Somatic Problems; Attention Deficit/Hyperactivity Problems; Oppositional Defiant Problems; and Conduct Problems.

For children too young for the CBCL/6-18, the Child Behavior Checklist/1-5 (CBCL/1-5) is used instead. Parents and other adults with close relationships to adults aged eighteen to fifty-nine can complete the Adult Behavior Checklist (ABCL).

The Child Attention Profile (CAP)

The Child Attention Profile (CAP) was developed by Craig Edelbrook. It is composed of twelve items taken from the Inattention and Nervous-Overactive scales of the Child Behavior Checklist Teacher Report Form (CBCL-TRF). The CAP has two primary factors: Inattention and Overactivity. This scale is useful in subtyping ADHD children into those with and without hyperactivity. The Child Attention Profile (and normative data) can be found in *Attention Deficit Hyperactivity Disorder: A Clinical Workbook* by Russell A Barkley and Kevin Murphy.

The Child Symptom Inventories (CSI)

The CSI was developed by Kenneth Gadow and Joyce Sprafkin. They are screening instruments for the behavioral, affective, and cognitive symptoms of over a dozen DSM-IV childhood disorders. Individual items are phrased in such a way as to be easily understood by parents and teachers. There are CSI for three different age groups, Early Childhood Inventory-4 (ages three to five years), Child Symptom Inventory-4 (ages five to twelve years), and Adolescent Symptom Inventory-4 (ages twelve to eighteen years), and a self-report measure for adolescent patients, Youth's Inventory-4 (ages twelve to eighteen years).

The clinician can either (a) ask the parent or teacher each question and record the respondent's answer, or more efficiently, (b) simply review the answers during the clinical interview and ask more detailed questions about those categories that the youth's care provider has indicated are problem areas. The items are grouped according to diagnostic category, which facilitates a thorough and orderly interview, helps in detecting co-morbid conditions, and simplifies making differential diagnoses.

In a school setting, the school psychologist can use the CSI to screen for the presence of emotional and behavioral symptoms in children who are being considered for special services. They can also help to determine whether a child should be referred to a qualified mental health professional for a more in-depth evaluation.

In a general medical practice, the CSI can help the physician to identify the specific emotional or behavioral problems that are of concern to parents. The physician can easily decide whether referral to a mental health professional is appropriate.

There are separate forms for different ages and for parents, teachers, and self-reports. The items of the CSI are scored on scales representing DSM-IV categories.

The Conners Teacher and Parent Rating Scales-Revised

The Conners Teacher Rating Scale was the first standardized rating scale designed to assess teacher perceptions of hyperactivity and other learning and behavioral problems. The CTRS was originally developed by C. Keith Conners in 1969 to evaluate changes in behavior for children being treated with medication. For over thirty-five years Conners rating scales have been used in numerous studies and are very widely used in clinical practice. Normative data is available on children as young as three years of age and up to age seventeen. With the quick-scoring forms these scales are very easy to use.

The CTRS-R forms assess problem behaviors reported by teachers. Both long and short versions are available. The fifty-nine-item long version (CTRS-R:L) consists of the following subscales: Oppositional, Cognitive Problems/Inattention, Hyperactivity, Anxious-Shy, Perfectionism, Social Problems, DSM-IV Symptom Subscales, ADHD Index, Conners' Global Index. The twenty-seven-item short version (CTRS-R:S) includes the following subscales: Oppositional, Cognitive Problems/Inattention, Hyperactivity, and ADHD Index.

The Conners' Global Index (CGI) is a ten-item scale that is ideal for treatment monitoring. It contains items found to be critical in assessing the severity of childhood problems. The CGI scale is incorporated into the CTRS-R:L forms as well as being available separately.

These scales contain descriptors of behavior which are rated by the teacher along a continuum of frequency from not at all, just a little, pretty much, very much.

The Conners Parent Rating Scales (CPRS-R) assess problem behaviors reported by parents. Both long and short versions are available. The eighty-item long version (CPRS-R:L) consists of the following subscales: Oppositional, Cognitive Problems/Inattention, Anxious-Shy, Perfectionism, Social Problems, Psychosomatic, DSM-IV Symptom Subscales, ADHD Index, Conners' Global Index. The twenty-seven-item short version (CTRS-R:S) includes the following subscales: Oppositional, Cognitive Problems/Inattention, Hyperactivity,

and ADHD Index. These scales contain descriptors of behavior that are rated by the parent or care-giver along a continuum of frequency.

The Home Situations Questionnaire

The Home Situations Questionnaire by Russell A. Barkley was developed as a means of assessing situational variability and severity of behavior problems in the home. The scale contains sixteen home situations and asks the parent to rate the degree to which the child demonstrates problems with behavior in each situation. The scale provides two scores: number of problem situations and severity of behavior problems. The Home Situations Questionnaire (and normative data) can be found in *Attention Deficit Hyperactivity Disorder: A Clinical Workbook* by Russell A. Barkley and Kevin Murphy.

The IOWA-Conners Rating Scale

The IOWA-Conners Rating Scale was developed in 1981 by Jan Loney and Richard Milich due to concerns that the original Conners was not able to sufficiently discriminate ADHD children from children with aggression or conduct disorders. The IOWA-Conners contains ten items from the original thirty-nine-item Conners, five of which measure attention/overactivity and five of which measure aggression, but which are not correlated with inattention.

The Personality Inventory for Children: Second Edition (PIC-2)

The Personality Inventory for Children: Second Edition (PIC-2), developed by David Lachar, Ph.D. and Chistian P. Gruber, Ph.D. is a recent revision of the PIC, a highly regarded test used for decades to evaluate the emotional, behavioral, cognitive, and interpersonal adjustment of children and teens. The PIC-2 provides the parent's description of the child and may be used in conjunction with the Personality Inventory for Youth, a self-report instrument for children, and the Student Behavior Survey (SBS), a teacher rating scale. The PIC-2 is appropriate for evaluating five through nineteen-year-olds and includes 275 True-False items on the following Adjustment Scales and Subscales: Cognitive Impairment; Impulsivity and Distractibility; Delinquency; Family Dysfunction; Reality Distortion; Somatic Concern; Psychological Discomfort; Social Withdrawal; and Social Skill Deficits. The PIC-2 offers a new Behavioral Summary which is comprised of the first ninety-five items on the test. The complete test takes about forty minutes to complete and the short version takes about fifteen minutes.

The School Situations Questionnaire

The School Situations Questionnaire was developed by Russell Barkley as a means of assessing situational variability and the severity of behavior problems in a school setting. The scale consists of twelve situations and teachers are asked to what degree the child exhibits behavior problems in each one. The scale provides two scores: the number of problem areas in which the child has trouble behaving, and the severity of behavior problems. The School Situations Questionnaire (and normative data) can be found in *Attention Deficit Hyperactivity Disorder: A Clinical Workbook (Second Edition)* by Russell A Barkley and Kevin Murphy.

The SNAP-IV Teacher and Parent Rating Scale

In 1984, a team of researchers developed the Swanson Nolan and Pelham (SNAP) Rating Scale as an alternative measure to the CTRS and the IOWA-Conners. This scale was updated for the DSM-IV criteria to an eighteen-item norm-referenced checklist that is designed to determine if symptoms of ADHD are present. This checklist by James Swanson can be completed by either a parent or other caregiver or an educator for use by a healthcare provider in performing an assessment. Automated scoring of the SNAP-IV is available to subscribers on www.myadhd.com or at www.adhd.net.

The SNAP-IV-C Rating Scale

The SNAP-IV-C Rating Scale is a revision of the SNAP Questionnaire. It contains eighty items that can be completed by parents, teachers, or other caregivers for use by a healthcare provider in performing an assessment. The items from the DSM-IV criteria for ADHD and Oppositional Defiant Disorder are included. In addition, the SNAP-IV-C contains ten items from the SKAMP. These ten items are classroom manifestations of inattention, hyperactivity, and impulsivity (i.e., getting started, staying on task, interactions with others, completing work, and shifting activities). The SKAMP may be used to estimate severity of impairment in the classroom. There are additional items from other DSM-IV disorders such as Conduct Disorder, Intermittent Explosive Disorder, Tourette's Disorder, Stereotypic Movement Disorder, Obsessive-Compulsive Disorder, Generalized Anxiety Disorder, Narcolepsy, Manic Episode, Major Depressive Episode, Dysthymic Disorder, etc. This scale is available to subscribers on www.myadhd.com or at www.adhd.net.

The Vanderbilt Assessment Scale (Teacher Informant and Parent Informant)

The Vanderbilt Rating Scales were developed by Mark Wolraich. The teacher version is a forty-three-item rating scale that has two components: symptom assessment and impairment of performance in school. This rating scale is widely used by healthcare professionals to screen for symptoms of ADHD, oppositional defiant disorder, conduct disorder, and anxiety and depression in children.

The parent version is a fifty-five-item rating scale that has two components: symptom assessment and impairment of performance at home, in school, and in social settings. This rating scale is widely used by healthcare professionals to screen for symptoms of ADHD, oppositional defiant disorder, conduct disorder, and anxiety and depression in children. Both the teacher and parent versions of the Vanderbilt Assessment Scale are available on the Internet. Automated scoring of these scales is available to subscribers on www.myadhd.com.

Psychometric Testing

For many children, psychometric testing is an important and necessary part of a diagnostic assessment of ADHD and related conditions. Data relevant to a child's intellectual ability, information processing skills, and academic achievement is obtained through psychometric testing. This information can be helpful in understanding the student's learning style, whether or not there are any signs of a learning disability, or if there are academic achievement deficits which could be the result of non-cognitive factors.

Psychometric testing may involve evaluating intellectual ability, attention span, visual-motor skills, paired-associate learning, impulsivity, short-term memory, and a number of other cognitive functions. These tests are frequently administered by clinical, school, or educational psychologists who are specially trained to administer such tests and interpret their results. Test findings are usually communicated in a written report that outlines information about the child's presenting problems, developmental and social history, test data, interpretation of the test results in terms of specific strengths and weaknesses of the child, and recommendations for interventions, when necessary. Teachers are frequently asked to read such reports for a better understanding of the student.

Intelligence Tests

Intelligence testing is frequently performed to obtain an overall measure of the student's intellectual ability. The two tests that are used most

often for this purpose are: Wechsler Preschool and Primary Scale of Intelligence-Third Edition (WPPSI-III) and the Wechsler Intelligence Scale for Children-Fourth Edition (WISC-IV) by David Wechsler.

The WISC-IV is an individually administered clinical instrument for assessing the cognitive ability of children aged six through sixteen. The WISC-IV provides subtest and composite scores that represent intellectual functioning in specific cognitive domains, as well as a composite score that represents general intellectual ability (i.e., Full Scale IQ). The WISC-IV is composed of fifteen subtests which will derive a total of five composite scores: Verbal Comprehension Index, Perceptual Reasoning Index, Working Memory Index, Processing Speed Index, and Full Scale IQ.

The Stanford-Binet Intelligence Scales, Fifth Edition (SB5) has a long and rich tradition that began in 1916 when Lewis M. Terman completed his American revision of the 1908 Binet-Simon Scale.

The Leiter International Performance Scale-Revised (Leiter-R) by Gale Roid and Lucy Miller avoids much of the dependence upon language to understand tests.

The Kaufman Assessment Battery for Children, Second Edition was developed by Alan S. Kaufman and Nadeen L. Kaufman. The KABC-II is firmly based on cognitive theory and especially on the distinction between sequential processing (involved in processing information that is ordered in time or space) and simultaneous processing (in which several pieces of information are integrated and processed as a whole). In practice, most "simultaneous" tasks are visual-perceptual and most "sequential" tasks are verbal or motor.

The Das-Naglieri Cognitive Assessment Scale (CAS) by Jack A. Naglieri and J. P. Das combines psychometric credibility with satisfying psychological theory and it yields subscales of planning, attention, simultaneous, and successive processes, as well as a Full Scale score.

Neuropsychological Tests

Neuropsychological test batteries evaluate strengths and weaknesses of cognitive function. The NEPSY, developed by Marit Korkman, Ursula Kirk, and Sally Kemp, for example, includes scores for language and communication, sensorimotor functions, visual-spatial abilities, learning and memory, and executive functions such as attention and planning.

The study of brain-behavior relationships in cognition is undergoing rapid change. The correlation of psychological test performance with underlying alterations of the brain can be seen using modern neuroimaging. Some tests have shown surprisingly strong associations, e.g., tests of attention with size of frontal structures and basal ganglia.

The most common neuropsychological functions assessed are: language, memory, visuo-spatial skills, attention, executive functioning, motor abilities, and adaptive function.

Executive Function Tests

Some tests have been developed to measure the high-level functions of planning, inhibiting immediate or inappropriate reactions, decision-making, and organization. For the most part their standardization is weak. The Stroop Color and Word Test by Charles Golden has its roots in the early published work of John Ridley Stroop. In this test a conflict of information is set up (e.g., the word "blue" being printed in red color), so that successful completion of the test requires one to suppress an "obvious" but wrong response. Like most neuropsychological tests, the Stroop is dependent upon a wide variety of cognitive processes. Color perception and reading ability may affect performance rendering so scores may not simply reflect problems with disinhibition. The Stroop Color and Word Test takes about five minutes to administer.

Other executive function tests purport to measure aspects of problem solving, [e.g., the Trail Making Test and Wisconsin Card Sort Tests (WCST) by David A. Grant and Esta A. Berg or the Tower of London (TOL) developed by T. Shallice]. "Executive function" is a weakly defined concept, therefore, tests that have been designed to measure different aspects of this concept have had difficulty doing so.

Motor Abilities and Adaptive Function

Children can have significant difficulties of organization and coordination of motor tasks (dyspraxia). With a clinical neurological examination, patterns of incoordination can be determined (such as cerebellar ataxia, motor overflow or ideomotor apraxia) as well as underlying causes (such as mild cerebral palsy). There are standardized tests available to precisely quantify levels of incoordination. Scales have also been developed that include items relating to self-care and independence skills. Quantifying these kinds of "adaptive function" is important in assessing the needs of children with global learning disabilities. The Vineland Adaptive Behavior Scales, Second Edition was developed by Sara Sparrow, Domenic Ciccetti, and David Balla. The Vineland is widely used and has a practical advantage in that information can be acquired by parental report as well as by direct examination of the child's abilities.

Achievement Tests

Tests of academic achievement are routinely incorporated in assessments of children and adolescents. Since many of the problems of children with ADHD are school related, and since a significant number of children with ADHD also have a co-existing learning disability, it is important to examine the child's achievement skills to assess weaknesses in areas of reading, arithmetic, and written language.

Standardized tests used for this purpose include such instruments as: Woodcock-Johnson III Tests of Achievement, Wide Range Achievement Test, Test of Written Language-3, Woodcock Reading Mastery Test-Revised, Gray Oral Reading Tests, Fourth Edition, and others.

Teachers usually are disappointed with the findings of psychoeducational testing because they are needing a prescriptive rather than diagnostic approach to guide curriculum and classroom practice for the individual student. Test results provide a good description of the student's strengths and weaknesses, but may not provide the educator with helpful remedial approaches. For this reason, many educators prefer the approach of curriculum-based assessment. This is criterion-based rather than based on what is average for the population. The goal is simply to describe whether or not a person has mastered what they are expected to learn. In curriculum-based assessment, test items are drawn directly from the curriculum, and assessment is closely tied with teaching. This type of testing is more concerned with the level of achievement than diagnosis of the reasons for any impairment.

Assessment Procedures for Social and Emotional Development

Assessment procedures to evaluate social and emotional development include: structured approaches to diagnostic interviewing; use of standardized measures including inventories and rating scales that are completed by parents and teachers and self-report; observation of the child; and other forms of testing.

Projective tests are still often used, in spite of having fared poorly against empirical tests of reliability and validity. The aim of projective testing is to provide a child with an ambiguous stimulus and then to interpret their responses to indicate underlying problems. They purposely lack structure and they are difficult to make quantitative sense out of the enormous number of possible responses. Clear and explicit rules for scoring often do not exist and when they do they are often inaptly applied. Tests such as the Thematic Apperception Test and the Rorschach Inkblot Test are examples.

The structured interview is the most often used procedure for assessment of social and emotional functioning and development in children and adolescents. The collection of information through the interview in a coherent, structured fashion provides valuable facts to the clinician. Interviews are often held with multiple informants (caregivers, other family members, teachers, and the child in question). Structured diagnostic interview procedures are preferred over unstructured interview formats. Examples of structured interview protocols are: the Child Assessment Schedule (CAS); the Diagnostic Interview Schedule for Children and Adolescents (DICA); the Interview Schedule for Children and Adolescents (ISCA); and the Kiddie Schedule for Affective Disorders and Schizophrenia (K-SADS).

Observations of behavior play a central role in helping clinicians evaluate social and emotional development. With some very disturbed children, observation, more than any other assessment procedure, may contribute the most important material. Observations may begin in the waiting room, while the child is being interviewed, during administration of psychological tests, in the classroom, or in less structured social settings. This gives the observer the opportunity to assess the child or adolescent in a variety of settings each of which may require different sets of behavior. Among the dimensions of behavior to observe are the ability of the child or adolescent to separate from family members, physical appearance, motor behavior, form and content of speech, quality of social interaction, affective behavior, level of self-control, developmental level, etc.

Standardized inventories and rating scales with parent and teacher informants and self-report are useful tools in an assessment of social and emotional development of the child or adolescent. The Millon Adolescent Clinical Inventory (MACI) by Theodore Millon with Carrie Millon and Roger Davis was created to address the unique concerns, pressures, and situations facing adolescents. The MACI test was designed with a focused sample that included adolescents in various clinical treatment settings. Through a series of questions, the test helps assess an adolescent's personality along with self-reported concerns and clinical symptoms.

The Minnesota Multiphasic Personality Inventory-Adolescent (MMPI-A) was adapted from the original MMPI. The MMPI-A helps identify personal, social, and behavioral problems in adolescents. An empirically based measure of adolescent psychopathology, the MMPI-A test contains adolescent-specific scales and other unique features designed to make the instrument especially appropriate for today's youth.

Computerized Attention Testing

Computerized assessment of attention span had been used for more than forty years in laboratories performing research on hyperactive children. The first such computerized assessment device was the Continuous Performance Test (CPT) (Rosvold, et al., 1956). This test required the child to attend to a screen and selectively respond to a specific pair of flashing letters presented in sequential combination over a fixed period of time. Many years of research indicated that children with attentional disorders tended to do less well on such a task. However, the CPT was too bulky and expensive to use in clinical practice.

Michael Gordon was one of the first to develop a portable CPT called the Gordon Diagnostic System (GDS). The GDS is a computerized instrument that can easily be programmed to administer any of three tasks to a child. The Delay Task, for example, provides a measure of impulse control. During this task, the child sits before the GDS and is instructed that he can earn points by repeatedly pressing a button on the GDS console. However, in order to earn points the child must press the button, wait awhile, and press it again. The child is not told how long he should wait between button presses, but if he waits long enough, he will earn additional points which accumulate on a visual display for feedback. The Vigilance Task measures sustained attention. During this task, the child sits before the GDS and is instructed to look at the display whereon numbers flash on and off. The child is told to press the button on the console when he sees a specific number (or sequence of numbers) come up on the display. Sustained attention is measured by number of correct responses the child is able to make when the targeted numbers appear and by the number of errors he makes either by neglecting to respond when he should have (errors of omission) or by not suppressing a response (errors of commission). The Distractibility Task measures sustained attention when distracting stimuli are present.

The T.O.V.A., Tests of Variables of Attention, is another continuous performance test that can be used as part of a multi-modal assessment for ADHD. It is also being used to determine response to medication and monitor pharmacotherapy in ADHD children. This easily administered test, programmed for use with Windows compatible and Macintosh personal computers, was developed Dr. Lawrence Greenberg at the University of Minnesota.

The Continuous Performance Test Computer Program II (CPT II), developed by C. Keith Conners, is also popular among clinicians for assessment of ADHD and medication effects. Similar to the other CPTs, results can be accessed by computer immediately after administration.

The Integrated Visual and Auditory Continuous Performance Test (IVA) was developed by Joseph A. Sanford and Ann Turner. This CPT combines visual and auditory stimuli, and assesses impulsivity, inattention, and hyperactivity in individuals from age five through adulthood. The client is instructed to click the mouse only when he or she sees or hears a "1" and not to click when he or she sees or hears a "2". Administration and scoring are fully automated.

Continuous performance tests such as the Gordon Diagnostic System, T.O.V.A., Conners CPT II, and IVA are often used as part of a larger battery of procedures in the assessment of ADHD and in determining responses to medication. While they may provide information that is useful to the assessment process, the data obtained from such tests should always be used in conjunction with other information in determining whether a child has ADHD.

Quantitative EEG

Quantitative Electroencephalographic (QEEG) scanning was approved by the Food and Drug Administration in 2005 as a method of diagnosing ADHD. QEEG is a technique used to measure electrophysiological activity in particular regions of the brain. Several studies have found that individuals with ADHD could be reliably distinguished from non-ADHD individuals by QEEG scan results of the prefrontal cortical areas. Specifically, ADHD individuals have been found to have an increase in low-frequency theta waves and a decrease in high-frequency beta waves in the prefrontal cortex. These brain wave changes can be captured in a single variable, the theta-beta ratio. This ratio is used to determine the presence or absence of children and adults with ADHD. Approximately ninety percent of individuals who had been carefully diagnosed with ADHD using standard diagnostic procedures showed a pattern of under activity or cortical slowing in these areas. In contrast, ninety-four percent of a control population did not. These data provided good initial evidence that QEEG scanning might be a useful "objective" procedure to assist in the diagnosis of

ADHD (Rabiner, 2001).

Sensors are first placed on the surface of a person's scalp. Then, EEG activity is measured under different states and real-world tasks that a person frequently encounters: eyes closed, eyes open, reading, writing, listening, and doing arithmetic. In QEEG assessments, a person's brainwave activity is measured during performance of tasks in which the brain is most active, which helps identify problems associated with everyday functioning in school or work.

In addition to studying the use of QEEG with ADHD, other conditions have been studied including depression and learning disabilities. QEEG may help clarify the underlying nature of deficits in behavior, learning, and emotional functioning, and may thus add useful data for diagnostic decisions and intervention strategies.

Direct Observation of the Student

Direct observation of the child's activities within the classroom may provide objective information for documenting the degree to which the child with ADHD exhibits symptoms. Direct observational data can confirm teacher's reports via interview or rating scale methods about a student's functioning and can add more information about the ecology of the classroom itself and its effect upon the student.

The advantage of direct observation procedures is that they reduce bias in ratings of students as data are unaffected by teacher perceptions. One disadvantage of direct observation procedures is that they are typically the most costly of school-based assessment methods because they involve a great deal of time in training and data collection. A second disadvantage is the lack of standardization of data collected.

Traditionally, classroom observation is often done in a casual, anecdotal fashion. The following excerpt from an observation of a kindergarten child illustrates typical anecdotal observational data:

10:00 a.m.

Charles is at the math center. He is standing at his seat using a geoboard. The other children at the center are using pattern blocks to create designs and/or figures. He uses rubber bands on the geoboard. One rubber band flies across the room. A girl from his table goes to Ms. Walker and tells her Charles is "shooting rubber bands". Ms. Walker tells Charles he is not supposed to be using the rubber bands and geoboard; she instructs him to put it away; he does.

10:12 a.m.

Charles begins playing with blocks. He builds and "flicks" his bombs (Here comes a bomb!") till his blocks knock into a neighbor's. A child tells the teacher that Charles is knocking over their buildings/designs. Ms. Walker monitors. Charles says to the children again, "Want to make a bomb?"

10:14 a.m.

Charles builds a three dimensional structure; moves it towards his neighbor's; talks with his neighbor; reaches to the center of the table for additional blocks. He stands and talks.

10:15 a.m.

Ms. Walker turns out the lights; Charles stands. When instructed to clean up, Charles argues with two other children at the table who were designated as the "cleanup people". As these two children begin putting away the blocks on the table, Charles argues with them. He continues building. Ms. Walker tells Charles he needs to come to the group on the floor. He knocks down his building in anger.

10:17 a.m.

Charles goes to the group area, does not sit, bounces up and down, bending at the knees. The children are told to find their own personal space.

He goes inside the "barn" area (he is the only child in the "barn"). The children begin moving around the room to the music on a CD. Charles appears to dance to the music rather than move around the room as the other children are doing. He freezes when the music stops (as he should do).

10:19 a.m.

When other children come to the "barn" area Charles leaves and moves very freely across the room. He continues to freeze when appropriate (and the observation continues).

Systematic behavioral observation techniques have become more popular. School psychologists have probably received more training in this procedure than other groups. Systematic direct observations can focus on the specific characteristics of ADHD (inattention, impulsivity, hyperactivity) that are manifested in the classroom during performance of independent seat work or during times when direct instruction is presented by the teacher. When using such a procedure, behavioral manifestations of ADHD in the classroom are typically coded as: off-task (e.g., not attending to work or instruction); fidgeting (e.g. repetitive, purposeless, task-irrelevant behavior); out of seat (e.g., gets up from chair without permission); vocalizes (e.g. talks without permission, makes noises); plays with objects (e.g., manipulating objects in a way which is not directly associated with assigned work).

The ADHD School Observation Code (ADHD-SOC) by Kenneth D. Gadow, Joyce Sprafkin, and Edith E. Nolan was developed to collect observational data. In more than a dozen studies using the ADHD-SOC, it has been shown that with a modest amount of training, it is possible to achieve a high degree of inter-rater reliability. The ADHD-SOC categories show a reasonably high degree of correspondence with actual psychiatric diagnoses (predictive validity), easily differentiates clinical and non-clinical populations (discriminant validity), correlates well with commonly used behavior rating scales (concurrent validity), and are sensitive for evaluating response to therapeutic interventions.

Trial Interventions

It is recommended that a program of trial interventions be planned and implemented for the child with ADHD in the regular classroom setting. Such interventions may result in improved academic performance and socialization. Trial interventions should be carefully documented, giving information about the objectives of the interventions, the strategies that will be utilized, the methods of implementation, and the process by which results will be evaluated to determine outcomes.

The outcome of such trial interventions could provide additional information as to the child's need for services. While successful outcomes from trial interventions should not rule out the child possibly being considered for special education services, an unsuccessful outcome could be a strong indication that the child's impairment may be significant enough to warrant consideration for special education services.

Evaluating the Severity of Impact on Academic Performance

In addition to determining if a child has ADHD, the assessment team must determine the degree to which the child is impaired as a result of this or any other disorder.

A recent article (Gordon, Antshel, Faraone, Barkley, Lewandowski, Hudziak, Biederman, & Cunningham, 2005) in *The ADHD Report* discusses the importance of determining the level of impairment caused by symptoms of ADHD. The authors contend that one cannot assume that symptoms of ADHD necessarily lead to impairment. In fact, they contend that someone can display the full range of ADHD symptoms without necessarily displaying significant impair-

ment.

They also point out that there is a lack of developmentally sensitive, standardized techniques for measuring impairment. There are few rating scales designed to assess childhood impairment, and those that do exist are rarely used. The Competence Scales of the Child Behavior Checklist and The Social Adjustment Inventory for Children and Adolescents (SAICA; John, Gammon, Prusoff, & Warner, 1987) are described in the article as impairment measures.

The Competence Scales of the Child Behavior Checklist contains three measures of adaptive functioning as rated by parents: 1) the Activities scale, which measures the amount and quality of the child's participation in sports, nonsport hobbies, leisure activities, games, jobs, and chores; 2) the Social scale, which measures membership and participation in organizations, number of friends and contacts with them, and behaviors with parents, siblings, and peers; and 3) the School scale, which measures the child's average performance in academic subjects, types of school placement, promotion status, and presence or absence of problems in school.

The Social Adjustment Inventory for Children and Adolescents is a semi-structured interview administered to the child or parent that measures social functioning in children ages six to eighteen years old. Areas measured include activities, peer relations, family relations, and academic performance.

The Academic Performance Rating Scale (APRS), developed by George J. DuPaul, Mark D. Rapport, and Lucy M. Perriello can also provide information about the quality of a student's academic performance in the classroom. The APRS provides important data as to the student's academic productivity in terms of amount of work completed and accuracy of work done. The following scores can be tabulated: Total Score, Learning Ability, Impulse Control, Academic Performance, and Social Withdrawal (Barkley, 1991). The APRS can be found in *Attention Defi-*

cit Hyperactivity Disorder: A Clinical Workbook (Second Edition) by Russell A. Barkley and Kevin Murphy.

Gordon and his esteemed colleagues point out that it is essential that evaluators identify children who are impaired enough to require the services of their school and of mental health providers. In systems of care that are already underfunded and overcrowded it becomes increasingly important to provide such services to those who have the greatest need.

After the Assessment

Ideally, assessment data should lead to a thorough understanding of the individual's strengths and areas of need. If a diagnosis of ADHD and/or other disorders is made, treatment planning should include all areas where interventions are recommended. The physician may discuss appropriate medical interventions. The psychologist or other mental health professionals may discuss counseling, behavior modification, or social and study skills training options. The school may set up classroom interventions to accommodate the adolescent's areas of need in school or may provide special education or related services. Some or all members of the assessment team may become part of the treatment team, which is responsible for managing the treatment of the individual. Once treatment is instituted, it is important to maintain periodic follow-up and monitoring.

As you will discover in the next chapter on treatment of ADHD, close follow-up and adjustment of medical and psychosocial interventions is quite important to obtain success for children with ADHD.

Summary

ADHD can be reliably assessed in children and adolescents and could be distinguished from other disorders that may produce symptoms of inattention, hyperactivity, and impulsivity. The American Academy of Pediatrics published guidelines for ADHD assessment and recommended that primary care physicians should initiate such an assessment when symptoms of ADHD were noted. Furthermore, assessment should follow the DSM-IV criteria, data should be gathered from the school and family of the child, and other co-existng conditions should be considered.

The assessment of ADHD may be clinic- or school-based and professionals involved may include physicians, psychologists, social workers, speech and language pathologists, occupational and physical therapists, and others. Multiple procedures involving the use of behavior rating scales, interviews, direct observation of the child, and psychoeducational assessment may be used. Quantitative electroencephalography (QEEG) was recently approved by the FDA as a method of diagnosing ADHD. Measures of severity of impairment in academic performance and socialization are important. Treatment for ADHD should follow comprehensive assessment and such treatment should be closely monitored and adjusted to the needs of the child.

Chapter 6
An Overview of Treatments for ADHD

A great deal is known about treating child-hood ADHD and the research literature on adult treatment is growing. There have been numerous studies to investigate the efficacy and safety of a number of different treatments. Three treatments have been proven to be the most effective for ADHD: behavior modification, medication, and the combination of the two. These treatments have been demonstrated to have short-term effects. No treatment has been shown to influence outcomes in children and adolescents with ADHD over the long term.

The NIMH Collaborative Multisite Multimodal Treatment of Children with ADHD (MTA)

There have been many treatment studies of children with ADHD. However, by far, the most comprehensive one was the MTA study. Initial results of this study were published in 1999. In this study, 579 children ages seven to nine years, nine months with ADHD, combined type were randomly assigned to one of four treatment groups.

One group, intended to serve as a control or contrast group for the other interventions, was the community care (CC) group. Subjects in this group were given the same evaluations as the treatment groups, but were not given the specific treatment procedures. They were referred to their communities and given a list of community mental health resources. About two-thirds of these subjects received some type of psychiatric medication during the study period.

A second group, the medication alone group (MED), received medication to treat ADHD symptoms. The titration process was quite a bit more detailed and rigorous in evaluating each group member's response to the medication and adjusting their doses than is typical in clinical practice. Children in this group were initially tested in a double-blind protocol for a twenty-eight-day period on methylphenidate and five drug conditions (placebo, 5, 10, 15, and 20 mg), randomly ordered across subjects. Medication doses were administered at breakfast and lunch with a half dose in the afternoon. Investigators reviewed graphs of the subject's response to these different doses and selected an optimal dose for each child, which then became their initial maintenance dose in the study. If the child did not have a satisfactory response to methylphenidate, they were tested on one of several other medications in the following order: dextroamphetamine, pemoline, imipramine, and, if needed, an alternative medication approved by a panel. All the children in the medication alone group were seen monthly for monitoring dosage/medication adjustments.

A third group received psychosocial treatments (BEH). The types of behavioral treatments they were given were based on those previously found to be effective with children who have ADHD. This included group parent training classes in child management (twenty-seven sessions) along with individual parent training classes (eight sessions); child-focused counseling, including an intensive all day summer treatment program based on William Pelham's approach; and school-based intervention. The school-based interventions were comprised of ten to sixteen bi-weekly teacher training and consultation sessions, twelve weeks of a classroom aide for the fall semester of school, and a daily school report card linked to home consequences throughout the academic year. During the eight week summer training program, the treatment group was given training in social skills, group problem solving, and sports skills. Point systems, time out, social reinforcement, and modeling were also used. These behavioral treatments were gradually reduced in intensity and frequency over the fourteen months of the treatment that all groups received.

The fourth treatment group (COMB) received a combination of the BEH and MED treatment procedures.

Outcome Measures

MTA study investigators used the following outcome measures to determine treatment efficacy:

1. ADHD symptoms
2. oppositional and aggressive behavior
3. social skills
4. anxiety and depression symptoms
5. parent-child relations
6. academic achievement

Findings

Initial findings from the MTA study were published in 1999 in the *Archives of General Psychiatry*, however, many papers have been written since then analyzing the data gathered from this study. Much of this analysis is beyond the scope of this book.

The primary conclusion of the study was that medication management was superior to behavioral treatment and that the combined (medication plus behavioral treatment) was slightly better than medication alone. The group that received both medication and behavior treatment received a modest advantage over the medication alone group in terms of improvement of non-ADHD symptoms. In addition, parents expressed greater satisfaction with the combination treatment than with the medication treatment alone.

The MTA study was a landmark study in that it provided strong evidence as to the efficacy of certain ADHD treatments (medication in combination with behavioral strategies) and it underscored the importance of frequent and careful monitoring by healthcare providers to ensure that treatment goals were reached.

American Academy of Pediatrics Guidelines for Treatment of ADHD

In 2001, the American Academy of Pediatrics (AAP) published clinical practice guidelines for the treatment of school-aged children with ADHD. The AAP recommended the following:

1. primary care clinicians should establish a treatment program that recognizes ADHD as a chronic condition;
2. appropriate target outcomes designed in collaboration with the clinician, parents, child, and school personnel should guide management;

3. stimulant medication and/or behavior therapy as appropriate should be used in the treatment;

4. if a child has not met the targeted outcomes, clinicians should evaluate the original diagnosis, use all appropriate treatments, and consider co-existing conditions; and

5. periodic, systematic follow-up for the child should be done with monitoring directed to target outcomes and adverse effects. Information for monitoring should be gathered from parents, teachers, and the child.

Behavioral Treatments

Behavioral treatments have been used for more than three decades to treat children who exhibit disruptive or aggressive behavior. An early paper published in 1967 by Daniel O'Leary and Wesley Becker described the successful use of a classroom token reinforcement system to manage disruptive classroom behavior. The system involved reviewing a list of classroom rules twice each day, praising appropriate behavior and ignoring disruptive behavior, as well as feedback to the children about how well they did academically and socially. In addition, the children received reinforcers in the form of prizes such as special pencils, rulers, and candy. The combination of these factors led to a significant decrease in disruptive behavior by the students.

Behavioral treatments have been successfully applied to children with ADHD to manage disruptive behavior, inattention, social skills building, improve academic performance, etc.

William Pelham, an expert in behavioral treatments for children with ADHD, describes five categories of behavioral treatment:

- cognitive-behavioral interventions
- clinical behavior therapy/parent training programs
- direct contingency management
- intensive, packaged behavioral treatments
- combined behavioral and pharmacological treatments

Each of these behavioral treatments will be briefly described below.

Cognitive-Behavioral Interventions (CBI)

The goal of this form of behavioral treatment is to teach self-control through verbal self-instructions, problem-solving strategies, cognitive modeling, self-monitoring, self-evaluation, self-reinforcement, and other strategies. Typically, a therapist meets with a client once or twice a week in an attempt to teach the client through modeling, role playing and practicing cognitive strategies, the person can use to control his or her inattention and impulsive behavior. As a simple example, a child may be taught to say "stop" to himself when he is about to call out in class. Children with ADHD seem to lack these internal cues and so it was thought that teaching them such cues would be helpful. While CBI was popular in the 1980's and early 1990's for treatment of ADHD, its popularity has waned in the absence of strong research to support its efficacy.

Clinical Behavior Therapy (CBT)/Parent Training Programs

The goal of this form of behavioral treatment is typically to train parents, teachers, or other caregivers to implement contingency management programs with children. Parents generally attend parent training programs where they are given assigned readings and instruction in standard behavioral techniques. Therapists using CBT often work with teachers in a consultation model to teach behavioral strategies for application in the classroom. The use of a daily report card system wherein the child receives tokens or points for certain target behaviors in the classroom is a popular example of an effective CBT program for children with ADHD.

Psychologists have been at the forefront in developing programs to train parents in the use of behavioral strategies to manage noncompliance. Traditional parent training programs have common features in that they teach parents skills related to attending, rewarding, ignoring, instructing, and using time-out. The programs make use of home practice assignments and exercises and use direct instruction and modeling as primary teaching methods. One of the best known of these traditional parent training programs is Russell Barkley's *Defiant Children*, which is suitable for children up to the age of twelve. In addition to the skills noted above, Barkley has incorporated a number of additional components to teach parents, including information specific to ADHD, a token reinforcement system, and a daily report card system for school problems.

Another well-known and widely used program for children between two and twelve years of age is Tom Phelan's *1-2-3 Magic*. This program focuses on the use of time-out as a consequence for noncompliance and teaches parents the appropriate ways to administer time-out and correct misbehavior.

Ross Greene has developed a program for difficult children who display noncompliance accompanied by angry and explosive behavior. Greene calls his approach Collaborative Problem Solving (CPS), and he describes it in detail in his best-selling book, *The Explosive Child*.

In their book, *Try and Make Me*, Ray Levy and Bill O'Hanlon teach parents to use an approach they call "Practice Academy" to manage non-compliant behavior. This approach incorporates the behavioral strategy referred to as "overcorrection" in an effort to teach the non-compliant child appropriate behavior. The Practice Academy approach contains four simple steps for parents to apply to correct misbehavior.

Contingency Management (CM)

Contingency management is a behavioral treatment that involves a more intensive program of behavior modification. Typically this type of program is implemented in a specialized treatment facility or specialized classroom. The techniques used in such programs include token economies set up to encourage specific behavior through the use of rewards and consequences earned by the child, time out, response cost and precise teacher responses to behavior through attention, reprimands and gain or loss of privileges.

Intensive Behavioral Treatments

The focus of intensive behavioral treatments is to combine clinical behavior therapy and contingency management into an intensive program to improve self-control and socialization. Children who attend the Children's Summer Treatment Program designed by William Pelham (1997), for example, attend an eight-week program for nine hours a day. Children have a "summer camp" experience and are placed in groups of twelve. Each group spends two hours daily in classrooms where behavioral interventions and other types of instruction are provided. The rest of the day consists of recreationally based group activities. The children's progress is tracked and rewarded at home by parents who attend classes to learn how to apply behavior management at home.

Combined Pharmacological and Behavioral Interventions

This form of treatment focuses on the combined use of medication and behavioral treatment. This combination has been shown to be quite effective in treating children with ADHD and has several advantages over medication alone or behavioral treatment alone. With the addition of medication, the behavioral component of treatment may be able to be scaled down, thereby reducing the amount of time parents and teachers need to spend on shaping behavior. The dose of medication can be reduced for children using a combined approach. Parents knowledgeable about the use of behavioral treatments can apply such treatments during times when the child is not taking medication (i.e., in the evenings for those on stimulant medication).

Medication Treatments for ADHD

The rate of medication treatment for elementary school students has increased from 1.07 percent in 1971 to nearly six percent in 1987; for middle school students, it increased from .59 percent in 1975 to nearly three percent in 1998; and for high school students it increased from .22 percent in 1983 to .70 percent in 1993 (Jensen and Cooper, 2002). A brief description of medication treatments for ADHD follows. See chapter eleven for more details.

Stimulant medications are the most often prescribed. They are the best studied medicines for ADHD. There are basically two classes of stimulants: methylphenidate and amphetamine products. With more than 200 controlled double-blind studies of stimulant use in children with ADHD, the findings are well documented that these medicines improve attention span, self-control, behavior, fine motor control, and social functioning. Stimulant preparations can be quick-acting (within thirty minutes) and short lasting (four to six hours) or longer lasting (eight to twelve hours). Preparations, such as Concerta, Adderall XR, Metadate CD, and Ritalin LA, promise once-a-day dosing lasting from eight to twelve hours depending on the brand used.

Atomoxetine, brand name, Strattera, a non-stimulant, was approved in November, 2002 and became available in the United States in early 2003 for children and adults with ADHD. It is a selective norepinephrine reuptake inhibitor. While the stimulants primarily affect the dopaminergic system, atomoxetine has its primary effect on the noradrenergic system. It has been shown to improve core symptoms of ADHD, namely, inattention, impulsivity, and hyperactivity. It has some weak antidepressant properties as well and may help improve and regulate mood. While stimulants start working within a half hour to an hour after ingestion, atomoxetine has a more gradual onset and the maximal effect may not be seen for several weeks.

Certain anti-hypertensive medications known as adrenergic agonists (Clonidine and Tenex) are used in combination with other medications to help very hyperactive and impulsive children.

Medication should never be given without an established system to monitor its effectiveness. The doctor prescribing the medication should obtain information from parents and teachers concerning their observation of any changes in behavior, attentiveness, mood or physical complaints the adolescent may have while taking medication. Typically, teachers are a good source of information about medication effects. Teachers may report information about the student's reactions to medication informally to the physician or they may complete similar forms as the parents for more systematic data collection. Use of behavior rating scales such as these can be extremely helpful in determining changes in behavior. The ADHD Monitoring System is a convenient program that parents can use to carefully monitor how their child is doing at school. By using this program, parents will be able to carefully track their child's progress in school and will be alerted to when any adjustments or modifications to their child's treatment need to be discussed with their physician. This and other rating scales to monitor performance are available on myADHD.com. They can be electronically sent for completion and review.

Educational Interventions— Programs and Accommodations

Educators understand the importance of providing assistance to students with ADHD. Under existing federal laws (IDEA 2004, ADA, Rehabilitation Act of 1973 [Section 504]), public schools are required to provide special education and related services to students with ADHD who need such assistance (Davila et al., 1991). Schools must meet the needs of those with ADHD who require accommodations in regular education classes. Such accommodations may "even the playing field" for those disabled by ADHD who must compete with other students in school.

Section 504 of the Rehabilitation Act of 1973 guarantees that no person "shall, solely by reason of her or his disability, be excluded from the participation in, be denied the benefits of, or be subjected to discrimination under any program or activity receiving Federal financial assistance."

To qualify for Section 504 services, there must be evidence of the existence of an identified physical or mental impairment that substantially limits a major life activity. Having a diagnosis of ADHD alone is not enough to qualify for accommodations under Section 504 unless the person's ADHD significantly impacts on learning or behavior.

Under Section 504, the definition of a disability is much broader than it is under the Individuals with Disabilities in Education Act (IDEA). While all IDEA students are covered by Section 504, not all Section 504 students would qualify for protection under IDEA. Under IDEA, the qualifying student will receive an Individual Education Plan (IEP) tailored to the child's unique needs. The child may receive special education and/or related services at public expense in accordance with the IEP. Later chapters will describe educational interventions for students with ADHD more thoroughly.

Unproven Treatments for ADHD

With the increased interest paid to ADHD in the past decade, there has also been an increase in claims made by vendors of products or services that purport to effectively treat symptoms of the disorder. Consumers need to know how to evaluate these claims so they can determine the efficacy of such treatments. ADHD experts (Ingersoll and Goldstein, 1993) warn consumers about controversial and unproven treatments. Typically they advise consumers to be wary of any company boasting "miracle" cures that work for everyone with ADHD, claims based on the results of just one study, or studies that lack a control group, claims that the product is a harmless, "natural" remedy with few or no adverse effects, and product ads that attack established, mainstream medical treatments.

ADHD experts often list the following treatments as either unproven, disproven, or controversial: dietary interventions, nutritional supplements, sensory integration training, anti-motion sickness medication, optometric visual training, applied kinesiology, treatment for lead toxicity, thyroid dysfunction, and candidas yeast therapy. Claims as to the effectiveness of EEG biofeedback training or interactive metronome training for ADHD have not yet lived up to the rigor of scientific investigation to be regarded as effective treatments. More information about unproven treatments can be found in chapter sixteen.

Summary

Over the past four decades the treatment of ADHD in children has been well studied. Only three treatments have been proven to be effective: behavior modification, medication, and the combination of the two. These treatments have been demonstrated to have short-term effects with improvements noted in core symptoms of inattention, hyperactivity, and impulsivity along with improvement in social functioning.

Results of the MTA study have been published over the past few years and have confirmed the importance of treating children with ADHD with a combination of procedures. Carefully administered and closely monitored medication treatment, parent training in child management, and school-based behavioral interventions can be combined to essentially "normalize" functioning in many children with ADHD.

The AAP published treatment guidelines that should be followed by physicians. The AAP emphasized a multimodal approach to treatment with careful monitoring of outcomes. Unproven treatments for ADHD abound and consumers should be cautious about using treatments that have not been rigorously tested.

Chapter 7
MyADHD.com
An Internet-based System to Facilitate Assessment and Treatment of ADHD

In the past forty years, the treatment of children and adolescents with ADHD has progressed substantially. In previous chapters, I reviewed assessment practices that lead to more accurate diagnosis and treatment options that can manage ADHD symptoms and improve functioning.

I have emphasized that, before a treatment is started, a comprehensive assessment of the child or adolescent must be performed. Parents and educators are usually asked to provide vital information for this assessment by being interviewed and by completing rating scales, checklists, history forms, etc. Once started, treatments should be closely monitored to improve outcomes. Without systematic monitoring, treatments can often be inadequate or inappropriate.

The AAP, NASP and other organizations have recommended that clinicians follow specific assessment and treatment guidelines when caring for children with ADHD. The AAP and National Initiative for Children's Healthcare Quality (NICHQ) published the ADHD Tool Kit which provides very useful forms to assess and treat affected children. They recognized the importance of comprehensive assessment and careful monitoring to ensure that children with

ADHD will achieve the maximal benefit from treatment.

In 2004, Michelle Frisch, Simon Frisch, Roberta Parker, Julia Parker, and I launched an Internet site (myADHD.com) to improve the way assessment and treatment for ADHD is performed. This site contains tools to make it easier for stakeholders—healthcare professionals, parents, educators, and adults with ADHD to provide information to one another. This is done through the use of myADHD.com assessment, treatment, tracking, and library tools. What follows is a brief description of this very comprehensive site. I would encourage you to visit the site and experience using it.

Assessment Tools

The assessment tools section of the site contains history forms, rating scales and checklists for adults with ADHD and parents and teachers of children with ADHD to complete. These instruments can be used in three ways: viewed on screen and printed; downloaded as a PDF document, printed, and completed; or transmitted to others electronically using myADHD.com's unique Subscriber Administration tool. The forms listed below are used by clinicians to evaluate the presence of ADHD symptoms and to determine whether the child or adult being assessed exhibits signs of other disorders.

SNAP IV Teacher and Parent Rating Scale

This is an eighteen-item norm-referenced checklist that is designed to determine if symptoms of ADHD are present. This checklist can be completed by either a parent or other caregiver or an educator for use by a healthcare provider in performing an assessment.

ADHD Symptom Checklist

This is a twenty-one-item checklist that is designed to determine if symptoms of ADHD are present—in what settings such symptoms appear, when symptoms began, and whether the child is impaired as a result of having such symptoms. This checklist can be completed by either a parent or other caregiver or an educator for use by a healthcare provider in performing an assessment.

ADHD Symptom Checklist (Adult Version—Self Report)

This is a twenty-one-item checklist that is designed to determine if symptoms of ADHD are present—in what settings such symptoms appear, when symptoms began, and whether the adult is impaired as a result of having such symptoms. This is the self-report form to be completed by the adult suspected of having ADHD.

ADHD Symptom Checklist (Adult Version—Observer Report)

This is a twenty-one-item checklist that is designed to determine if symptoms of ADHD are present—in what settings such symptoms appear, when symptoms began, and whether the adult is impaired as a result of having such symptoms. This is the observer form to be completed by an observer.

Childhood Disorders Checklist

This is a listing of disorders described in the Diagnostic and Statistical Manual of Mental Disorders: Fourth Edition (DSM-IV-TR). This checklist can be completed by a parent or other caregiver for use by a healthcare provider in performing an assessment.

Child and Adolescent Developmental History Form

This form asks about the child or adolescent's history and includes questions about family composition, current concerns, developmental and medical information, family information, school information, child management techniques used in the home, and the child's strengths and accomplishments. This form can be completed by a parent or other caregiver for use by a healthcare provider in performing an assessment.

Adult Psychosocial History Form

This form asks adults to provide information about early child and adolescent history, past and present employment history, schooling, and history of any social, emotional, or behavioral problems. The form also contains scales for measuring ADHD symptoms and symptoms of anxiety and mood disorders. This form can be completed by an adult who suspects they may have ADHD.

Novotni Social Skills Checklist

This checklist was designed by Michele Novotni, Ph.D. to evaluate social traits and social skills of adolescents and adults. The social skills that are evaluated include: basic manners, verbal communication skills, nonverbal communication skills, communication road blocks, organizational skills-trustworthiness, self-control, knowledge of social interaction, relationship skills and self-care. This form can be completed by an adolescent or adult or by an observer.

Tracking Tools

Tracking tools are brief forms, checklists, and rating scales designed to monitor the progress of children or adults who are receiving interventions and treatment. Healthcare professionals may request that educators and parents regularly complete one of these scales to evaluate the child's progress in school and at home. Healthcare professionals may request that adults with ADHD, or persons whom they know, regularly complete one of these scales to evaluate progress in various settings such as school, work, family, or social activities. Treatments and interventions can then be adjusted to achieve maximal improvement. These instruments can be used in three ways: viewed on screen and printed; downloaded as a PDF document, printed, and completed; or transmitted electronically for completion online using myADHD.com's Subscriber Administration tool

A number of the scales in the assessment tools section of the site are also available as tracking tools. In addition, the ADHD Monitoring System is available as a tracking tool.

The ADHD Monitoring System

This twenty-one-item instrument was designed by David Rabiner, Ph.D. to carefully track a student's progress in school so that parents and health care professionals will be alerted as to when any adjustments or modifications to treatment need to be made. Items on the scale not only evaluate the presence and severity of core ADHD symptoms, but also evaluate the quality of classwork and homework the student is doing and compares performance at different points during the day.

Treatment Tools

Treatment tools are very brief programs designed to teach or reinforce specific skills to improve behavior, socialization, study skills, and academic performance in children and adolescents. There are also a variety of treatment tools for adults. These focus on job or career-related issues, organization, planning, social behavior, etc.

Parents can use these tools at home and teachers can use them at school. Treatment tools to improve behavior at home and at school include a variety of daily report card systems, home and school token economy programs, self-monitoring work sheets, cognitive behavioral work sheets, and guides for family communication and problem-solving. Treatment Tools to provide tips on organization of study areas, bedrooms, school supplies, and time management are included. There are a variety of organization tools for different age levels, youngsters and adults. Study skills treatment tools provide help with note-taking, reading comprehension, preparation of research reports, book reports, etc.

A partial list of treatment tools for children and adolescents is listed below:

3001	Daily Report Card—Primary Version
7006	Using Abbreviation in Notes
3002	Daily Report Card—Elementary Version
7007	Improving Reading Comprehension
3003	Daily Report Card—Middle School Version
7008	Comprehension Exercise
3004	Home Token Economy
7009	Using Paraphrasing
3005	Behavior Contract
7010	Paraphrasing Exercises
3006	Homework Contract
7011	Taking Notes in Simple Outlines
3007	How Did You Do in School Today Checklist
7012	Notes Using Mind Mapping
3009	Practice Raising Your Hand Before Speaking
6004	School Supplies Checklist
2010	Weekly Progress Report
6006	Organizing Your Study Area

2020   Homework Self-Check
6009   Evaluating Your Time
2021   Using a Homework Planner
6011   Using a To Do List
2023   Monthly Planner
6013   Keeping Track of Grades
2024   Start a Study Buddy Club
6015   Organizing Long Term Projects
2026   The Learning Station™
7005   Using a Weekly Planner
2028   My Perfect Study Area
7002   Steps to Problem Solving
2031   Following Directions
7001   Overcoming Roadblocks to Family
       Communication

A partial list of treatment tools for adults is listed below:

9001   Problem Solving Activity Sheet
9002   Matching Your Interests and Your Career
       Choice 1
9003   Matching Your Interests and Your Career
       Choice 2
9004   Matching Your Interests and Your Career
       Choice 3
9004   Identify You Work Skills
9006   Preparing Your Job Resume
9007   Types of Resumes
9008   Preparing a Cover Letter
9009   Pros and Cons of Medication
9010   Keeping Track of Medication
       Side-Effects
1101   Using a To-Do List
1102   Housecleaning Tips
1103   Travel Checklist
1104   Time Management Tips
1105   Organizing Your Workplace
1106   Computer Scheduling Programs

Library Tools

These are resources designed to provide more information for parents, educators, health professionals, and adults. Articles, links to other sites to get additional information, and resources are part of the library tools offered.

Visitors can register to receive a bi-weekly newsletter, *myADHD.com News*. Each edition of the newsletter contains sample assessment or treatment tools, research updates, and current articles written by ADHD experts.

Stay Connected to Be Effective

As the MTA study results indicated, to reach maximum improvement, children treated for ADHD must be followed closely by their healthcare provider. Inadequate monitoring of the effects of medication can result in under-treatment and insufficient progress. To track effectively, parents and teachers must communicate with doctors who can determine if target symptoms are responding to the treatments provided. If not, treatments may need to be modified and/or the treating professional may need to consider other factors that can be causing or exacerbating symptoms. MyADHD.com endeavors to make tools easily available to all of the stakeholders in this process. Tools can be printed, saved, faxed, or e-mailed.

Summary

Effective treatment of ADHD in children, adolescents, or adults will require a combination of procedures that can be accessed through myADHD.com. This site was developed to provide opportunities for stakeholders such as healthcare professionals, families, adults with ADHD, and educators to exchange information electronically to optimize assessment and treatment. The collection of tools on the site provides forms for assessment, tracking, treatment of ADHD as well as library tools to provide information on current research findings.

Visitors to the site can subscribe to a newsletter and receive bi-weekly updates on research findings and other interesting articles.

Chapter 8
The School's Role in Providing Services for Students with ADHD

Prior to the 1990's, few people seemed to have the answers to help students with ADHD in a school setting. Daily reports of poor school performance created heartache and misery for children with ADHD and their parents, who faced each new school day with the discouraging thought that it would offer no more hope than the day before. Unfortunately, most teachers were not sure how to help these inattentive, hyperactive children who needed supervision to stay on task and to complete work. Back then, many teachers had little or no training in their undergraduate education programs about ADHD and probably had received only minimal ADHD-related in-service training during their teaching careers. Books about ADHD were not readily available before 1990, and those that were had been written more for healthcare professionals and parents than for teachers. With an average of one to two children with ADHD in every classroom and with teachers unaware of how to reach them, children with ADHD were in trouble and their parents and teachers knew it.

One of the reasons so few educators knew about ADHD was because, for many years, ADHD had not been considered a handicapping condition in our nation's public schools. There was little if no mention of ADHD or its cardinal symptoms of inattention, impulsivity, and hyperactivity in the Education of the Handicapped Act (EHA; PL 94-142) or in its reauthorized form, the Individuals with Disabilities Education Act (IDEA; PL 101-476). Before 1991, ADHD was not considered, in and of itself, a disabling condition, despite the fact that many children with ADHD experienced substantial problems in school.

Concern and desperation drove parents of children with ADHD to meet and organize support groups. The support group movement had unprecedented growth in the late 1980's and 1990's. With a strong conviction to find help for their children and to secure a place for them in our country's educational system, parents and professionals worked tirelessly together to develop support groups and to spread information about ADHD in their communities, around the country, and throughout the world. Starting in 1989, parents began to tell members of the United States Congress their stories of heartache and discouragement in trying to obtain educational help for their children with ADHD. Their timing was right because the Individuals with Disabilities in Education Act (IDEA) had to come before the legislature for reauthorization.

While considering the reauthorization of this act, the United States Senate became aware that children with ADHD were not receiving a free appropriate public education as the law required. Attempting to remedy this situation, the Senate Committee on Labor and Human Resources passed a bill in November 1989 which added ADHD to the act under the definition of specific learning disability (SLD). While categorizing children with ADHD within the definition of learning disabled looked like a workable solution to members of the Senate, ADHD experts knew that this step would not only be technically inaccurate, but would not help the majority of children with ADHD who do not have learning disabilities. The Senate's remedy would have been a solution in name only, with little practical benefit to most children with ADHD who needed special help. Trying to apply an SLD definition to children with ADHD would not work. In the Spring of 1990, the United States House of Representatives' Committee on Education and Labor was also considering their reauthorization bill. Parents Sandra F. Thomas and Mary C. Fowler and ADHD expert, Dr. James Swanson, prepared testimony which was heard by the Subcommittee on Select Education. Their testimony led the Subcommittee to recognize, as the Senate did, that children with ADHD were being denied a free appropriate public education. They were also made aware of the fact that ADHD and SLD were different disorders. The drawbacks of the Senate bill, which was passed six months earlier, became evident. Taking this testimony into consideration, the House passed a bill which would have included ADHD in the act as a handicapping condition under the existing category of Other Health Impairments (OHI). By doing so, children with ADHD would have a better chance of receiving help if needed.

As soon as the House bill was passed in May 1990, opposition to the ADHD language in the bill was heard from a number of advocacy groups. These groups opposed the inclusion of ADHD as a special education disability. They created enough uncertainty about the issue to cause a joint House and Senate conference committee to meet to discuss the issue further and arrive at a consensus as to what should be done. To resolve the controversy, the conference committee decided to ask the Department of Education to issue a public Notice of Inquiry that would provide Congress with the widest possible range of advice on the issue.

Policy Memorandum Clarifies That ADHD Can Fall Under OHI Category

Nearly 3,000 responses to the Notice of Inquiry were submitted to the Department of Education by parents and professionals. In May 1991, the Office of Special Education and Rehabilitative Services (OSERS) provided a summary of these responses to Congress. Overall, the Department found that there was a great deal of confusion as to how children with ADHD were being understood and taught in schools. With the Notice of Inquiry responses in mind, the Department of Education sought to clarify to state departments of education whether children with ADHD could be eligible for special education services.

OSERS announced that, "Children with ADHD may be considered disabled solely on the basis of this disorder within the Other Health Impaired category in situations where special education and related services are needed because of ADHD." (OSERS News Update, March-April 1991, p. 2). On September 16, 1991 the Department of Education more fully explained its policy on ADHD in a memorandum to chief state school officers. This memorandum was signed by the Assistant Secretaries of OSERS, the Office for Civil Rights, and the Office of Elementary and

Secondary Education. The memorandum was far reaching in its content and emphasized state and local education agencies' responsibility to address the needs of children with ADHD both within general and special education.

With respect to special education, the memorandum indicated that children with ADHD may be considered disabled solely on the basis of this disorder within the OHI category. This category includes chronic or acute impairments that result in limited alertness, which adversely affects educational performance.

The policy memorandum stated that children with ADHD are also eligible for services under Part B (IDEA) if the children satisfy the criteria applicable to other disability categories. For example, children with ADHD are also eligible for services under the "specific learning disability" category or Part B if they meet criteria and under the "seriously emotionally disturbed" category of Part B if they meet criteria for that category.

Furthermore, it was made clear that state and local education agencies are obligated to evaluate the possible need for special education services for children with a prior medical diagnosis of ADHD and for those children who are suspected of having ADHD.

Not all students with ADHD will qualify for special education and related services under IDEA. It must be determined that the disability significantly impairs the child's educational performance and results in a need for special education and related services. The impact on educational performance is not limited to academics alone, but can include impairments in other areas of school functioning such as impairments in socialization, emotional functioning, or behavior can be reason to need special education or related services as can deficits in study skills and work production that affects learning. Failing grades and low test scores are not a prerequisite for special education and related services.

The final regulations of IDEA 1997 were published in 1999. ADHD was specifically named on the list of chronic health problems. This eliminated any ambiguity that school districts may have had about serving students with ADHD under IDEA. IDEA has been amended several times, most recently in 2004.

Policy Memorandum Emphasizes Regular Classroom Accommodations

The 1991 policy memorandum pointed out that state and local education agencies should offer protections to ADHD students even if such students were found not to be eligible for services under Part B of IDEA. The Department encouraged such education agencies to take necessary steps to make accommodations within the classroom to meet the needs of students with ADHD in the regular education setting and emphasized that education agencies must consider the provisions of Section 504 of the Rehabilitation Act of 1973 in doing so.

Section 504 is a federal law that requires public school districts to provide a free appropriate public education to every "qualified handicapped person" residing within their jurisdiction. The Office of Civil Rights (OCR) is the federal agency within the Department of Education that enforces Section 504. OCR has ruled that Children with ADHD are "qualified handicapped persons" under Section 504 if their ability to learn or to otherwise benefit from their education is substantially limited due to ADHD.

Thus, regardless of whether a child with ADHD meets eligibility guidelines to receive federally funded special education programs (under IDEA), Section 504 guarantees the ADHD child the right to receive a free appropriate public education.

The policy memorandum emphasized the important role that teachers in regular education have in providing help to students with ADHD. It directed state education agencies to take steps to train regular education teachers and other personnel to develop their awareness about ADHD and its manifestations. Educators were to become aware of adaptations that could be implemented in regular education programs to address the instructional needs of these children. The Department felt that through the use of appropriate adaptations and interventions in regular classes, many of which may be required by Section 504, that local education agencies will be able to effectively address the instructional needs of many children with ADHD.

The Americans with Disabilities Act of 1990 (ADA)

The ADA guarantees disabled people access to employment, transportation, telecommunications, public accommodations, and public services. The ADA expands on the concepts and protections introduced by Section 504 of the Rehabilitation Act of 1973. It provides comprehensive federal civil rights protections for people with disabilities in the private and public sectors.

How Has All This Been Working Out?

There is insufficient data regarding how children with ADHD have actually been served in public schools in the United States since this policy memorandum was issued in 1991. Peter Jensen and James Cooper (2002) estimated that of the children with ADHD who are in special education, about twenty-six percent have been placed in the learning disability category, about forty-three percent have been placed in the emotional disturbance category, and about forty percent have been placed under the OHI category.

There is no way to identify the number of children in the OHI category who are receiving special education on the basis of having ADHD, but enrollment in the OHI category has been growing steadily. There was a three-fold increase in the number of children in OHI within the first four years after the 1991-1992 school year and the activation of the new policy. The category more than doubled in size during that time from 56,335 to 133,354. Many of these children have ADHD. Nevertheless, parents of children with ADHD in 2005 are still having difficulty getting appropriate services for their children. However, they are not alone as parents of children with other disabilities report similar difficulty.

In the past fourteen years, since the initial policy memorandum, schools have recognized the significance that ADHD plays in how students learn and perform in school. Undergraduate schools of education are focusing on ADHD in their curriculum for new teachers. Special issues of major education journals have been devoted to ADHD. Professional education associations such as the Council for Exceptional Children (CEC) and the National Association of School Psychologists (NASP) and many others, along with the Department of Education, have developed resources for educators on how to help students with ADHD.

Steps to Identifying and Serving Children in Need of Special Education and Related Services

1. The child is identified as possibly needing special education and related services.

The "Child Find" program requires states to identify, locate, and evaluate all children with disabilities in the state who need special education and related services. To accomplish this, states conduct "Child Find" activities in which a child may be identified, and parents may be asked if the child can be evaluated. Parents who suspect that their child has a disability can also call the "Child Find" system and request an evaluation. A school professional may also ask that a child be evaluated to see if he has a disability.

Parents may also contact the child's teacher or other school professional to ask that their child be evaluated. The request may be verbal or in writing. Evaluations need to be completed within a reasonable time after the parent gives consent.

2. The evaluation.

A multi-disciplinary team will be involved in the evaluation. The evaluation must assess the child in all areas related to the child's suspected disability. The results of the evaluation will be used to determine if the child is eligible for special education and related services and to make decisions about an appropriate educational program for the child based on the child's educational needs. If the parents disagree with the results of an evaluation, they have the right to take their child for an Independent Educational Evaluation (IEE). They can ask that the school system pay for this IEE. The team must consider the findings of any evaluation the student may have had by an outside source.

3. Eligibility is decided.

The evaluation team and the parents look at the results of the child's evaluation. Together, they decide if the child is a "child with a disability," as defined by IDEA. If the parents disagree with the district's findings they may ask for a hearing to challenge the eligibility decision.

4. Child is found eligible for services.

Once it is determined that a child is eligible for special education and related services, within thirty calendar days, the Individual Education Program (IEP) team must meet to write an IEP for the child.

5. An IEP meeting is scheduled.

The school district schedules and conducts the IEP meeting. The school staff must do the following: contact the participants including the parents; notify parents early enough to make sure they have the opportunity to attend; schedule the meeting at a time and place agreeable to parents and the school; tell the parents the purpose, time, and location of the meeting; tell the parents who will be attending; and tell the parents that they may invite people to the meeting who have knowledge or special expertise about the child.

6. The IEP meeting is held and the IEP is written.

At the IEP meeting the team talks about the child's needs and writes the IEP. Parents and the student (when appropriate) are part of the meeting. If the child's placement is decided by a different group, the parents must be part of that group as well. The parents must give consent before the school system may provide special education and related services to the child for the first time. As soon after the meeting as possible, the child begins to receive services. Parents who do not agree with the IEP and placement may discuss their concerns with other members of the IEP team and try to work out an agreement. If they cannot resolve their differences, parents can ask for mediation, or the school may offer mediation. Parents may file a complaint with the state education agency and may request a hearing for due process, at which time mediation must be available.

7. Services are provided.

The child's IEP must be implemented by the school as it was written. Parents are given a copy of the IEP and each of the child's teachers and service providers has access to the IEP and is aware of his or her responsibilities for implementing the IEP. This includes accommodations, modifications, and supports that must be provided to the child.

8. Progress is measured and reported to parents.

The school must ensure that the child's

progress toward the annual goals stated in the IEP is measured. The parents are regularly informed of the child's progress and whether that progress is enough for the child to achieve the goals by the end of the year. These progress reports must be given to parents at least as often as parents are informed of a non-disabled child's progress.

9. IEP is reviewed.

The IEP team reviews the IEP at least once each year, or more often if the parents or school ask for a review. The IEP may be revised if necessary. Parents must be invited to attend these meetings and can make suggestions for changes within the IEP and can agree or disagree with the placement.

10. Child is reevaluated.

Every three years, the child must be re-evaluated. The purpose of this evaluation is to find out if the child continues to be a "child with a disability," as defined by IDEA, and what the child's educational needs are. More frequent re-evaluations can be done if conditions warrant them or if the child's parents or teacher asks for a new evaluation.

What Are the Contents of the IEP?

The IEP must include certain information about the child and the educational program that is designed to meet the child's unique needs.

- *Current performance.* The classroom teacher, parents, service providers, and school staff provide information about the child's current educational performance.
- *Annual goals.* These are goals that the child can reasonably accomplish in one year. The goals are broken down into short-term objectives. Goals may be academic, social, behavioral, relate to physical needs, or address other educational needs. They must be measurable to enable others to evaluate if the student has achieved them.

- *Special education and related services.* There must be a list of the special education and related services to be provided to the child or on behalf of the child.
- *Participation with non-disabled children.* The IEP must explain the extent (if any) to which the child will not participate with non-disabled children in the regular class and other school activities.
- *Participation in state and district-wide tests.* The IEP must state what modifications in the administration of state and district-wide tests the child will need. In cases where a test is not appropriate for a child, the IEP must state why the test is not appropriate and how the child will be tested instead.
- *Dates and places.* The IEP must state when services will start, how often they will be provided, where they will be provided, and how long they will last.
- *Transition service needs.* When the child is fourteen years of age (or younger, if appropriate), the IEP must address the courses he needs to take to reach his post-school goals. There must be a statement of transition service needs in each of the child's subsequent IEPs.
- *Needed transition services.* Starting when the child is sixteen years of age (or younger, if appropriate), the IEP must state the transition services needed to help him prepare for leaving school.
- *Age of majority.* Starting at least one year before the child reaches the age of majority, the IEP must include a statement that the student has been told of any rights that will transfer to him or her at the age of majority.
- *Measuring progress.* The IEP must state how the child's progress will be measured and how parents will be informed of that

progress.
Related Services

In order to benefit from special education, a child may require any of the following related services:

- Audiology services
- Counseling services
- Early identification and assessment of disabilities in children
- Medical services
- Occupational therapy
- Orientation and mobility services
- Parent counseling and training
- Physical therapy
- Psychological services
- Recreation
- Rehabilitation counseling services
- School health services
- Social work services in schools
- Speech-language pathology services
- Transportation

Section 504 of the Rehabilitation Act of 1973

In 1973, the Vocational Rehabilitation Act became law. As part of the act, Congress enacted Section 504, which provided that individuals cannot be discriminated against solely on the basis of their disability. Section 504 became the first federal civil rights law to protect the rights of persons with disabilities.

Section 504 applies to all divisions of state government and all public or private agencies, institutions, and organizations that are the recipients of federal financial assistance. All local school systems in the United States are subject to Section 504 regulations if they receive federal aid through grant programs such as vocational education, Chapter 1, special education, and food/nutrition programs.

To be eligible for protection under Section

504 an individual with a disability means any person who (1) has a physical or mental impairment that substantially limits one or more of such person's major life activities; or (2) has a record of such an impairment; or (3) is regarded as having such an impairment.

If the school team determines that the child's ADHD does significantly limit his or her learning, then the child would be eligible for a 504 Plan that would specify reasonable accommodations in the educational program and related aids and services, if deemed necessary (e.g., counseling, assistive technology). School personnel involved in general education, not special education, typically implement the 504 Plan. Students who receive services under 504 are not limited to only being able to receive accommodations and supports within the general education program. In fact, Section 504 does not limit the services provided or where the services may be provided, in regular or special education classrooms.

Sample Classroom Accommodations.

Below is a list of accommodations that can be put in a 504 Plan to accommodate students with ADHD.

Assignments/Worksheets
- extra time to complete tasks
- simplify directions
- hand worksheets one at a time
- shorten assignments
- allow use of word processor
- use self-monitoring devices or programs
- provide training in study skills
- break work into small parts
- allow use of tape recorder
- don't grade handwriting

Behaviors
- praise specific behaviors
- use self-monitoring devices or programs
- give extra privileges/rewards

- cue students to stay on task
- increase immediacy of rewards
- mark correct answers not incorrect ones
- use classroom behavior management program
- allow legitimate movement
- allow student time out of seat to run errands
- ignore minor, inappropriate behavior
- use time-out procedure for misbehavior
- seat student near good role model
- set up behavior contract
- ignore calling out without raising hand
- praise student when hand raised

Lesson Presentation
- pair students to check work
- write major points on chalkboard
- ask student to repeat instructions
- use computer assisted instruction
- break longer presentations into shorter ones
- provide written outline
- make frequent eye contact with student
- include a variety of activities during each lesson

Physical Arrangement of Room
- seat student near teacher
- seat student near positive role model
- avoid distracting stimuli (window, air conditioner noise, etc.)
- increase distance between desks
- stand near student when giving directions

Organization
- provide peer assistance with organizational skills
- assign volunteer homework buddy
- allow student to have an extra set of books at home
- send daily/weekly progress notes home

for parents
- provide homework assignment book
- review rules of neatness on written assignments
- help student organize materials in desk/backpack,
- develop reward system for completion of classwork/homework
- teach time management principles
- help student organize long-term projects by setting shorter goals

Test Taking
- allow open book exams
- give exams orally if written language is difficult
- give take home tests
- use more objective tests as opposed to essays
- allow student to give test answers on tape recorder
- allow extra time for tests

Academic Skill
- if skill weaknesses are suspected refer for academic achievement assessment
- if reading is weak: provide previewing strategies; select text with less on a page; shorten amount of required reading
- if oral expression is weak: accept all oral responses; substitute display for oral report; encourage expression of new ideas; pick topics that are easy for student to talk about
- if written language is weak: accept non-written forms for reports; accept use of typewriter, word processor, tape recorder; do not assign large quantity of written work; give multiple choice tests rather than essay tests
- if math is weak: allow use of calculator; use graph paper to space numbers; provide additional math time; provide im-

mediate correctness feedback and instruction via modeling of the correct computational procedure; teach steps to solve type of math problem; encourage use of "self-talk" to proceed through problem solving

Special Considerations

- alert bus driver to needs of student
- suggest parenting program
- monitor closely on field trips
- communicate with physician regarding effects of medication and other treatments the student may be receiving
- suggest other agency involvement as needed
- social skills training
- counseling
- establish procedure for dispensing medication
- consult with other outside professionals, i.e., counselor
- monitor medication side-effects

Section 504 or IDEA! How Should a Student with ADHD Be Served?

Section 504 provides a quicker procedure for obtaining accommodations and services for children with disabilities than with IDEA. The eligibility criteria are broader, less information is usually required to determine eligibility, and less bureaucratic "red tape" exists to get services for the child. This may be quite satisfactory for children who have less serious disabilities. The more formal and rigorous procedures under IDEA, although time-consuming, offer better protections and safeguards for families than Section 504. Under IDEA, parent or guardian participation is required at each step of the evaluation, placement, or change of placement. These safeguards, with respect to due process and discipline, are particularly important when a change in placement of the child is being considered. The ADA

provides an extra layer of protections for persons with disabilities in addition to those outlined in IDEA and Section 504.

For children whose disability is less serious, many school districts will encourage the use of Section 504 rather than IDEA. It is quicker, more flexible, and the district has greater latitude and less accountability for decision-making and enforcement. Since the early 1990's, school districts have focused heavily on procedures to better serve students under Section 504. Plans have been implemented to ensure that the student with ADHD will receive appropriate accommodations in the regular classroom. Commonly used interventions are: change seating, behavior modification, time-out, shortened assignments, one-to-one instruction, consultation with an educational specialist, peer tutoring, frequent breaks, and helping with organization. These and other accommodations and intervention strategies have been more fully discussed elsewhere in this book.

Many parents find that districts are reluctant to place children with ADHD in special education under IDEA within the OHI category. Parents and guardians must evaluate their individual child's situation, the track record of the school and district in providing services under a 504 Plan, and then determine the best option for their child.

Disciplining Students with Disabilities Under IDEA

Continued behavior problems is often a sign that the program that the child is receiving is not effective in addressing his educational needs. If parents or teachers believe that this is the case, they should request an IEP team meeting.

IDEA offers protections to students with behavior problems who are receiving special education services. The school must make sure that the student is not punished for conduct he or she cannot control; that such students get the services that he or she needs to behave properly; and that

Differences Between IDEA, Section 504, and the ADA

IDEA	Section 504	ADA
Purpose		
To provide financial aid to the states in their efforts to ensure adequate and appropriate services for children with disabilities.	A civil rights law to protect the rights of individuals with disabilities in programs and activities that receive federal financial assistance from the U.S. Department of Education	A federal statute that requires businesses and other entities to provide reasonable accommodations to individuals who are protected by the Act.
Who is Protected?		
All children ages birth through 21 who are determined to be eligible within one or more of 13 categories and who need special education and related services.	All school-age children who meet the broader definition of qualified handicapped person; i.e., (1) has or (2) has had a physical or mental impairment which substantially limits a major life activity or (3) is regarded as handicapped by others. Major life activities include walking, seeing, hearing, speaking, breathing, learning, working, caring for oneself, and performing manual tasks.	Same broad definition as 504.
Responsibility to Provide a Free Appropriate Public Education		
Both IDEA and Section 504 require the provision of a free appropriate public education (FAPE) to eligible students covered under them. IDEA requires a written IEP document with specific content and required number of specific participants at the IEP meeting.	Section 504 does not require a document such as an IEP, but does require a plan. It is recommended that a group of persons knowledgeable about the student convene and specify the agreed upon services.	ADA does provide for FAPE to eligible students. The ADA has two provisions and services for eligible students with a disability. First, the ADHD applies its protections to cover nonsectarian private schools. Second, the ADA provides an additional layer of protection in combination with actions brought uner Section 504. and IDEA.
Funding		
IDEA provides additional federal funding for eligible students.	No additional funds are provided by Section 504.	No additional funds are provided by the ADA.
Regular vs Special Education		
A student is eligible for services under IDEA if it is determined that the student is disabled under one or more of the specific qualifying disabilities and requires special education and related services. The student must be provided services within the least restrictive environment. Special education and related services included within the IEP must be provided at no cost to parents. In addition, a full continuum of placement alternatives, including the regular classroom must be available for providing special education and related services required in the IEP.	A student is eligible as long as he or she meets the definition of a broadly defined qualified person. It is not required that the disability adversely affect education performance, or that the student need special education in order to be protected. The student's education must be provided in the regular classroom unless it is demonstrated that education in the regular environment with the use of aids and services cannot be achieved satisfactorily.	ADA does not address the provision of services within the regular or special education classroom. It broadens the policies set forth in Section 504. The public schools must provide appropriate accommodations. Related aids and services may be appropriate modifications.

IDEA	Section 504	ADA
Program Accessibility		
Requires appropriate modifications for eligible students.	Has detailed regulations regarding building and program accessibility.	Requires modification be made if necessary to provide access to FAPE.
Procedural Safeguards		
IDEA and 504 require notice to the parent or guardian with respect to identification, evaluation, and/or placement.	IDEA and 504 require notice ot the parent or guardian with respect to identification, evaluation and/or placement.	Does not specify procedural safeguards for special education.
Requires written notice with specifies required components of written notice.	Written notice is not required.	
Requires written notice prior to any change of placement.	Requires notification only before a "significant change" in placement.	
Evaluations		
A comprehensive evaluation which assesses all areas related to the suspected disability is required. The child must be evaluated by a multidisciplinary team or group.	Evaluation must draw on information from a variety of sources in the area of concern. Decisions made by a group knowledgeable about the student, evaluation data, and placement options.	Does not delineate specific evaluation requirements. However, appropriate modifications must be provided during an evaluation such as modifying entrance exams or providing readers or interpreters.
Informed consent required before an initial evaluation is conducted.	No consent from parent or guardian required—only notice is required.	
Re-evaluation to be conducted at least every 3 years.	Requires periodic re-evaluations.	
Re-evaluation may be necessary before a significant change in placement.	Re-evaluation is required before a significant change in placement.	
Provides for independent educational evaluation at district's expense if parents disagee with evaluation obtained by school and hearing officer agrees.	No provision for independent evaluations at district's expense.	
Procedures for Placement		
IDEA and 504 require districts when interpreting evaluation data and making decisions regarding placement to: • Draw upon information from a variety of sources. • Assure that all information is documented and considered. • Ensure that decisions regarding eligibility are made by persons who are knowledgeable about the child, the meaning of the evaluation data, and placement options. • Ensure that the student is educated with his/her non-disabled peers to the maximum extent appropriate (least restrictive environment).	IDEA and 504 require districts when interpreting evaluation data and making decisions regarding placement to: • Draw upon information from a variety of sources. • Assure that all information is documented and considered. • Ensure that decisions regarding eligibility are made by persons who are knowledgeable about the child, the meaning of the evaluation data, and placement options. • Ensure that the student is educated with his/her non-disabled peers to the maximum extent appropriate (least restrictive environment).	No specific placement procedures are required. However, appropriate modifications are required.

IDEA	Section 504	ADA
Enforcement		
Enforced by the U.S. Department of Education, Office of Special Education Programs (OSEP). The districts response is monitored by the Staate Department of Education and OSEP. Potentially, federal funding could be withheld or a payback required should the district not be in compliance.	Enforced by the U.S. Department of Education, Office of Civil Rights. Potentially, all federal funding could be withheld should a state education agency or district not come into compliance.	Enforced by the Equal Employment Opportunity commission and the Department of Justice.
Grievance Procedures		
Does not require a grievance procedure nor a compliance officer. Citizen complaints, however, may be filed with state department of education.	Districts with 15 employees required to (1) designate an employee to be responsible for assuring district is in compliance with Section 504 and (2) provides a grievance procedure for parents, students, and employees.	Does not require specific grievance procedures related to education.
Due Process		
Parents have the right to participate in all IEP meetings and to receive notice of all procedural safeguards when the school district intends or refuses to take action or when a proposed change of placement or services is considered. Districts are required to provide impartial hearings for parents or guardians who disagree with the identification, evaluation, and/or placement, or any change of placement. The parent or guardian has the right to an independent hearing officer, present testimony and cross examine witnesses, and exclude evidence not presented by the opposing side at least five days prior to the hearing. The parent or guardian also has the right to be represented by counsel, and the right to a written decision within 10 days. IDEA has a "stay-put" provision. When the parent requests an impartial due process hearing, the child must remain in the current educational placement until all administrative and legal proceedings are finished. Suspensions or expulsions of a chid from school may trigger the "stay-put" placement provision if the parent requires a due process hearing to challenge the proposed suspension or expulsion. There is no similar "stay-put" provision in Section 504.	Section 504 requires notice to the parent or guardian with respect to identification, evaluation, and/or placement. Such notification does not have to be written. Notice is required before a "significant change" in placement is being made. Allows for the school district to appoint an impartial hearing officer. Requires that the parent or guardian have an opportunity to participate and be represented by counsel. Other details are left to the discretion of the local school district.	Does not delineate specific due process procedures. Individuals with disabilities have the same remedies which are available under Title VII of the Civil Rights Act of 1964, as amended by the Civil Rights Act of 1991.

the student is not unfairly disciplined. This becomes quite important for students with ADHD whose behavior can lead to disciplinary action.

A "Manifestations Determination Review" must be conducted before a student with a disability is suspended for more than ten days, expelled, or placed in another setting due to behavioral issues and violations of school rules. This review must take place within ten school days from the time the school decides to change the placement of the child because of a violation of a code of student conduct. The reviewers must consider each of these questions:

- Is the student's IEP correct?
- Is the student's school placement correct?
- Was the school following the IEP?
- Did the student's disability limit his or her understanding of the behavior in question or the consequences of such behavior?
- Did the student have trouble controlling the behavior due to his or her disability?

If the reviewers decide that the student did not receive all required services, or that the child's disability affected his or her ability to understand or control the misbehavior, they must find that the misbehavior was a "manifestation" of the disability. If the reviewers decide that the misbehavior was not a manifestation of the disability, they can recommend that the student be subject to exclusion from school, including expulsion, on the same basis as students who are not disabled. The parents may challenge this decision through the special education procedural safeguard system.

If the conduct in question was caused by or had a direct relationship to the child's disability or the school's failure to implement the IEP, the student's conduct shall be determined to be a manifestation of the child's disability. Then, the IEP team must conduct a functional behavioral assessment (FBA) and implement a behavioral intervention plan (BIP). It must also review and modify any existing BIP and return the child to the placement from which the child was removed. In addition, if the reviewers identify deficiencies in the child's IEP, the implementation of the IEP or the child's placement, immediate steps must be taken to fix the problems.

These same protections are available to students who are being considered for eligibility for special education even though they have not yet been determined to be eligible. Schools can remove a student with disabilities for up to forty-five school days without regard to whether the behavior is determined to be a manifestation of the child's disability in cases of: carrying or possessing a weapon; knowingly using, selling, or soliciting illegal drugs or controlled substances at school or school functions; or inflicting serious bodily injury on another person while at school, on school premises, or at a school function.

Summary

Beginning in the 1980's, advocacy efforts have been underway to ensure that students with ADHD are properly identified and receive appropriate educational services in this country's public school. In 1991 the Department of Education took a giant step to ensure such protections by issuing a policy memorandum that addressed the needs of students with ADHD. This memorandum directed state education agencies to provide special education and related services to students with ADHD who qualified for such services under the OHI category of special education. It also reaffirmed the protections under Section 504 of the Rehabilitation Act of 1973 provided for those students with ADHD who did not need special education but who needed accommodations in regular classrooms. The Americans with Disabilities Act of 1990 strengthened these protections.

Since then, many school districts have implemented programs to serve students with ADHD.

Higher education teacher training programs have incorporated more information about ADHD in their curricula. In-service training on ADHD has become more available to teachers. Assessment teams are watchful for signs of ADHD in students who are needing psychoeducational evaluations as part of a determination for eligibility for special education. Schools are providing assistance to parents of children with ADHD and are reaching out to community health care providers.

The number of children receiving help under OHI on the basis of having ADHD has increased substantially over the past several years since the incorporation of the policy memorandum into IDEA.

Chapter 9
Twenty Critical Ideas for Teaching Students with ADHD

As we discussed in chapter one, schools play a vital role in identifying children with mental health needs, providing treatment and services to those identified, and in helping children develop mentally healthy ways of functioning. Classroom teachers have the most contact with students and are often the first to notice when problems occur. They can be a catalyst for the implementation of assessment and intervention services.

Along with parents, classroom teachers teach children positive behavior, social competence, and emotional well-being in addition to academics. Teachers can build a child's self-confidence. They can create a sense of belonging and connectedness for the child. They can encourage children to explore their talents and abilities leading to a sense of accomplishment and pride.

Children with ADHD have their greatest problems in school. Most students with ADHD can be taught successfully in regular classroom settings, provided teachers are able to modify teaching practices to accommodate students' special needs. Small changes in how a teacher approaches the student, or in what the teacher expects, can often be the difference between success or failure for the student. This chapter provides twenty ideas that are critical to helping children with ADHD in the classroom. Crowded classrooms, limited teacher planning time, lack of available support staff, and other factors make it difficult for classroom teachers to give special attention to individual students. The following ideas do not take a great deal of additional time to implement and, for the most part, they are just good instructional practices that can benefit all students. However, for those students who have ADHD and other special needs these ideas can be critical for success.

1. **Develop a relationship with the student that shows caring, respect, and understanding.**

Teachers who act in a positive, supportive, and collaborative way with students will often get the best results from them. It can be difficult to maintain a positive attitude with students who exhibit disruptive behavior. Teachers who resort to confrontational or punitive approaches to managing disruptive behavior may not get the desired result. Punishment usually has a negative effect on the teacher-student relationship.

Students who violate the rules need to be dealt with in a constructive way. Punishment alone is ineffective and, in fact, may be highly destructive. Teachers should find ways to discipline that will be beneficial in both the short and the long-term.

- Find more behavior to praise than you do to criticize.
- Discuss problem behavior with the student in a private, scheduled conversation.
- Ask the student's parent to help out.
- Don't judge negative behavior until you speak with the student to get all sides of the story.
- Stand close to children who are off task.
- Look for ways to enhance the self-esteem of troublesome students. Find things they are good at and give them responsibility in areas that they may be able to excel.
- Smile rather than frown at students who are about to misbehave. Keep things light.
- Send fidgety students on errands to channel their hyperactivity.
- Discuss repetitive problem behavior with the student and seek his ideas for solutions and consequences.
- Give second chances with good humor.
- Speak softly and politely to engender an atmosphere of calm and respect.
- Don't discipline when you are angry. Instead set up a time later to speak with the student.
- Post classroom rules and review them.
- Make sure your students are busy working all the time. Idle time can lead to troublesome behavior.
- Stay moving so you visit all parts of the classroom.
- Always treat the student in a respectful way when reprimanding.
- Be prepared to "drop" an issue even if you have to lose some "face" from time to time.

2. Form effective partnerships with parents and other professionals helping the child with ADHD.

If teachers could make a wish list of what they would like to have most to help them do their job effectively, they would probably ask for smaller class sizes, more time for planning and preparation, less administrative responsibilities, and more motivated students. Near the top of the list, however, would also be the wish to have more parents involved in their child's education. Teachers know that parent involvement makes their job easier and it encourages the student to be more successful in school. Students whose parents are involved are more motivated to perform. Parents can back up teachers' learning expectations and can supervise homework and long-term projects better because of the clear communication between the school and the home. Try these ideas to form effective partnerships with parents whose children have ADHD.

- Schedule parent-teacher conferences more frequently than you generally do to address the needs of the student.
- Discuss the student's strengths as well as his weaknesses during such conferences.
- Understand what treatments the student may be receiving to help manage ADHD symptoms and offer to work with other professionals involved in providing such treatment.
- Brainstorm ideas with parents to find solutions for problems with homework, behavior, organization, work completion, motivation, and attention.
- Inquire about strategies past teachers used to help the student.
- Direct the parent to other resources in the school or community that might be helpful.

It will also be important for the teacher to communicate with other community professionals. Physicians prescribing ADHD medication may need the teacher's input as to how the medication is working. School-based or community-based counselors working with the child on behavioral interventions or tutors and therapists may need your help in implementing strategies in the classroom to improve learning and behavior.

3. Keep your classroom highly structured with clear rules and expectations about performance.

Most children function best in structured environments wherein expectations are clearly set by the teacher. Children with ADHD seem to need this even more. Classroom rules are an important part of this structure. To be effective, rules cannot just be posted and forgotten, they should serve as a framework for guiding the student and teacher behavior throughout the year. However, rules alone will not develop and maintain appropriate student behavior, especially for students with ADHD. Rules will be most effective when combined with a system of rewards and consequences.

- Discuss appropriate classroom rules with students.
- Write lists of rules on the chalkboard as students offer them.
- Choose four to six rules that are the most important and phrase them positively, e.g. Cooperate with others; Raise your hand to ask permission to talk; Complete work neatly and on time; Work at your desk quietly; Be prepared each day with your work.
- Print rules on poster board and display them in the front of the room.
- Develop a system of rewards and consequences that can be used when rules are followed or broken.
- Provide rewards and consequences as soon as possible after a desired or undesired behavior.

- Use behavioral programs such as contracts, daily report cards, token economy systems, and self-monitoring strategies to help students conform to expectations and rules (see the next chapter for forms).

4. Develop routines for repetitive activities.

In every classroom, like in every home, there are routine activities that are performed daily. Like most elementary and secondary students, those with ADHD, perform better in highly structured classrooms with set procedures for carrying out activities. Having routines will diminish off-task or disruptive behavior and will help establish discipline in your classroom. Being consistent in following routines will save you time and will eliminate many of the discipline headaches that can otherwise occur.

- Develop structured routines to start the day off in a consistent manner. Students get on-task from the minute they come into your room and continue to be focused throughout the period.
- Design a method of handing out and collecting papers.
- Designate a specific place the teacher keeps collected papers.
- Have students keep completed work in specific locations, e.g. notebooks, folders, etc.
- Use established procedures to check homework and classroom assignments.
- Establish routines for dismissal.
- Design procedures for dealing with transitions, e.g. short breaks, introduce new lessons with interesting joke or story, etc.
- Develop strategies for discipline and for administering consequences.

5. Make organization a priority and provide help to students with ADHD who have trouble staying organized.

As most teachers will readily attest, students with ADHD are generally not well organized. Their desks, lockers, book bags, or notebooks can be in shambles within days, if not hours, of just having been cleaned up and straightened out. Parents of children with ADHD also have their hands full trying to keep their kids organized. Teachers (and parents) should place a high priority on being organized even though the child may have a hard time doing so.

- Establish rules for neatness early on so that students appreciate your concern for quality work.
- Direct students with organizational problems to straighten up belongings and work area daily. For elementary students, spot check their desks to encourage cleanliness and order.
- Schedule regular times for students to clean out their desks, notebooks, and backpacks.
- Check that notebooks have proper dividers for different subjects or activities and that the student uses clearly identified folders to store papers.
- Have the student write notes to himself for helpful reminders. Reinforce note writing strategies.
- Insist the student use a homework journal or assignment pad each day.
- Keep extra supplies on hand for the student to borrow.
- Have the student clear his desk of unnecessary material when working.
- Write assignments on chalkboard for the student to copy.
- Compliment the student when you note improvements in neatness and organization.
- When providing handouts, make sure they are three-hole punched ahead of time so students can easily put them in notebooks for storage.

- Some students will benefit from you checking at the end of the day to make sure they are bringing home all the materials to complete homework.
- Some students with ADHD may need an extra set of books at home because they have too much difficulty organizing their supplies.
- Encourage parents to help the student stay organized. Parents can help the child set up a filing system at home. Use an accordion file to organize papers. Organize the child's backpack every day. Check that homework is done each day and put completed homework in a separate folder to give to the teacher. Set up a routine each morning to check that the child has all the supplies needed for school that day. Put a bookshelf in the child's bedroom. Keep school supplies in plastic bins with lids.

6. **State directions clearly and follow up to make sure the student is on task.**

Students with ADHD are often poor listeners. They distract easily and frequently miss important information said by the teacher. A common reason children with ADHD don't follow directions is they are often unaware that directions have been given.

- Before giving directions, get the full attention of the class. This can be done by changing the tone of your voice, flicking the lights on and off, closing the classroom door, or saying cue phrases like, "May I have your attention please?" to which the class has been conditioned to respond by listening for directions.
- Use short, simple sentences when speaking to the student. Be sure to give verbal instructions at the student's vocabulary level.
- Stand near the inattentive student when

giving directions.

- Organize directions in sequence to avoid confusion.
- Give one instruction at a time. Avoid multiple commands.
- Give examples of what you expect the student to do.
- Check to be sure the student understands the directions. Repeat directions as many times as necessary.
- Ask the student to repeat the directions back.
- Write a summary of the directions on the chalkboard for easy reference or prepare assignments written on index cards.
- Provide practice at the appropriate level of difficulty. Precede independent practice with supervised practice.
- To reinforce a direction to an individual student, first make eye contact, then call the child by name and give the direction.
- Follow-up after giving directions to make sure the student is on-task. Enlist the help of peer tutors or volunteer.

7. Arrange classroom seating so that you can teach most effectively. Seat students with ADHD in distraction-free areas of the classroom and in close proximity to you.

Arranging classroom seating seems simple. Just assign students seats to sit in within nice neat rows and you're all done. Right? Not necessarily so. Experts in classroom management say decisions teachers make about whether students will be allowed to select their own seats and about physical arrangement of the classroom can have an effect on discipline and the effectiveness of teacher instruction. While nicely formed rows may help the custodian do his job, it may be an obstacle to effective teaching. When arranging your classroom, it is best to do it in a way that allows you to move around the room

freely and easily. This allows you to check on students as they are working. There is a lot less fooling around and a lot more time on-task when students know the teacher might be coming to their desk to check on their work. I was giving a talk in Phoenix a few years ago and a teacher in the audience remarked that everyone in her "halo" did well in her class. By "halo" she meant everyone that was sitting within arm's length of her as she passed by them.

Considering that many classrooms are overcrowded, teachers need to think about how they can arrange students' desks so broad walkways run from the front to the back of the class and also from side to side. Some teachers prefer to group desks together, others like to seat in semicircles, and others in rows. There are pros and cons to any seating arrangement you pick. You will need to find one that works for you.

What about assigning seats for students? It doesn't take long to figure out who the student with ADHD should be sitting near. Teachers rearrange seats constantly to find the right mix for students, especially those who are prone to being overly sociable or disruptive. Try to avoid seating students with ADHD near each other, near windows, by bulletin boards, or close to areas of the room where they are subject to more distractions. The best seating is probably in close proximity to the teacher so that the student is easily accessible for teacher prompting, correction, or reinforcement, or near a good peer role model.

8. Design your classroom and your teaching style with motivation in mind.

The physical structure of a classroom can have a negative or positive effect on the performance of students. Early theories that children who are distractible will perform better in sterile, distraction-free learning environments led special educators to seat students with learning disabilities and ADHD in isolated study carrels, free of distracting stimuli or in classrooms with minimal room decorations, etc. Working on the "horse with blinders" theory to learning, these early educators were hopeful that with fewer distractions, the ADHD child would be more able to attend to work and complete tasks. Unfortunately, many of these children were just as off task in this type of setting as in more normal ones. What distractions the environment doesn't immediately provide to the child, the child will create for himself as desk chairs could easily become rockers, scraps of paper interesting toys to fiddle with, etc. Children with ADHD manufacture distractions.

Teachers need to compete for the attention of their students with ADHD by creating as enriching and exciting a learning environment as possible, thereby increasing the child's motivation to attend. Sydney Zentall, Ph.D. (1990) stresses the importance of using colorful worksheets to stimulate the attention of students with ADHD and for teachers to incorporate into their instructional program creative learning experiences that fit the student's interests.

- Design your classroom with motivation in mind. Stimulating classroom decor with colorful and interesting surroundings has more of a chance at capturing the ADHD child's attention than does blank walls.
- Bulletin boards shouldn't be just classroom decorations. They should augment the learning experiences that are going on in the classroom. Bulletin boards can be teacher made, student made, or a combined effort of teacher and student. The best ones are interactive and give the students a sense of ownership by displaying their work.
- Your classroom should have centers of interest filled with ideas to stimulate creativity and independent learning. Learning centers are stations set up throughout the classroom where children can go

to engage in some learning activity. Children with ADHD, in particular, may do well in learning centers. They have the opportunity to find activities that are of interest to them leading to greater task completion. During learning center time children can explore and practice skills to their own satisfaction. Centers also provide opportunities for hands-on learning, cooperative learning, and social interaction that may be very important for some children with ADHD. Some examples of learning centers are: reading areas (a place for students to read independently); writing center (where students can work on writing independently as well as collaboratively); computer center (an area for computer use in writing, math, reading, keyboard practice, research); creative arts center (where students can get involved in visual art and dramatic play); listening center (where students listen to tapes and CDs of books, songs, stories, and poems).

- Spend time motivating your students to learn. Use an experiential approach to get the point of your lessons across. Find out what interests the students and go from there. Use the students' interests as a starting point and try to build on them.
- Students who lack intrinsic motivation can be motivated by praise or rewards. You can give reward certificates for good work (free homework pass; center time certificate; eat lunch with a friend certificate).
- One of the most successful ways to motivate is the active involvement of students in their own learning. Standing in front of a room and lecturing to them is usually not good enough (especially for students with ADHD who are probably not listening to you). It is better to get

students involved in activities through group problem solving exercises, helping to decide what to do and the best way to do it, helping the teacher, working with each other, or in some other way getting physically involved in the lesson.

- Make learning visual. Incorporate drawings, diagrams, pictures, charts, graphs, bulleted lists, even three-dimensional objects you can bring to class to help students anchor the idea to an image.

- Incorporate emotions into your teaching. If you can make something fun, exciting, happy, loving, or perhaps even a bit frightening, students will learn more readily and the learning will last much longer. Emotions can be created by classroom attitudes, by doing something unexpected or outrageous, by praise, and by many other means.

- Maintain a high level of energy and enthusiasm. Energy is motivating (and entertaining). Action movies hold our interest. Energy sells and if you want to "sell" your students on an idea or concept, do it with an energetic and enthusiastic teaching style.

- Be approachable and friendly. Students are motivated to learn when they sense their teachers truly care about them and can be approached to provide help if needed. Many students lose motivation to complete work when they don't understand what it is they have to do. This happens quite often and many times students don't ask for extra help or clarification. Create an approachable atmosphere in the classroom so your students feel comfortable coming to you for help.

9. Use computers to motivate learning.

If your classroom is like most, you probably have a few computers set up in a learning pod.

This arrangement works well for setting up an independent activity center where students complete tasks you've assigned.

Teachers may find that computer assisted learning materials are better able to hold the interest of the ADHD student. Colorful graphics, interactive learning, and immediate feedback for responses act like magnets to attract attention.

- Plan with students the procedures that they should follow for moving to and from the computer center as well as how they should hand in completed center activities.

- Write directions for computer activities on index cards or poster board and laminate them so you don't have to repeat them every day.

- Design a schedule for using the computer center and post this schedule with times for each student. This helps keep the "Is it my turn yet?" questions to a minimum.

- If a small group of students will be using computers while the rest are at their desks, make sure the computers don't become a distraction. Rotate monitors away from the classroom and get some headphones to restrict noise.

- Use computer time as a reinforcement for good behavior and academic performance.

10. Gear assignments to attention span as well as ability level.

While students with ADHD sometimes have trouble getting started on assignments, they almost always have trouble finishing assignments. As one mother remarked:

"My child spent so much time in third grade in the nurse's office finishing his work, I don't know when he began anything new, because he had to keep finishing everything."

Closure is important to all of us, and satisfaction comes from a job well done. How good could a child feel about himself if he is always "finishing" his work and trying to catch up to others in class? Try these strategies to help students with ADHD pay attention:

- Make allowances for the ADHD child's short attention span by shortening assignments when necessary.
- Give the child extra time to complete work if necessary.
- After giving directions provide an opportunity to practice. Supervised practice should always precede independent practice.
- Provide breaks within a long work period.
- Use prompting, self-monitoring, contracting or other behavioral strategies to help the ADHD child to stay on task.
- Praise the child for staying on task.
- Homework can be a nightmare for many children and their parents. Kids with ADHD will often spend hours on assignments you think should just take minutes. If homework is a problem for a student in your class, check with parents and see if you could work together to find solutions to reduce homework stress.

11. Plan ahead for transitions.

Transitions can be exceedingly time consuming activities in the classroom. They can also be disruptive, interrupting what otherwise might have been a productive class period. Students probably make more than a dozen transitions each day. Transitions occur when:

- Students stay in their seats and change from one subject to another.
- Students change their seat to go to an activity in another part of the classroom.
- Students complete an activity and move back to their seat.
- Students leave the classroom and go to another part of the school.

- Students come back to their classroom after being in another part of the school.

Such times are often difficult for students with ADHD due to problems with disorganization and impulsivity. They have trouble settling down and getting their things together to proceed to a new activity. Particularly difficult for the ADHD student is the move from an unstructured activity (e.g., physical education, lunch) to a more structured one which requires them to have self-restraint and work quietly. To assist students with transition the teacher should:

- Maintain a predictable class structure. Set up classroom routines for transitions such as entering and exiting the classroom and handing in homework. Decide how you want students to prepare for classroom activities (getting into groups, sitting quietly at their desks).
- Rehearse routines and rules for transitions, e.g., gather the materials you need, move quietly, keep your hands and feet to yourselves, get ready for the next activity.
- Review transition rules with your class until the routine is established.
- Announce transitions ahead of time. "Class, we will be clearing our desks and getting ready for recess in a few minutes."
- Supervise students closely during transition times.
- Provide immediate and consistent feedback to students who are doing well.
- Set time limits for transitions, e.g., try to complete a transition within three minutes, etc.
- Get students started on a task during transition times so those that transition quickly can get focused on work.

12. Help the student set realistic goals for work.

Students with ADHD often have trouble setting goals and carrying out assignments, especially long-term projects. Book reports, science projects, term papers, etc., can present a challenge to the student and a headache to his parents. In order to set goals and finish assignments, the student with ADHD will very likely need your help.

- Divide large projects into bite-size parts.
- Communicate with parents to let them know what is expected and when things are due. Using Internet-based communication sites such as schoolnotes.com to post homework assignments, grades, and other information can be extremely helpful.
- Use homework journals and assignment time-lines for long term projects.
- Monitor student's work carefully so he doesn't fall behind and get discouraged.
- Reinforce progress as work gets completed.

13. Provide frequent praise.

By the time most students with ADHD have completed two or three grades in school, they have often had a stream of negative experiences with teachers. Students with ADHD usually have a hard time winning teacher approval and developing a positive relationship. As every teacher knows, the building of a positive teacher-student relationship is essential both to facilitate learning and to encourage the development of positive self-esteem in the student. Such a relationship, like any other positive, meaningful interaction, must contain ingredients of caring, understanding, respect, and encouragement. In addition to bolstering shaky self-esteem, a teacher's positive regard will encourage students to put more effort into their work both to satisfy their teacher and themselves.

The first few days and weeks of school can be important as a tone-setter for the remainder of the school year. Many, although not all, chil-

dren with ADHD are fairly well behaved in new situations and will generally show a honeymoon effect in school during the first few weeks. Teachers could take advantage of this positive display of behavior.

- Attend to the student's pro-learning behavior, recognizing efforts at achievement, and praising attempts as well as successes.
- Ignore minor negative behaviors and quickly attend to incompatible positive behaviors (ignore blurting out, praise hand-raising).
- Maintain close proximity to the child throughout the day by preferential seating close to the teacher or by the teacher walking near the student's desk.
- Spend one or two minutes each day to have a brief "heart-to-heart" talk with the child.
- Keep a mental note of what kind of attention the child likes. When does his face brighten with pride? What words work to encourage? Does he respond to nonverbal reinforcers such as a smile, a wink, or a nod? Is he most proud when recognized publicly by verbal acknowledgments of his efforts or is he more motivated by the promise of tangible rewards?

14. Use teacher attention to motivate.

Teacher attention is an extremely powerful force in shaping behavior. Attention motivates students to perform, and the teacher is in a position to give positive attention to students contingent on their behavior. Most often, teachers will use attention to manage student behavior while students are involved in seat work activities. However, attention can be used to manage other activities, such as those during instructional lessons, transition times, or unstructured class activities. In providing attention to students, teachers should consider the following procedures:

- Move about the room looking for opportunities to attend to positive behavior with praise.
- Scan the classroom frequently. Scanning lets children know you are watching.
- Spot check the work of children who are good at looking busy but who may not be working.
- Praise the ADHD student frequently when you notice that he is complying with class rules.

15. Use prudent reprimands when correcting misbehavior.

Teacher reprimands for misbehavior are frequently used for classroom control. Prudent reprimands provide immediate negative feedback to the student and are delivered unemotionally and briefly. They may be backed up with a mild punishment such as loss of privilege, time-out, or loss of points, if a token system is used. Less successful in changing student behavior are teacher reprimands that are delayed, long-winded, and delivered in an emotionally charged style with empty threats of consequences.

Students with ADHD will probably receive more reprimands than others due to disruptive behavior or because they are not staying on task. Be sure to find plenty of opportunities to praise the student also. If the number of reprimands received in a day outweighs the number of compliments given, this can be a recipe for discouragement. Try to keep things more on the positive than negative side in your communication with students.

16. Recognize that students with motor coordination problems may have difficulty with writing.

Up to sixty percent of students with ADHD have problems with fine-motor coordination. This results in handwriting problems. They have trouble forming letters, maintaining consistent spacing, staying within margins, writing quickly, etc. Writing letters and words is a complex process that involves eye-hand coordination, being able to mentally picture and recall how a letter is shaped, awareness of size constancy , sequencing of letters properly to form words, motor planning, and speed of production.

Students with serious handwriting difficulties may benefit from working with an occupational therapist. The occupational therapist can help by: teaching the child to maintain appropriate posture that supports the proper use of arms, hands, head, and eyes; improving the child's level of physical strength and endurance; help the child develop adequate fine-motor control, which includes holding a pencil, and visual and perceptual abilities that influence the form of letters and shapes; provide teachers with strategies to help the child improve classroom performance; and suggest home activities that promote the development of needed skills.

- When teaching students with handwriting deficits you should be aware that the student may need additional time to complete written work.
- If the amount of written work is too great, the student may become overwhelmed and may need fewer writing assignments.
- Minimize the amount of work the student needs to copy from the chalkboard or from books.
- Substitute oral responses for written responses.
- Be understanding of the student's difficulty with neatness. Encourage neat work but don't penalize the student unnecessarily.
- Some students will do better on a keyboard and should be encouraged to learn keyboarding skills to replace handwriting.
- Allow students to partner with a peer who

can share notes, etc.

- Refer to the handwriting self-monitoring forms for elementary students found in chapter ten.

17. Teach study strategies.

Study strategies can be taught to students in elementary as well as secondary schools. Study strategies refer to those things that individuals do when they have to locate, organize, and remember information. Helping students learn to use study strategies is the responsibility of all teachers in all grades and subject areas, not just the reading or language arts teacher. The overall goal of literacy learning is to help students become independent in their learning. Learning to use a variety of study skills helps students to achieve this goal.

By teaching study strategies, students can improve organization, note-taking, test-taking, listening, reading comprehension, time-management, memory, vocabulary, writing, using references and resources, and completing reports and research projects.

Sandra Rief describes numerous study strategies for elementary and secondary students in *How to Reach and Teach Children with ADD/ADHD.* Leslie Davis, Sandi Sirotowitz, and I provide study strategies and worksheets for elementary students and secondary students in our books: *Study Strategies for Early School Success* and *Study Strategies Made Easy.*

Refer to chapter thirteen in this book for a broader discussion of study strategies and for sample forms and exercises that can be used with elementary and secondary students to improve organization, time management, planning, reading comprehension, note-taking, and test-taking.

18. Give the student with ADHD responsibility.

Giving the ADHD student responsibilities that assist the teacher in managing the classroom can help the child feel like an important contributor to the class. Assigning him leadership positions on teams, giving him jobs at which he can be successful, and showing the other students that you respect him by trusting him to do a job well can promote acceptance from others and build confidence within the child.

19. Treat the student with ADHD as a whole child, not just a label.

When students are diagnosed as having a disorder, there is a tendency to see them as they have been labeled rather than to view them as you do others. One can make arguments in either direction about the pros and cons of labeling children. Advocates for labeling would assert that labels drive services. Opponents point out that labeling of disabled children may make them even more "dis-labeled" in the eyes of those trying to help them. Clearly, we must appreciate the advantages and disadvantages of using labels to categorize students, and we must always be cognizant that regardless of a common label, every child is different. Each has his or her own strengths and weaknesses and should be seen as uniquely individual.

What makes the student with ADHD exceptional is not his disability, but his ability. Teachers, through accommodating the student's needs by modifying the environment alone, will have only done part of the job. To do the rest, they must focus on the child's strengths and teach to his abilities not to his disabilities.

20. Collaborate with other professionals in your school to get ideas for teaching and discipline.

Schools are communities of learning that contain many different resources to help students. Some of the best teaching ideas you use will come from colleagues in your school community: other teachers, guidance counselors, school psychologists, technical assistance staff, remediation specialists, behavioral specialists, vocational counselors, media specialists, para-professionals, police liaison staff, security guards, drug rehabilitation counselors, technology specialists, etc. When you need help coming up with strategies to improve a student's learning or behavior, check with your colleagues to see what has worked for them with similar students. Take advantage of systems within your school for collaborative consultation.

Summary

Children with ADHD have their greatest problems in school. Inattention, impulsivity, and hyperactivity can result in problems with incomplete work, time management, organization, self-control, and social difficulties. A child's teacher can make a big difference in how well he does in school.

This chapter provided twenty principles for teaching children with ADHD. Of course there are probably many more. In part, these principles emphasize the importance of showing respect for students and demonstrating a caring, concerned attitude toward their progress in school. Several principals encourage classrooms to be highly structured with clear expectations and established routines. Teaching styles that motivate students and keeps their attention are particularly important for students with ADHD as they seem to lack intrinsic motivation. Teacher attention and tight discipline can help troublesome students maintain focus and self-control.

The goal of literacy training is to help students become independent learners. Teaching study strategies can improve reading comprehension, organization, test-taking, vocabulary, listening, time-management, etc.

Collaboration with colleagues in your school community can strengthen your skills as a teacher and provide you with interesting ideas to apply in your classroom.

Chapter 10
Classroom Interventions to Improve Behavior and Attention

While the strategies and accommodations described in the previous chapter can be helpful for many students with ADHD, often additional interventions will be needed to improve attention and student behavior. This chapter is designed to provide teachers with the step-by-step information they will need to be able to implement a variety of helpful interventions in their classrooms.

Some of the strategies to be reviewed in this chapter are behavioral interventions. Behavioral interventions are commonly used by teachers to modify student behavior. The goals of behavioral interventions are generally to increase appropriate or adaptive behavior and to decrease inappropriate or maladaptive behavior. The success of behavioral interventions for students with ADHD has been well documented in reducing rates of disruptive, off-task behavior and in improving compliance, organization, attention, and work production. Behavior modification programs are particularly helpful with students with ADHD because they motivate, provide structure, and establish clearly defined goals and objectives for students to reach. Many students with ADHD, not sufficiently motivated by the typi-

cal rewards in school that naturally motivate most other students, require additional incentives.

Teachers familiar with general behavioral principles tend to like using behavior modification programs in their classrooms. Generally, such interventions are relatively easy to implement and provide fairly quick results. Several non-behavioral strategies are also discussed, including the utilization of students as peer teachers.

No teacher can be an expert in everything needed to run an efficient and effective classroom. Especially when individual differences in students are so varied. Best results will be seen when members of a school's faculty collaborate with one another in order to share knowledge and expertise about the student's needs and to formulate creative and practical ideas to help meet the needs of students..

Throughout this chapter, the reader will find a number of student worksheets. Copies of these worksheets are contained in the Appendix and can be reproduced for classroom use. These worksheets were designed for self-monitoring and recording behavior, contracting with students, and setting up classroom token economy systems as well as daily report card programs. Most classroom teachers have used similar forms to assist their students in charting their behavior or to motivate student performance. The following interventions will be reviewed:

- Behavioral Contracting
- Token Economy Systems
- Daily Report Cards
- Behavioral Principles
- Self-Monitoring
- Time-Out
- Modeling
- Peer Teaching
- Pre-referral Strategies

The reader is referred to The ADAPT Program for additional forms and worksheets useful in the design and implementation of accommodations and behavioral interventions for students in elementary through middle school. Teachers can use ADAPT forms found in The ADAPT Teacher Planbook to assess the need for specific accommodations and interventions and can monitor student progress after an accommodation plan is implemented. In addition, many of the worksheets discussed in this chapter are also found in The ADAPT Student Planbook. Those already using ADAPT forms will benefit from reviewing the behavioral interventions which are discussed in this chapter.

Behavioral Contracting

A behavioral contract is an agreement drawn up between two or more parties, in this case a teacher, a parent, and a student, wherein the student agrees to behave in a specified manner in exchange for some specific reciprocal behavior from the teacher or parent. The purpose of the contract is to restructure the environment to provide a consistent set of expectations and consequences to the student, based upon certain pre-defined performance criteria.

Behavioral contracts, whether written or oral, should clearly delineate the expectations of all parties, should contain well-defined methods of assessing student performance, and should specify precise rewards and/or penalties to be provided based on student performance. Written behavioral contracts tend to be more official than oral contracts and should contain the signatures of all parties, the date when the contract was entered into, and the signature of a witnessing party (see samples on pages 97 and 98).

Behavioral contracts have been used successfully for many years to motivate students to perform. Contracts are often successful because they provide a "win-win" approach to helping the student and take into consideration the personal goals of each party.

The use of behavioral contracts with students with ADHD may require certain modifications that may not normally be needed with students who do not have problems of impulsivity and hyperactivity.

Young students, in general, may lack adequate language development to understand the essential meaning of a contract and the implication that this is an agreement, promise, or "deal" which is meant to be kept by both the teacher and the student. A young student with ADHD, in particular, may have such a lack of impulse control that contracting is ineffective, since the student is just unable to manifest enough self-control even for very short periods of time to fulfill his end of the agreement. This is especially true of very hyperactive youngsters who are in preschool through first or second grade.

Contracting with children who have ADHD, in general, may require the teacher or parent to emphasize immediacy of reinforcement. Non-ADHD youngsters are more likely able to wait a day or longer to "cash-in" on their positive performance as per the terms of their behavioral contracts. Many students with ADHD will probably need shorter periods of time and more opportunities to receive reinforcement than will their non-ADHD counterparts. Every student with ADHD will respond differently with respect to the length of time between reinforcement, as some will require reinforcement at the end of each period, some at the end of the morning or afternoon, and some will be able to wait until the end of the day or week before "cashing-in."

How To Use Behavioral Contracting with Students with ADHD

1. Explain what a behavior contract is. For young children, the contract can be described as a "game" which gives the student an opportunity to win things from the teacher. For older children, explain that contracts are used throughout society in business, in social relationships, and between countries. Equate the idea of a contract to the notion of a promise or an agreement between two people who give their word to exchange one thing for another.

2. Explain that contracts can be used in school to help motivate students to improve their performance.

3. For young children, select one or two "target" behaviors on which you would like the student to focus. Demonstrate the behavior so that the child clearly understands what you mean. For instance, if you are asking the child to pay attention to you when you are talking, you might sit at the desk, show the child that paying attention means to look at the person talking, listen to that person, and do what they say to do. If your goal is to increase work production, then you should tell the child exactly how this will be measured (e.g., by counting problems completed).

For older students, discuss with the student general behaviors that he exhibits which need improving. Specify these behaviors as "target" behaviors as specifically as possible. Encourage student input in defining the "target" behaviors.

4. Write down one or two target behaviors for younger students while older students may be able to work on four or more such target behaviors: e.g. raises hand before asking a question or giving an answer, copies homework assignments from board each day in an assignment journal, pays attention for fifteen minutes at the start of every math lesson, etc.

5. Specify how each target behavior will be measured and when (e.g., mark down every time the child raises his hand instead of calling out; challenge him to pay attention for fifteen minutes during a math lesson and record his performance).

6. With student input, decide on an appropriate reward (or penalty) to be given for performing (or not performing) the target behavior(s). Specify when the reward (or penalty) is to be given. Remember, students with ADHD may need more frequent rewards. Make a menu of such rewards or change the reward regularly to maintain motivation.

7. Write down the specifics of the contract and have it signed by the student. Make a copy for both the teacher and student.

8. Review the contract daily. When target behaviors are demonstrated by the student, use social praise with consistent administration of pre-determined reinforc-

ers when performance levels have met or exceeded criteria.

Token Economy Systems

Token economy systems are a form of behavioral contracting that uses tokens as an immediate reward for certain behavior or task performance. Tokens generally have no intrinsic value other than their worth when exchanged for valued objects, activities, or privileges. Teachers are often unable to provide more tangible reinforcers "on the spot" and, therefore, utilize token systems to motivate students to reach certain behavioral or performance criteria. Token systems have an additional advantage over simple behavioral contracts in that they offer the promise of a hierarchal reward system and teach the student to delay gratification.

How To Use Token Economy Systems with Students with ADHD

1. Explain the concept of a token economy system to the student. Tell the student that he will receive or lose tokens based upon his performance throughout the school day.

2. Select an appropriate token. Commonly used tokens may be points on a card or chart (for older students age eight and up) or poker chips, fake money, stamps, etc. (for students below eight). Make sure the student could not reproduce the token on his own. For example if you are using points on a card use a pen to tally points, etc.

3. Discuss with the student the specific goals that you had in mind for the student to reach. Decide which school behavior is important for the student to demonstrate in order to reach these goals. List two to five behaviors targeted for change

on a daily or weekly chart (see sample). Make sure the target behaviors are positively phrased and described in a way that is observable and measurable.

4. Assign a token value for each behavior. Simple behaviors, or those that are frequently demonstrated by the student, should have a smaller token value than behaviors that are more complicated or infrequently demonstrated by the student.

5. Fines can be a part of the token system as well. Select one negative behavior which is particularly problematic and remove tokens when that behavior is displayed. While it is better to have a positively oriented token program than a negatively oriented one, the judicious use of fines can be effective in discouraging inappropriate behavior.

6. Determine rewards for which the tokens can be exchanged. A large variety of rewards should be listed so to motivate the student. Rewards may be activities that the student likes (free time, homework pass, food, objects).

7. Decide when tokens will be given and when they might be exchanged for rewards. Again, younger students with ADHD or students with ADHD who have serious performance problems, may need tokens delivered immediately upon demonstrating a behavior, while others may be able to wait for the period to end or for the end of the morning or day to receive tokens. Similarly, some students may prefer to "cash in" tokens for rewards from their list more frequently than others.

Homework Contract

Name:_____ Date:_____

Use this homework contract to set goals for yourself and earn rewards and privileges.

I, _____ (child's name), do hereby declare that I will copy

all assignments that I am given in class and that I will do all my homework and turn it in

when it is due. Furthermore, I will only ask for help if and when I don't understand what

I am supposed to do. I will work as neatly as I can and I will check my work to make sure

it is done correctly. When I finish my homework I will put it away in a safe place to bring

to school the following day.

In WITNESS WHEREOF, we have subscribed our names on this date.

Date:_____

Child's signature:_____

Witness's signature_____

Behavior Contract

Name:_____ Date:_____

Use this behavior contract to set goals for yourself and earn rewards and privileges.

I, _____ (child's name), do hereby declare that I will:

_____

_____

I, _____ (teacher/parent), do hereby declare that in exchange

for _____(child's name) fulfilling his/her promise I will

_____.

In WITNESS WHEREOF, we have subscribed our names on this date.

Date:_____

Child's signature:_____

Teacher's/parent's signature:_____

Generally speaking, when starting a new program, try to reward new target behaviors frequently by administering tokens often and by offering the student frequent opportunities to cash-in the tokens for rewards. Some students may want to save up their tokens for a larger, more special predetermined privilege to be awarded at the end of the week.

8. Construct a daily or weekly chart (see sample on page 101) on which the target behaviors will be listed along with their respective token value. Also list the rewards, the value of each reward, and when the reward may be received by the student.

9. Using the daily or weekly chart, discuss with the student his performance on a daily basis. Praise success and encourage better performance in weak areas. Make suggestions to the student on ways he can better succeed. Offer to use verbal or non-verbal prompts to remind the student to perform certain behaviors. Maintain a positive, encouraging attitude.

The Attention Training System

Dr. Michael Gordon invented the Attention Training System (ATS) to be used along with a classroom token economy to help motivate students to pay attention. The ATS is a small electronic counter that is placed on the student's desk. The ATS automatically awards the child a point every sixty seconds. If the student wanders off task, the teacher uses a remote control to deduct a point and activate a small warning light on the student's module. The ATS delivers unobtrusive, but effective feedback and functions during regular classroom activities. Each teacher module can control four student modules. Points earned on the ATS may be exchanged for rewards or

free time activities within the token economy system.

Although some teachers initially express concern that an electronic device such as the ATS may cause a distraction in the classroom, most classes adapt to the novelty of the ATS in a few days and teachers find it to be a very helpful way to promote attention-to-task.

The Daily Report Card

The Daily Report Card program involves the collaboration between school and home in the assessment of student behavior by the teacher, and the administration of rewards and consequences at home, based upon the teacher's assessment.

Unlike a token economy system or behavioral contract, the Daily Report Card has the advantage of incorporating the student's parents into the behavioral program that is being used in school. Parents of students with ADHD, used to working with teachers, quickly adapt to the program and often appreciate having daily feedback as to their child's school performance. Daily reporting generally facilitates better parent-teacher communication and encourages the development of home-school partnerships. Parents don't have to wait for parent-teacher conferences or report cards to learn about their child's progress.

While the Daily Report Card program is effective for a good many students with ADHD, there are some problems which can develop when it is implemented.

First, some students cannot delay gratification long enough to receive reinforcements later that day when they return home. This is particularly true when working with students with ADHD in the primary grades who may need more immediate reinforcement.

Second, some students will be irresponsible in bringing the Daily Report Card home or returning it to school. Students can be trained to use their cards daily. Teachers should establish routines for scoring of cards in school and parents should have consistent routines for daily review of the card at home. Mild consequences for not bringing the card to or from school may sometimes need to be implemented to encourage reluctant or forgetful students.

Third, parental compliance in reviewing the Daily Report Card and in delivery of contingencies is generally out of the teacher's control. Poor parental compliance will inevitably cause the system to fail.

How To Use the Daily Report Card

The Daily Report Card can be adapted for individual students' needs. One of the sample Daily Report Cards shown targets five behaviors commonly found to be problematic for children with ADHD in the classroom. There are two forms of the program: a rating by day card, on which the child is evaluated once per day each day for the entire week, and a rating by subject (period) card, whereon the child is evaluated several times per day either by subject, activity, period, or teacher (see pages 104-107).

Most children in elementary school will be able to use a rating by day Daily Report Card because they will be evaluated by one teacher one time per day. Those elementary school students who require more frequent daily ratings, due to high rates of inappropriate behavior, or because they are evaluated by more than one teacher each day, will need a rating by subject card. Middle school students, who usually have several teachers in one day, will need to use the rating by subject card.

Regardless of whether the child is evaluated one or more times a day the target behaviors can remain the same and may include the following (as listed on the samples on pages 104 and 106):

- Paid Attention
- Completed Work
- Completed Homework
- Was Well Behaved
- Desk and Notebook Neat

The student is rated on a five point scale (1=Poor, 2=Improved, 3=Fair, 4=Good, 5=Excellent). When a category of behavior does not apply for the student for that day (e.g., no homework assigned, the teacher marks N/A and the student is automatically awarded five points).

STEP 1: Explaining the Program to the Child

The Daily Report Card may be introduced to the child by his parents alone, together with his teacher, or with the assistance of a health care professional. The program should be described in a positive manner as a method by which to help the child achieve more success in school.

1. The child is instructed to give the Daily Report Card to his teacher(s) each day for scoring.

2. The teacher(s) scores the card, initials it and returns it to the student to bring home to his parents for review.

3. Each evening, the parents review the total points earned for the day. If the child is using the single rating Daily Report Card, it is to be brought to school each day for the rest of the week to be completed by the teacher. If a multiple rating Daily Report Card is used, then the child should be given a new card to bring to school for use the following day.

4. Encouragement is offered to the child by the parents in the form of verbal praise and tangible rewards for his successes, while loss of privileges is applied for point totals below a prescribed amount each day (see below). It is important that a combination of rewards and consequences be utilized since children with ADHD are noted to have a high reinforcement tolerance. That is, they seem to re-

Classroom Token Economy

START BEHAVIORS	Value	Mo	Tu	We	Th	Fr
Extra Credit!_____						
TOTAL TOKENS EARNED						

STOP BEHAVIORS	Value	Mo	Tu	We	Th	Fr
Extra Loss!_____						
TOTAL TOKENS LOST						

TOTAL TOKENS AVAILABLE					

REWARDS	Value	Mo	Tu	We	Th	Fr
TOTAL TOKENS REMAINING						

quire larger reinforcers and stronger consequences other children.

5. Explain to the child that if he forgets, loses, or destroys the Daily Report Card he is given zero points for the day and appropriate consequences should follow.

If we are to expect complete cooperation from the child then both parents and teachers need to demonstrate a strong involvement with the program through daily evaluation by the teacher and nightly review by the parents.

STEP 2: Setting Up Rewards and Consequences

When using the Daily Report Card be careful to set your reinforcement and punishment cut-off scores at a realistic level so that the child can be successful on the card provided that he is making a reasonable effort in school. Although individual differences need to be considered, I have found that a Daily Report Card score of 17 points or more per day is an effective cut-off score for starting the program if five behaviors are targeted.

As the child improves in performance, the cut-off score can be raised a little at a time in accordance with the child's progress. If the child receives less than the cut-off number of points on any given day then a mild punishment (e.g., removal of a privilege, earlier bed time, etc.) should be provided, however, for points at or above the amount expected, a reward should be forthcoming.

Constructing a List of Rewards

The child and parents should construct a list of rewards that the child would like to receive for bringing home a good Daily Report Card. Some sample rewards are:
- Additional time for television in the evening after homework

- Staying up later than usual
- Time on video game
- A trip to the store for ice-cream, etc.
- Playing a game with mom or dad
- Going to a friend's house after school
- Earning money to buy something or to add to savings
- Exchanging points for tokens to save up for a larger reward at some future time.

Constructing Negative Consequences

The child and parents should construct a list of negative consequences one of which could be imposed upon the child for failure to earn a specified number of points on the Daily Report Card. Negative consequences should be applied judiciously given consideration for the student with ADHD who has inherent difficulties. Some examples are:
- Early bedtime for not reaching a set number of points
- Missing dessert
- Reduction in length of play time or television time
- Removal of video game for the day

STEP 3: Using the Program

During the first three days of the program, baseline data should be collected. This is the breaking-in phase wherein points earned by the student will count toward rewards, but not toward loss of privileges. As with any new procedure, it is likely that either the child or teacher will occasionally forget to have the Daily Report Card completed. Such mistakes should be overlooked during this breaking-in phase.

After this brief period, it is essential that the teacher score the Daily Report Card each day. The teacher should ask the child for the card even when the child forgets to bring it up for scoring and should reinforce the child for remembering on his own to hand in the card for scoring. If the child repeatedly does not bring the card to the teacher for scoring the teacher should explain the importance of daily review of the card to the child. A mild consequence may be applied if the child continues to forget the card.

Generally the best time to score the card for elementary school students who are on a single rating system is at the end of the day. Middle school students, of course, should obtain scores after each period. Ignore any arguing or negotiating on the part of the student regarding points earned. Simply encourage the child to try harder the next day.

Parents should be certain to review the Daily Report Card on a nightly basis. It is not wise to review the card immediately upon seeing the child that afternoon or evening. Set some time aside before dinner to review the card thoroughly and dispense appropriate rewards or remove privileges if necessary. After reviewing the card parents should enter the child's daily score on a monthly calendar to track points earned each day for that month. This will serve as a permanent record and can be used for students who are earning points for long term rewards.

STEP 4: Self-Evaluation Training

The self-evaluation phase of the Daily Report Card program is important in that it offers the child the opportunity to evaluate his own performance in school and creates greater self-awareness of behavior. After the child has been successful on the program for at least one month, the teacher should ask the child to complete his own Daily Report Card each day and to compare his ratings with that of the teacher's for the day. When child and teacher ratings for a particular behavior are substantially different, the teacher should explain why the child received the teacher rating.

Continue with the self-evaluation phase if the child's performance continues to be positive.

STEP 5: Phasing Out the Program

Initially, the delivery of rewards and the pru-

dent use of negative consequences drives the Daily Report Card program and provides the initial motivation to the child to succeed. When the program is working well and the child consistently brings home good marks on the Daily Report Card, he gains a sense of pride about his performance. The joy of a job well done becomes an even more powerful incentive to the child than extrinsic rewards or the fear of negative consequences. When such a result is achieved, the parents and teacher should discuss phasing out the program so as not to build reliance on the Daily Report Card.

Begin the phasing out procedures as soon as the student's behavior is consistently positive for a six-week period. Partial phasing out has already been instituted by the child's self-evaluating behavior (Step 4). Additional phasing out of the program can be accomplished by using the card less frequently (every other day or every other week). Teachers need to continue to positively reinforce the child for demonstration of appropriate target behaviors, even well after the program is discontinued.

After daily reports are phased out, you can use a weekly progress report to maintain communication between school and home regarding the student's academic performance. A sample Weekly Progress Report is included in the following pages. This one tracks the child's behavior, effort, overall progress, completion of homework, test scores, quality of work, and attention span.

Through a combined program of daily then weekly reports, teachers, parents, and the student can stay abreast of areas that are improving and those that will continue to be worked on for improvement.

Behavioral Principles

Teachers have applied the principles of behavior modification in classrooms for many years. Behavior modification is based on the as-

Daily Report Card

Rating By Day

Instructions: Please use the report card for one week. Evaluate the student's daily performance on each behavior listed below. Using the guide below, write a number in each space that indicates the student's performance in that area for the day. Use the space at the bottom for comments.

Name_____   Grade_____

Teacher_____   Week of _____

Days of the Week	MON	TUE	WED	THU	FRI
Behaviors:					
1. Paid attention in class	___	___	___	___	___
2. Completed work in class	___	___	___	___	___
3. Completed homework	___	___	___	___	___
4. Was well behaved	___	___	___	___	___
5. Desk and notebook neat	___	___	___	___	___
TOTALS	___	___	___	___	___

Teacher's Initials
5 = Excellent
4 = Good
3 = Fair
2 = Needs Improvement
1 = Poor
N/A = not applicable

Comments

Daily Report Card

Rating By Day

Instructions: Please use the report card for one week. Evaluate the student's daily performance on each behavior listed below (parent or teacher insert). Using the guide below, write a number in each space that indicates the student's performance in that area for the day. Use the space at the bottom for comments.

Name_____   Grade_____

Teacher_____   Week of _____

Days of the Week   MON TUE WED THU FRI

Behaviors

1._____   ___ ___ ___ ___ ___

2._____   ___ ___ ___ ___ ___

3._____   ___ ___ ___ ___ ___

4._____   ___ ___ ___ ___ ___

5._____   ___ ___ ___ ___ ___

TOTALS   ___ ___ ___ ___ ___

Teacher's Initials

5= Excellent

4= Good

3 = Fair

2 = Needs Improvement

1 = Poor

N/A = not applicable

Comments

Daily Report Card

Rating By Subject

Instructions: Please use the report card for one day. Evaluate the student's performance on each behavior listed below. Using the guide below, write a number in each space that indicates the student's performance in each subject for the day. Use the space at the bottom for comments.

Name_____   Grade_____

Teacher_____   Week of _____

Subject: ____ ____ ____ ____ ____

Behaviors:

1. Paid attention in class   ____ ____ ____ ____ ____

2. Completed work in class   ____ ____ ____ ____ ____

3. Completed homework   ____ ____ ____ ____ ____

4. Was well behaved   ____ ____ ____ ____ ____

5. Desk and notebook neat   ____ ____ ____ ____ ____

TOTALS   ____ ____ ____ ____ ____

Teacher's Initials
5= Excellent
4= Good
3 = Fair
2 = Needs Improvement
1 = Poor
N/A = not applicable

Comments

Daily Report Card

Rating By Subject

Instructions: Please use the report card for one day. Evaluate the student's performance on each behavior listed below (parent or teacher insert). Using the guide below, write a number in each space that indicates the student's performance in each subject for the day. Use the space at the bottom for comments.

Name_____   Grade_____

Teacher_____   Week of _____

<u>Behaviors</u>   <u>Subject:</u>   ____ ____ ____ ____ ____

1._____   ____ ____ ____ ____ ____

2._____   ____ ____ ____ ____ ____

3._____   ____ ____ ____ ____ ____

4._____   ____ ____ ____ ____ ____

5._____   ____ ____ ____ ____ ____

TOTALS   ____ ____ ____ ____ ____

Teacher's Initials
5= Excellent
4= Good
3 = Fair
2 = Needs Improvement
1 = Poor
N/A = not applicable

Comments

sumption that teachers can increase, decrease, or eliminate specific behaviors of their students by manipulating responses that follow those behaviors. Three types of responses can affect behavior: positive reinforcement, negative reinforcement, and punishment or response-cost.

Positive reinforcement involves the administration of a pleasurable or rewarding response to the student following the demonstration of a specific behavior. Positive reinforcers increase the likelihood of a behavior re-occurring. By using positive reinforcement to strengthen an appropriate behavior, we can simultaneously weaken another, incompatible, inappropriate behavior. For example, a teacher will strengthen in-seat behavior by praising a student for sitting at his desk, while at the same time weakening out-of-seat behavior, since the two behaviors are incompatible.

Negative reinforcement involves the removal of an aversive or uncomfortable event following the demonstration of a specific behavior. Negative reinforcers also increase the likelihood of a behavior re-occurring.

Punishment, or response-cost, involves the presentation of an aversive or uncomfortable consequence to the student or the removal of the student from a positive situation following the demonstration of a specific behavior. Punishment, or response cost, decreases the likelihood of a behavior re-occurring.

Applying principles of positive reinforcement, negative reinforcement, and punishment properly requires the teacher to evaluate what is rewarding and what is not rewarding to the individual student. Students differ greatly in their response to consequences. For example, social praise may be rewarding to some students, but embarrassing to others, just as punishments may vary in their effectiveness from student to student. Determining how rewarding or punishing a consequence is for a student can be accomplished by questioning the student or by applying such consequences and observing the effects on the student's behavior.

How To Use Behavioral Principles for Students with ADHD

1. Select a specific behavior that you want to increase.

2. Record each time the behavior occurs over a given period of time (e.g., how often the student starts a task within two minutes after the task is given, how often the student blurts out without asking for permission to speak, how long the student stays on task during an independent math assignment).

3. Analyze the events that are currently preceding and following the behavior. These are called antecedents and consequences. They are usually the events which precipitate and maintain a behavior.

Determining the antecedent events gives the teacher a clue as to what might precipitate a targeted behavior. In certain circumstances, removing antecedents alone may eliminate a behavior. For instance, the off task behavior of a student may be the result of the student looking out the window. Changing the student's seat away from the window will remove the antecedent. In other circumstances, by providing an antecedent you may increase the likelihood of the student displaying a behavior. For instance, walking by a student immediately after giving an instruction to complete a task may prompt the student to get to work.

Furthermore, determining the consequences which follow a targeted behavior gives the teacher an idea as to what might maintain the behavior. For example, a student's blurting out may be followed by pleasantly perceived laughter from other students, thereby reinforcing the student's behavior. Asking other students to ignore such behavior or punishing it when it occurs may alter the consequences enough to reduce the behavior.

4. If your goal is to improve the frequency of a targeted behavior then select a reinforcer which you think the student might like. Often good reinforcers can be determined by asking the student what they would like or by watching to see their preferred interests. Built-in reinforcers are common to the classroom environment. For instance, attention and praise, awarding of jobs, offerings of free time, reduction in amount of work required, good notes sent home, being first to do a valued activity, etc. Decide on how much of a reinforcer is needed to motivate the student. If behavior does not improve think about increasing the size of the reinforcement, for instance, fifteen minutes of free time instead of ten minutes, or see if another reinforcer would be more attractive to the student. A reinforcer may need to be changed after a while as it may lose appeal for the student.

5. Initially, when teaching a new behavior, it is important to present positive reinforcements immediately and continuously. That is, reinforce right after you see the behavior and every time the behavior occurs. At first, the child may not demonstrate the target behavior you are looking for. In that case you would have to reinforce behaviors that approximate the target behavior. This is called shaping behavior. For instance, in the case of a student who doesn't complete independent assignments, he might never obtain a reinforcement for completed work. However, he could be reinforced for doing a certain amount and then reinforced again for doing more, and so on until his behavior was shaped to complete entire assignments.

6. If positive reinforcement is not effective in improving a behavior, even after several different reinforcers have been tried, then the teacher might need to use negative reinforcement or punishment to change behavior. It is usually best, however, to give the positive reinforcement program a good chance to work before applying negative methods.

Negative reinforcement allows the child to avoid an aversive consequence by behaving in a specific way. For instance, "If you do your math work now, you will not have to do it for homework." ; or "Be quiet or you will lose recess." In using negative reinforcement, tell the student what they can do to avoid the aversive consequence. If they don't do what they are supposed to, provide the consequence in a firm, business-like way without emotion, lectures, or long-winded explanations to the student.

Punishment involves the removal of the student from having a positive experience or the application of an aversive consequence. The aversive consequence or punishment is presented after the inappropriate behavior is demonstrated with the expectation that the behavior will decrease after it is punished. When using punishment, it is important to make sure that the consequence delivered to the student is indeed aversive. For instance, teacher attention, even negative attention, may be reinforcing to a student

Weekly Progess Report

Name: _____   Week of:_____

Teacher: _____   Subject: _____

Behavior
___ Positive
___ Satisfactory
___ Occasionally poor
___ Frequently poor

Effort
___ Good, working well
___ Satisfactory
___ Minimal
___ Declining

Progress
___ Satisfactory
___ Unsatisfactory
___ Improving
___ Declining

Homework
___ Thoroughly completed
___ Adequately completed
___ Sometimes unprepared
___ Often unprepared

Test Scores
___ Good
___ Average
___ Poor

Work Quality
___ Exceptional
___ Adequate
___ Poor

Attention Span
___ Good
___ Fair
___ Poor

Additional Comments
Note specific areas of improvement or problems with classwork/ homework or test scores.

rather. Getting in trouble may be amusing to the student, it may create popularity with other students, and it may get the student out of being in class or out of having to do unpleasant work.

While an aversive consequence may seem aversive to the teacher, it may not be negative to the student and, therefore, will not carry the weight of a punishment and will not result in a decline in inappropriate behavior. The teacher needs to find the right punishment for the behavior and for the child. Over punishing or delivering punishments in an emotionally harsh manner discourages, angers, and demoralizes students, and can produce more negative than positive effects. Punishment, when used, should be administered sparingly and judiciously.

Sample Compliments:

Great job!
Way to go!
You made it look easy.
Now you're cookin'!
Good thinking!
Keep up the good work!
FANTASTIC!
I like your style.
You really catch on quick.
That's terrific.
I'm proud of you.
That's good.
OUTSTANDING!
You figured that one out!
Much better.
Keep at it.
Good for you.
I knew you could do it.
A fine job.
Right on!
Couldn't be better.
Wow, you are good.
Good listening.
Keep up the good work.

Well, aren't you something.
GREAT!
SENSATIONAL!
Right on target.
Looking great.
You must be proud of yourself.
SUPERB!
That's right.
Good answer.
Nice try.
You got it right!
You did very well today.
You don't miss anything.
PERFECT!
That was great.
I'm impressed with you.
You keep improving.
UNBELIEVABLE!
OUT OF SIGHT!

Self-Monitoring

Self-monitoring is a method of teaching students self-control over their behavior. Self-monitoring requires that the student act as an observer for his or her own behavior and record their observations. In doing so students usually achieve better self-control.

Researchers have demonstrated that self-monitoring procedures can be used successfully in classrooms for students varying in ages and abilities and in both regular and special education settings. The bulk of classroom use of self-monitoring procedures has focused on increasing rates of positive behavior, for instance, attention-to-task, academic productivity, and academic accuracy.

When learning self-monitoring, students must perform a routine in which they stop what they are doing, evaluate their behavior, and record whether a specific target behavior has occurred or is occurring. Most self-monitoring procedures have been targeted at improving attention to tasks and employing cueing of the student when to initiate the self-monitoring routine. Popular cueing techniques involve tape-recorded tones presented at irregular intervals (mean intertone interval of forty-five seconds). Each tone serves to prompt the student to evaluate whether they were performing the target behavior, for instance, paying attention to their work, and to self-record their performance on a data sheet. In using this procedure, teachers frequently ask if it would be more effective to provide students with auditory cues through earphones so that they would not be audible to other students in the classroom. There is some limited evidence suggesting that when other students who are not the targets of the self-monitoring intervention hear the cues, their behavior improves as well.

How To Use Self-Monitoring To Improve Attention-To-Task

1. Explain to the student that you would like to help him learn to pay attention better. Explain to younger students that paying attention to work means that they should keep their eyes on their work, think about what they are doing, and follow instructions to complete the assignment. Teachers should demonstrate examples of off-task behavior such as daydreaming, drawing or doodling at the desk, talking to a nearby student, etc.

2. The teacher should have a signalling tape which will provide an audible tone to the student and cue the student to self-monitor. A self-recording form is provided(see page 116) on which the student could mark whether or not he was paying attention when he heard the audible tone. You can make your own signalling tape by recording a tone at irregular intervals (mean interval approximately 45 seconds) or by purchasing commercially

available signalling tapes. The Listen, Look and Think Program (Parker, 1992) is available through the ADD WareHouse and contains a continuous-play self-recording tape, instruction booklet, and self-evaluation forms for students to record and assess their performance.

3. Demonstrate the signalling tape and recording forms to a group of students who have trouble paying attention. In this way it will be less embarrassing for any one student to use the procedure. Eventually, as the self-monitoring procedure becomes more of an established routine in the classroom, it may be used more with individual students when needed.

4. Decide with the student(s) when it would be best for the student(s) to self-monitor attentiveness. Usually self-monitoring is done when independent seat work is required. Students will vary in their attentiveness to a task depending on the characteristics of the task. Some students will be more interested in one subject over another and may benefit from using a self-monitoring procedure only on low-interest tasks or on tasks on which they find it difficult to keep their minds set.

5. Set up the signalling tape and give each student using the procedure a self-recording form which includes a self-evaluation section. Review the procedures for self-recording and self-evaluation. Do not be concerned whether the student records his attention-to-task correctly. Research indicates that even when a student's assessment of on-task behavior is found to be exaggerated in comparison with independent observational data, improvement in attention is still noted.

6. After some period of noticeable improvement in attention-to-task with the self-monitoring procedure, the teacher can begin to withdraw elements of the procedure either by withdrawing the audible tone first, or by withdrawing the self-recording form first. It will be important, however, for the teacher to continue to positively reinforce on-task behavior in some manner. Attention-to-task usually continues without these aids, but if the positive effects begin to lessen, the teacher can provide "booster" training sessions by re-introducing the self-monitoring procedures periodically.

How To Use Self-Monitoring To Improve Attention, Self-Control, and Organization

1. Explain to the student the importance of paying attention, maintaining self-control, and keeping organized.

2. Review the self-monitoring record form (see pages 118-121) and instruct the student to check himself at the end of each morning and afternoon (or adapt for specific subjects) whether he was paying attention, controlling his behavior, and keeping his things in order.

3. Discuss with the student, activities the student would like to earn, based upon his performance on the "I Can Do It" record form.

4. The teacher should rate the child each morning and afternoon on a separate recording form and should ask the student to compare his ratings to those of the teachers. The student should try to match the teacher's twice daily ratings.

5. The student should be allowed to participate in a preselected activity, based upon the number of check marks he tallied for the morning and/or afternoon.

6. Some students will have difficulty waiting until the end of the morning or afternoon to rate their behavior. In such cases the student may need a modified version of the form that would allow for more frequent self-monitoring.

How To Use Self-Monitoring To Improve Handwriting

1. Explain to the student that you would like him to pay more attention to his handwriting. For younger students, explain that paying attention to handwriting means that they should keep their eyes on their work, think about what they are doing, and try to write as neatly as they can. Teachers should model behaviors that have been associated with poor handwriting such as poor pencil grip, awkward posture, poor paper orientation relative to body position, and rushing through work.

2. The teacher should ask the student to write four samples of a short paragraph of three or four lines showing their "best" penmanship, " good" penmanship, "fair" penmanship and "poor" penmanship on four separate large index cards. These writing samples should then be labeled as Best, Good, Fair, and Poor.

Remember, students with fine-motor handicaps will not be able to write as neatly. When making up penmanship samples, accept what they can do and rate their sample productions as Best, Good,

Fair, and Poor relative to their ability. Such students may need Additional help for handwriting problems. Discontinue if this self-monitoring procedure becomes too taxing or frustrating for them. Consider a referral to a specialist who can help the student further with handwriting difficulties.

3. Immediately after giving a writing assignment the teacher should review the rules of good handwriting with the student. These rules are on the handwriting recording form (next page) in the form of questions to cue appropriate behavior. For example:
   - Is my pencil sharp?
   - Am I holding the pencil correctly?
   - Am I sitting properly?
   - Is my paper where it should be?
   - Am I paying attention to neatness?
   - Am I taking my time when I write?

4. After finishing the assignment the student should fill out the handwriting recording form (see page 120) by circling the correct answer to each of the six questions. The student then should compare his handwriting to the writing samples he created earlier and rate the neatness of his current work.

How To Use Self-Monitoring and Self-Timing To Improve Productivity

1. Have student break assignment into three sections.

2. Train student to estimate the amount of time which he will need to complete each section.

3. Advise student to be cautious and to avoid careless errors that could result

from rushing through assignments. This is particularly important for those children who have attention deficits and who tend to do their work too quickly.

4. Provide student with a timing device (e.g., clock or alarm which will signal when estimated time is up).

5. Ask student to keep track whether he reached his goals in completing sections of work within the estimated time frame.

How To Use Self-Monitoring To Improve Social Skills in the Classroom

1. Train students in the use of appropriate social interaction skills through didactic teaching procedures and through role-playing.

2. With the student, select a specific social skill for the student to practice for the day. Model the skill for the student and ask him to identify when others in the class exhibit that particular skill.

3. Use the social skills recording form (see page 123) on which the student could self-monitor his performance of the skill periodically throughout the day.

Sample social skills:

Giving others a turn
Cooperating with others
Respecting the rights of others
Doing someone a favor
Starting a conversation
Leading a group
Expressing your ideas or feelings
Saying you're sorry
Ignoring someone's behavior
Being polite

Introducing yourself
Handling failure
Rewarding yourself
Asking for help
Saying thank you
Giving a compliment
Listening

How To Use Self-Monitoring To Transfer Self-Control Learning from a Resource Classroom To a Regular Classroom

1. The resource room teacher should teach appropriate target behaviors in a resource setting by using a token economy system and awarding points for demonstration of appropriate behaviors that are targeted for change.

2. The resource room teacher instructs the student to evaluate his own behavior by awarding himself points and compares his self-evaluations with the resource teacher's evaluations at the end of each period in the resource room.

3. Students are awarded points for demonstrating appropriate behavior and can earn additional points for matching the teacher's ratings of their behavior with their own ratings. Self-evaluations of behavior are recorded on a separate evaluation card.

4. The resource room teacher's ratings of the student's behavior are gradually faded out and the student is asked to evaluate his own behavior on the self-evaluation card with no external teacher evaluation.

5. Generalization to the regular education class is accomplished by having the student carry with him to the mainstream class the self-evaluation card on which

he has been recording his points. Regular classroom teachers then instruct the student to engage in the same self-evaluating routine that he has learned in the resource setting.

How To Use Self-Monitoring To Improve Hand-Raising Behavior

1. Review with student the rules regarding the appropriate use of hand-raising to ask permission to talk.

2. Explain the problems that result in the classroom when a student calls out an answer or speaks out of turn (e.g., disrupts other students, does not give a turn to others)..

3. Model appropriate hand-raising behavior. Encourage student who has difficulty waiting for recognition to repeat what he wants to say silently to himself while his hand is raised (e.g., student should say to himself over and over while waiting, "The answer is...", or "I want to ask the teacher if ...").

4. When training this new behavior, the teacher should make an effort to call on the student immediately after the student raises his hand. Accompany this with positive reinforcement (e.g., "Thank you for raising your hand.").

5. Remind student to mark a circle on his self-monitoring record form (se page 125) whenever he raises his hand before talking.

How To Use Self-Monitoring To Improve Proofreading Skills

1. Review with the student the importance of proofreading written work.

Was I Paying Attention?

Name: _____   Date:_____

Instructions:
Listen to the beep tape * as you do your work. Whenever you hear a beep, stop working for a moment and ask yourself, "Was I paying attention?" Mark your answer (√) and go right back to work. Answer the questions on the bottom of the page when you finish.

Was I Paying Attention?

Start here

YES	NO

Was I Paying Attention?

YES	NO

Did I follow the directions?	Yes	No
Did I pay attention?	Yes	No
Did I finish my work?	Yes	No
Did I check my answers?	Yes	No

* Beep tape available in Listen, Look and Think Program by Harvey C. Parker, Ph.D. (800) ADD-WARE

2. Go over the important elements of proof-reading. Explain that the following items should be checked:
   - Heading
   - Margins
   - Proper spacing between words
   - Neatness of handwriting
   - Starting sentences with capitals
   - Using punctuation correctly
   - Crossing out mistakes with only one line
   - Spelling correctly

3. Explain how to use the Proofreading Checklist form (see page 126).

Time-Out

Time-out is a mild punishment technique whereby the student is asked to leave a setting after committing an inappropriate act. Time-out has been used by teachers for years. Sending children to the hallway, asking them to sit by themselves in the room, or withdrawing attention from them in the classroom are all examples of time-out. Based upon the fact that inappropriate behaviors are weakened by punishment, time-out offers the teacher a sensible way to respond to the student.

How To Use Time-Out with Students with ADHD

1. Determine a place in the classroom that could be used as a time-out place. The time-out place could be a specific desk away from the other students, a place in the room that is marked off by strips of tape, etc. If a separate room is being used make sure it is well lit, ventilated, free of any material that could hurt the student, and that the student can be observable by the teacher or another adult.

2. Review the classroom rules with stu-dents, explain what time-out means, and when it will be applied.

3. Use a consistent method to warn the student whose behavior is inappropriate that he may be sent to time out if he continues to misbehave. Be brief. Don't lecture, scold, or repetitively remind the student to behave. One warning, administered calmly and tactfully, is best.

4. If the student continues to display the inappropriate behavior tell him he must go to time-out. Again, deliver the time-out instruction in a firm, calm, and uncritical manner. Do not give long-winded explanations or debate with the student about your reasons for directing him to time-out.

   Lack of consistent follow-through by the teacher and/or excessive warnings administered without action taken, will weaken the teacher's credibility and will render the time out procedure ineffective.

5. Usually time-out is brief, from one to ten minutes, with younger children requiring less time. Tell the student how long his time-out is. Begin timing when all inappropriate behavior stops. Tell the student that he cannot be released from time-out unless he is behaving appropriately during time-out.

6. Time-out is time out from reinforcement so all potential reinforcers should be removed from the student while he is in time-out. When in time-out the student should be ignored by the teacher and by classmates.

7. If a separate room has been used for time-

I Can Do My Best In Class

Name: _____   Date:_____

Instructions:
Students who are well behaved, and organized often do well in school. Read each line and circle either "YES" or "NO" to describe how you did today in one of the subjects you underline below.

English   Math   Reading   Social Studies   Science   Other

I CAN PAY ATTENTION

1.	I paid attention to the teacher today.	YES	NO
2.	I concentrated on my work and not on other students.	YES	NO
3.	I followed directions.	YES	NO
4.	I finished all my work.	YES	NO

I CAN KEEP MY THINGS IN ORDER

5.	My desk was neat.	YES	NO
6.	My work was put away in its place.	YES	NO
7.	My writing was neat.	YES	NO

I CAN CONTROL MY BEHAVIOR

8.	I raised my hand.	YES	NO
9.	I asked permission before getting up.	YES	NO
10.	I cooperated with others.	YES	NO

Add up the number of times you circled "YES" _____

How did you do?   GREAT   PRETTY GOOD   ROOM FOR IMPROVEMENT
                        8-10   5-7   1-4

Just as with attention, you can improve your organization and behavior by working on one "NO" answer each week.

I Can Pay Attention TODAY

Name: _____   Date:_____

Instructions:
For some people, paying attention is easy. They have no trouble focusing. For other people, paying attention is hard. They get distracted easily and find it hard to concentrate. Read each line and circle either "YES" or "NO" to describe how you did in class today.

1. I paid attention to the teacher today. YES   NO
2. I looked at the teacher while a lesson was being taught. YES   NO
3. I thought about what was important to remember while the teacher was teaching. YES   NO
4. I followed directions I was told. YES   NO
5. I read all the directions on written work. YES   NO
6. I asked questions if I didn't understand. YES   NO
7. I answered a question. YES   NO
8. I wrote all my homework in my assignment book. YES   NO
9. I remembered to take home what I needed. YES   NO
10. I reminded myself to pay attention if I got distracted. YES   NO
11. I finished all my work. YES   NO

Add up the number of times you circled "YES" _____

How did you do today?   GREAT   PRETTY GOOD   ROOM FOR IMPROVEMENT
                          9-11   6-10   1-5

Now it is time to work on the ones you answered "NO." Each week select a new behavior to practice in class. Soon you'll see improvement in your attention and your grades as well.

Writing Reminders

Name: _____   Date:_____

Instructions:
Good posture, a proper grip on your pencil, and the paper placed correctly in front of you are important habits to get into for good handwriting. Take your time while writiing and pay attention to neatness. Use this list below to remind you to be careful with your handwriting.

Assignment: _____

1. Is my pencil sharp?   YES   NO

2. Am I holding the pencil correctly?   YES   NO

3. Am I sitting properly?   YES   NO

4. Is my paper on the desk where it should be?   YES   NO

5. Am I paying attention to neatness?   YES   NO

6. Am I taking my time when I write?   YES   NO

Self-Evaluation Form

Name: _____   Date:_____

Instructions:
Complete this form and evaluate yourself on how you worked in school today.

1. Did I pay attention and follow directions today?   YES   NO

2. Did I put my heading on my papers today?   YES   NO

3. Did I finish all my work on time today?   YES   NO

4. Were my papers and my desk organized today?   YES   NO

5. Did I compy my homework in my assignment planner?   YES   NO

6. Did I use my time wisely today?   YES   NO

7. Did I have all my homework completed from last night?   YES   NO

out the teacher should keep a record of when the student was sent to time-out, for how long, and for what reason.

8. After the student is released from time-out, look for signs of appropriate behavior and reinforce it consistently. Remember, punishment only suppresses negative behaviors; it doesn't strengthen positive behaviors.

9. Do not use time-out as a way of keeping disruptive students segregated from the rest of the class.

Modeling

Modeling is a method of learning through observation and imitation. The student is encouraged to watch someone who exhibits a specific skill with the intention of their eventually being able to emulate that same skill. The student may be asked to just observe the model, observe and rehearse the modeled behavior, or observe and recite to themselves a description of the modeled behavior, and then rehearse the behavior.

How To Use Modeling with Students

1. Choose a behavior that you would like the student to emulate.

2. Describe the elements of the behavior that you would like the child to emulate and provide coaching for the child so he understands how to perform the behavior you are expecting. For example, if your goal is to teach attending behavior you might review the important elements of attending, namely: maintaining eye contact with the person who is speaking, focusing concentration, subvocalizing, etc.

    If the goal was related to acquisition of a social skill, such as making plans with another child, the teacher would review the important elements of doing so, namely: acting friendly, smiling, starting a conversation, and inviting the child to do something. It might help to write the elements of a behavior down so that they are clear to the child.

3. The teacher should then serve as the model for the behavior and should recite aloud the elements and demonstrate them. The teacher should practice this process with the student.

4. Throughout the day, the teacher should cue the student to practice the newly learned behavior. The student should be encouraged to subvocalize the elements of the behavior as they have been written down for him.

5. The teacher may point out other students in the class who also demonstrate the targeted behavior and should ask the student to observe them.

6. The teacher should provide incentives to the student for successful modeling and should praise the student for approximate successes so as to encourage skill building.

Peer Teaching

Peer teaching is a technique wherein one student works with another student under the supervision of a teacher. The peer teacher may be assigned to assist in teaching an academic skill or social skill: to be a study partner, a companion during lunch, a behavior manager, or to serve as a sounding board for another student.

Peer teaching can benefit both the student who receives the instruction and the provider of such instruction. Not only can bright, achieving

Getting Along

Name: _____   Date:_____

> **Instructions:**
> Choose one of the skills listed below to practice today or select one of your own
> and write it below.

I will practice: _____

Where (circle all areas):   In Class   At Lunch or Recess   After School

How did you get along with others today? _____ Great _____ Good _____ I could do better

Sample Social Skills

1. Giving others a turn.

2. Cooperating with others

3. Expressing my ideas and feelings.

4. Doing someone a favor.

5. Starting a conversation.

6. Telling the teacher when someone bothers me.

7. Leading a group.

8. Respecting the rights of others.

9. Saying I'm sorry.

10. Ignoring someone's behavior.

11. Being polite.

12. Controlling my temper.

students serve as peer teachers, but those students who are not excelling well and whose self-esteem is lacking may benefit by serving as peer teachers.

How To Use Peer Teaching with Students
The Student with ADHD as a Peer Teacher

1. The teacher decides that the student with ADHD would benefit from being a peer teacher. Such teaching would likely utilize the student who has ADHD as either an academic tutor or a behavior manager. As an academic tutor, the student will instruct another student in an academic skill during a prescribed time period under the supervision of the teacher.

   As a behavior manager, the student with ADHD might explain a behavior management program to another student, may keep track of behaviors, may dispense reinforcement, etc. during a prescribed period of time. The teacher determines the strengths of the student and finds another student, either in the same grade or younger, who might benefit from his assistance.

2. The teacher must select a tutoring place either in the classroom or in a nearby room.

3. The teacher should notify the parents of both students so that neither set of parents will be surprised if their child reports that they are helping or receiving help from another student.

4. Peer teachers should be taught basic teaching skills such as giving praise to correct responses, listening patiently, querying as to whether their student needs additional explanation or practice, and avoiding criticism. Teachers should role play situations so that the peer teacher can "get the feel" of tutoring another student.

5. The teacher should periodically question both the peer teacher and student about the peer teaching process to obtain continuous feedback and make adjustments accordingly. Personalities may conflict, academic skills may be hard to explain, behavioral programs may meet with limited success, etc. The supervising teacher needs to be alert to potential problems so that solutions can be applied early in the process, thereby reducing any wasted time or frustration to the parties involved.

The Student with ADHD as a Recipient of Peer Teaching

1. The teacher decides what the goals of having a peer teacher would be for the student with ADHD. As discussed above, the goal could be one of academic skill or behavioral improvement. The selection of the peer teacher is extremely important in that it should be someone who will be sensitive and understanding of the student's difficulties and one who will encourage a positive attitude and build up self-esteem.

2. The teacher must select a tutoring place either in the classroom or in a nearby room.

3. The teacher should notify the parents of both students so that neither set of parents will be surprised if their child reports that they are helping or receiving help from another student.

4. Peer teachers should be taught basic teaching skills such as giving praise to correct responses, listening patiently,

Hand Raising Record Form

Name: _____   Date:_____

Instructions:
Find the hidden dog bone and fill it in each time you remember to RAISE YOUR HAND to ask permission to talk.

Proofreading Checklist

Name: _____   Date:_____

Instructions:
After you have finished your writing assignment, check your work for neatness, spelling and organization. Circle either YES or NO. Or, if you like, ask another student in your class to look over your work and complete this proofreading checklist.

Assignment: _____

1. Heading on paper?	YES NO
2. Margins correct?	YES NO
3. Proper spacing between words?	YES NO
4. Handwriting neat?	YES NO
5. Sentences start with capital letters?	YES NO
6. Sentences end with correct punctuation?	YES NO
7. Crossed out mistakes with only one line?	YES NO
8. Spelling is correct?	YES NO

querying as to whether their student needs additional explanation or practice, and avoiding criticism. Teachers should role-play situations so that the peer teacher can "get the feel" of tutoring another student.

5. The teacher should periodically question both the peer teacher and student about the peer teaching process to obtain continuous feedback and make adjustments accordingly. Personalities may conflict, academic skills may be hard to explain, behavioral programs may meet with limited success, etc. The supervising teacher needs to be alert to potential problems so that solutions can be applied early in the process.

Pre-referral Strategies

Pre-referral consultation refers to a process whereby regular and special educators meet and collaborate to plan interventions for at-risk or hard-to-teach students in regular academic settings. In this model, the special educator serves as a resource for the regular classroom teacher. Various people within the district who have areas of expertise in teaching difficult students may serve as prereferral consultants to the regular education teacher.

How To Use Pre-referral Consultation

There are several stages to be followed in using a pre-referral intervention model.

Stage One: Informal Pre-consultation

Informal pre-consultation refers to the process by which a teacher collects problem-solving ideas from a variety of sources to help a student. Pre-consultation is initiated when the regular classroom teacher runs across a problem which she cannot solve. Often, initial help is sought from peers as teachers discuss strategies

informally with one another. Frequently, a teacher will seek assistance from the student's prior teacher and will try to find out what was helpful to the student in the past. Additionally, teachers at the same grade level who each have the student for a class may confer with one another as to what strategies each finds to be effective for the student. Informal consultation with other teachers can offer many ideas which will lead to implementing effective strategies.

If this informal pre-consultation with other teachers is not helpful, the teacher may ask for the assistance of a school administrator. The administrator and teacher may arrive at other ideas or may decide to request the assistance of a consultant who has expertise of the kind that may be helpful in solving the student's problem.

Stage Two: Collaborative Problem-Solving

Collaborative problem-solving refers to the process by which consultants are asked to collaborate with the regular teacher to find ways to solve the student's problem. Regular meetings may be held between the consultant and teacher for several weeks, months, or throughout the school year. The focus of these meetings will be to identify strategies that could be implemented in the classroom to assist the student. To do so, the collaborative problem-solving process will likely take several steps:

1. Identification and analysis of the student's problem through informal procedures such as: assessment checklists, classroom observations, review of cumulative records, discussion with previous teachers, etc.

2. Setting goals for what the student should accomplish as a result of the problem solving process.

3. Review of previous interventions that have been applied and determination as

to why they may not have been successful, or, if they were successful for a short
time, why success was not maintained.

4. Brainstorming of potential new interven-
    tions which may assist the student.

5. Selection of a most-likely-to-succeed in-
    tervention plan which will be clearly de-
    scribed, and determination of how the in-
    tervention plan will be monitored and its
    effectiveness measured.

6. Determination of how long the interven-
    tion plan should be tried before planning
    another collaborative problem-solving
    meeting to discuss the results.

**Stage Three: Implementation and
Evaluation**

During this stage, the regular education
teacher will implement the intervention plan and
the data-gathering process by which to judge results. At future meetings with the consultant,
the teacher will review the plan's effectiveness
to determine whether alternative strategies are
needed or, if the plan is working well, how long
it should be in effect and how best to increase
maintenance, and generalization of the desired
outcome.

Summary

There are many classroom interventions that
teachers could implement to improve the behavior and academic performance of children with
ADHD. These interventions include contracting,
use of token economy systems, daily report cards,
self-monitoring strategies, time-out, peer tutoring, and collaborative problem solving. These
strategies are generally easy to implement and
are often preferred by teachers.

Chapter 11
Medical Management of ADHD

This chapter will focus on medical management of ADHD. Medication alone is not typically used to treat children with ADHD. A multimodal plan including medical management, behavior modification, educational planning, counseling, and parent education is usually recommended.

Medicine has been used to treat children with ADHD for nearly seven decades. The research on medical treatments for ADHD is abundant, and it clearly shows the efficacy of ADHD medications. In most cases, medication will be the most effective treatment the child with ADHD will receive.

This chapter will discuss the common types of medications used to treat ADHD—stimulants and non-stimulants, how they work to improve ADHD symptoms, the safety and efficacy of these medications, adverse effects, and recommendations for their use. Information about commonly used medications to treat children with ADHD who have co-morbid disorders (anxiety, mood disorders, etc.) will also be presented because co-morbidity is quite common. This chapter is meant to serve only as an introduction to medication management. For more information,

the reader is referred to an excellent book by Dr. Timothy E. Wilens, *Straight Talk About Psychiatric Medications for Kids*. Please also note that while this chapter provides basic information about medications that are useful in treating ADHD, parents should consult their child's physician before making *any* decisions about the use of such medications.

Physicians need the cooperation of parents and school personnel to ensure that the medication is needed, that main effects and side effects are monitored, and that it is available and is taken by the child as prescribed. Parents and school personnel should be responsible for giving medication to the child while in school. Some youngsters will forget to take scheduled doses of medication. Others may be resistant to taking medication because they don't like the way it tastes, they have trouble swallowing a pill, or they don't like the way it makes them feel. Teachers should be discreet when reminding a child to take medication in school. Long-acting medications have greatly reduced the need for in-school dosing.

Medication should never be given without an established system to monitor its effectiveness. The doctor prescribing the medication should obtain information from parents and teachers. Typically, teachers are the best source of information about medication effects in school. Teachers may report information about the child's reactions to medication informally to the physician, or they may complete monitoring forms for more systematic data collection. Use of behavior rating scales can be extremely helpful in determining changes in behavior. The ADHD Monitoring System (described earlier) is a convenient program that parents can use to carefully monitor how their child is doing at school. By using this system, parents will be able to carefully track their child's progress in school and will be alerted as to when any adjustments or modifications to their child's treatment need to be discussed with their physician.

Parents and professionals can have access to the ADHD Monitoring System, the Vanderbilt Assessment Scales, and many other rating scales and history forms useful for assessment and monitoring by subscribing to myADHD.com (www.myadhd.com). Using this site, scales can be sent electronically by health care professionals, parents, educators, and others to easily obtain information about the child's progress.

Some physicians recommend a trial of temporarily stopping the use of ADHD medication for a week or so each year to determine if it is still needed. For children on a stimulant medication, it is best to do this about a month or two into the start of a new school year. This gives the teacher(s) a chance to have seen the child perform while on medication and compare the child's performance when no medication is given. For children taking non-stimulants, such as Strattera, or other medications that take time to build-up to a therapeutic level, it may not be advisable to do a trial of this sort. These medications take time to build up in the bloodstream and medication-effects will take more time to diminish.

Stimulants

The stimulants are the drugs that are most commonly used to treat ADHD. This group of medications includes methylphenidate (Ritalin, Ritalin LA, Focalin, Focalin XR, Concerta, Metadate CD, and Methylin) and amphetamine (Dexedrine, Adderall, and Adderall XR). The use of stimulants with children who have ADHD has been widely publicized, hotly debated, and often questioned. Are stimulants overprescribed? Do they cause long-term problems? Are they not just covering up the real, underlying psychological problems that children with ADHD have? Are physicians rushing to put children on medication without first doing an adequate assessment? Will stimulant use lead to substance abuse in the future? Why is the use of these medications so much higher in the United States than in other countries around the world?

Stimulant use has increased five-fold over the past dozen years, and production of methylphenidate has tripled over a ten-year period. More than ninety percent of the methylphenidate produced in the United States is used domestically. The increase in use of stimulants has led to concerns about identification of ADHD in children, prescription for profit, and abuse of these medications. What explains this increase? Certainly more children are being diagnosed with ADHD than before. Prevalence estimates of the disorder were between three and five percent in the 1980's and now have reached as high as seven to twelve percent in children. However, ADHD may still be under-diagnosed and under-treated. One survey in four different communities found that only about twelve percent of diagnosed ADHD children received adequate stimulant treatment (Jensen, et al., 1999). In contrast, another study in rural North Carolina found that many school-aged children on stimulants did not meet criteria for a diagnosis of ADHD (Angold, et al., 2000). Also pushing the rise in methylphenidate use is the fact that stimulants are being dosed at higher levels and more frequently than before as clinicians realize the benefits of having kids on medication after school, on weekends, and during holidays. More diagnosis of adult ADHD has contributed to the rise in use as well since it is estimated that about one to three percent of adults suffer from ADHD and more are being treated than ever before.

The media has expressed concern about this dramatic increase in medication use. Fringe religious groups have prepared media campaigns designed to mislead, alarm, and provide biased information about stimulant medication. As a result, controversy continues to abound in the use of these medications. The public is often confused by conflicting reports about safety and efficacy.

How do Stimulants Work?

Stimulant medications increase activity or arousal in areas of the brain that are responsible for inhibiting behavior and maintaining effort or attention. They work by influencing the action of certain brain neurotransmitters, primarily dopamine and norepinephrine, both of which occur naturally throughout the brain, but are found in higher concentrations in the frontal region. The stimulants increase the amount of these chemicals that are available in the brain. Their action enhances executive functioning. These effects are observed in both ADHD and non-ADHD children, so the fact that a child improves when taking such medication should not be used to confirm a diagnosis of ADHD.

Stimulant medications are rapidly absorbed in the body, often within the first thirty minutes after taking them. Short-acting forms of stimulants (Ritalin, Methylin, Metadate, Focalin, Adderall, Dextrostat, and Dexedrine) last three to four hours while mid- to long-acting stimulants (Ritalin LA, Focalin XR, Concerta, Methylin ER, Metadate CD, and Adderall XR) last six to twelve hours. Thus, short-acting forms of the

medication are often given two to three times per day. The longer-acting forms not only have the advantage of once-a-day dosing for many children, but they reduce the likelihood of multiple withdrawals from the medication per day due to wear off. They also reduce the inconvenience and stigma of in-school dosing. With long-acting medications, there is also greater likelihood of compliance and a lower risk of abuse.

Parents often consider the school hours as the most important time when children should be on medication, but children with ADHD can benefit from taking medication that will last after school as well. Consider problems settling down and paying attention to homework, difficulties participating in sports after school, problems related to social behavior, noncompliance at home, difficulty waiting in restaurants or on long car rides, etc. All of these areas of functioning are important and stimulant medication may benefit the child in each of them. The final decision of whether to administer stimulants continuously during the day and throughout the evenings, on weekends, and holidays should be made by the parent in consultation with the child's physician as the risks versus benefits of medication are weighed.

There have been hundreds of studies on thousands of children with ADHD to support the fact that stimulants improve symptoms of ADHD. In general, seventy to ninety percent of children with ADHD will respond. That still leaves ten to thirty percent who may respond poorly or not at all, or who might have significant adverse side effects to the stimulants and cannot take them. A parent cannot assume that their child will benefit from stimulants. The only way to know is to try and see. Furthermore, while overall, methylphenidate and amphetamine compounds are similar, they do vary in terms of specific action in the brain. Different stimulants may affect the child's ADHD symptoms to different degrees. If the child does not do well on Ritalin or Concerta, for example, he may respond very well to Dexedrine or Adderall XR.

Parents should be patient and keep a scientific mind about them. Systematically trying a medication at different doses and/or trying different medications to achieve the optimal response is recommended. Parents will need to work closely with their child's physician to find the right medication and dosing and close communication with the child's teacher(s) will be necessary to determine optimal response.

Documented Effects of Stimulants

To follow is a list of documented effects of stimulant medicines on children with ADHD.

- reduced activity level to normal
- decreased excessive talking and disruption in classroom
- improved handwriting and neatness of written work
- improved fine motor control
- improved attention to tasks
- reduced distractibility
- improved short-term memory
- decreased impulsivity
- increased academic productivity (i.e., work produced)
- increased accuracy of academic work
- reduced off-task behavior in classroom
- decreased anger, better self-control
- improved participation in organized sports (i.e., baseball)
- reduced bossy behavior with peers
- reduced verbal and physical aggression with peers
- improved peer social status
- reduced non-compliant, defiant, and oppositional behavior
- improved parent-child interactions
- improved teacher-student interactions

Dosing of Stimulants

The dose of stimulant prescribed is not related to body weight, but to how rapidly it is metabolized. A 180-pound adult may derive substantial benefit from five mg of Ritalin given three times a day, while a seventy-five pound child may need three times as much.

Usually the child's physician will start with a low dose and gradually increase it until caregivers (parents and teachers) note optimal levels of improvement in behavior and attention. Refer to the charts in the following pages to see recommended dosing of stimulants and other medications for ADHD.

Irritability or hyperfocused (spacey) behavior seen within thirty minutes or a couple of hours after taking the medication may suggest that the dose is too high for that child. On the other hand, if the dose is not sufficient, the physician may increase it every five days or so until the child is functioning at the optimal level, until adverse side-effects become a concern, or until the maximum recommended dose is reached. With each adjustment in dose, the physician should obtain information from a caregiver (parent and teacher) as to how the child is functioning.

For short-acting stimulants, the average length of action is about four hours. However, for some children the medication may last only two or three hours, and for others, it may last five or six hours. Thus, the dose interval must be established for each child.

Using feedback from parents and teachers, the physician may be able to determine when the medication is "wearing off" and when another dose should be given. Long-acting stimulants can take a child through the entire school-day, but an additional short-acting tablet may be needed to get through homework and after school activities, hopefully, without significantly affecting appetite and sleep.

Long-Term Effects of Stimulants

The long-term effects of stimulants have not been carefully studied, but in the MTA study, the behavioral and cognitive effects of stimulants were monitored over a twenty-four month period. This is a relatively short term considering people with ADHD take stimulants for years. Nevertheless, findings from the MTA study showed significant reduction in the core symptoms of ADHD and associated problems of aggression and oppositional behavior as measured by teacher and parent ratings.

There is no evidence that children build up a significant tolerance to stimulants, even after taking them for years throughout childhood and adolescence.

Side Effects of Stimulants

Common side effects of the stimulants are: headaches, irritability, stomachaches, appetite loss, insomnia, and weight loss. About half of the children started on a stimulant will experience one or more of the common side effects noted above. Interestingly, this same percentage of ADHD children will complain about similar side effects when they take a placebo pill without any active medication. Stomachaches and headaches occur in about one-third of children taking a stimulant.

Loss of Appetite. Decreased appetite occurs often and usually results in the child eating little for lunch due to the morning dose of medication. If a second or third dose is taken mid-day or later, this could affect appetite at dinner as well. For most children, however, their appetite returns after school, and they make up for the missed lunchtime meal. Parents should consult their doctor if appetite suppression is chronic and weight loss is significant. Medication dose or timing may need to be modified. Give the stimulant medication with meals. Nutritional supplements can be added to the diet. Serving a hearty breakfast, late night snack, or high-calorie snacks, like ice cream may help.

Some of the infrequent side effects that can be caused by stimulant use include rebound effects, difficulty falling asleep, irritable mood, and tics. These side effects are well understood in children.

Rebound. Some parents report that at the end of the school day, their child becomes more hyperactive, excitable, talkative, and irritable. This phenomena is referred to as "rebound," and it can affect many children with ADHD who take stimulant medication during the school day. When rebound occurs, it usually begins after the last dose of medication is wearing off. The doctor may recommend a smaller dose of medication be given or use of another medication to reduce the child's excitability. Rebound may be less common when using long-acting stimulants such as Ritalin LA, Concerta, Adderall XR, or Metadate CD.

Difficulty falling asleep. Children taking stimulants may have trouble falling asleep. They may be experiencing a drug rebound, which makes it difficult for them to quiet down and become restful. In some cases the doctor may recommend reducing or eliminating the mid-day dose of medication or may prescribe a small dose of stimulant medication before bedtime. You might try administering the medication earlier in the day so it is completely worn off by bedtime. If the child is taking a long-acting form of the medicine, try a short-acting form so that is completely worn off by bedtime. Other medications, such as Clonidine or Benadryl, may be prescribed to help the child fall asleep.

Non-medical interventions parents can try are: establish sleep routines in the home; avoid excessive activity or stimulation before bedtime; set a fixed bedtime and adhere to it; and teach the child how to relax in bed while trying to fall asleep.

Irritability. Clinicians and researchers have noted that stimulant usage in ADHD children may worsen the child's mood. The child may exhibit more frequent temper outbursts and may become more moody and more easily frustrated than usual. Moodiness could lead to oppositional behavior at home. Stimulants can also produce dysphoria (sadness) in some children. If irritability, sadness, moodiness, or agitation become evident during the first one to two hours after the medication is taken the doctor may lower the dose. If irritability, sadness, moodiness, or agitation worsen as the medication wears off, the doctor may change to an extended-release form of the stimulant, overlap stimulant dosing (usually by thirty minutes), combine long-and short-acting forms, or consider using an additional medication. If irritability persists, the child should be assessed for other psychiatric problems.

Tics and Tourette's syndrome. Simple motor tics consist of small, abrupt muscle movements usually around the face and upper body. Common simple motor tics include eye blinking, neck jerking, shoulder shrugging, and facial grimacing. Common simple vocal tics include throat clearing, grunting, sniffing, and snorting. Stimulants should be used with caution in patients with motor or vocal tics or in patients with a family history of tics. A little more than half of the ADHD children who start treatment with a stimulant medication will develop a subtle, transient motor or vocal tic. The tic might begin immediately or months after the medication is started. It might disappear on its own while the child is taking stimulants or it might worsen. Some physicians prefer to discontinue, reduce, or change the stimulant medication if tics appear.

A child who has either a motor or a vocal tic (but not both), which occurs many times a day, nearly every day, for a period of at least one year (without stopping for more than three months) may be diagnosed as having a chronic tic disorder. Tourette's syndrome is a chronic tic disorder characterized by both multiple motor tics and one or more vocal tics. These tics are more severe than the simple motor tics described above.

They involve the head and, frequently, other parts of the body such as the torso, arms, and legs. Vocal tics may include the production of sounds like clucking, grunting, yelping, barking, snorting, and coughing. Coprolalia, the utterance of obscenities, is rare and occurs in about ten percent of children with Tourette's. Stimulants should be used cautiously with children who have chronic tic disorder or Tourette's syndrome and ADHD as the medication may exacerbate the problem.

Cardiovascular effects and seizure threshold. There has been some speculation and concern that stimulant medications may produce adverse cardiovascular effects in children, particularly with long term use. While stimulants may cause some elevation of the heart rate in some children with ADHD, there is no evidence of any long term cardiovascular effects. Furthermore, there is no evidence that stimulants lower the seizure threshold putting the child at greater risk for having a seizure.

Abuse and dependency. Parents and teachers should not be overly concerned that the use of a stimulant medication would lead to dependence, addiction, or drug abuse. However, misuse/abuse of stimulants can and does occur, and parents and teachers should be aware of this. There have been fairly frequent reports of elementary and secondary school children giving away or selling stimulants, reports of diversion of stimulants into the hands of family members and school officials, and attempts by people to secure stimulants through unlawful prescriptions. Parents should maintain possession of any stimulant medication at home and carefully monitor the supply. The school should do so as well for medication dispensed during the school day. Hopefully, use of long-acting stimulants given once a day will reduce this problem.

Non-Stimulants to Treat ADHD

There is general consensus among experts treating children with ADHD that stimulants are relatively safe and very effective. For these reasons, they are generally considered the first-line medication to use. However, not all children will show an adequate response to stimulants. Some may develop adverse side effects, and others may benefit from a medication that has twenty-four hour effectiveness rather than the limited coverage that stimulants can provide. In addition, the fact that stimulants are controlled substances worries some parents who would like an alternative medication.

Atomoxetine (Strattera) has been marketed for the past few years as an FDA approved treatment for ADHD in children and in adults. It is a selective norepinephrine reuptake inhibitor (SNRI), and, as such, it blocks the reuptake of norepinephrine in certain regions of the brain. It is administered in the morning (or at night if the child becomes too sedated) and the dose is based on body weight. The starting dose is 0.5 mg/kg and the target daily dose might be 1.2 mg/kg. Strattera comes in capsules of 10, 18, 25, 40, and 60 mg strengths. It could take four to six weeks (or more) to reach maximal effect, however, the effects last twenty-four hours a day. It is sometimes used in combination with stimulants. In children, the side effects most likely to be seen with Strattera include stomach aches, sedation, nausea and vomiting, loss of appetite, and headaches.

Tricyclic Antidepressants

Tricyclic antidepressants (TCAs) are primarily used in children for ADHD and tic disorders. They are regarded as alternatives for children who have not succeeded with stimulants, for whom stimulants produced unacceptable side effects, or who suffer from other conditions (such as depression, anxiety, Tourette's syndrome, tics), or aggressive behavior and irritability along with ADHD. Imipramine (Tofranil), desipramine (Norpramin), amytriptyline (Elavil), and nortriptyline (Pamelor or Vivactyl), doxepin, and clomipramine (Anafranil) are TCAs.

TCAs have the advantage of longer duration of action (all day) as opposed to four to twelve hours common to stimulants. This avoids the troublesome and even embarrassing mid-day stimulant dose taken at school. Unfortunately, TCAs may not be as effective as the stimulants in improving attention and concentration or reducing hyperactive-impulsive symptoms of ADHD. TCAs also can produce adverse side effects, the most common of which are drowsiness, dry mouth, constipation, and abdominal discomfort. More concern, however, has been expressed at possible adverse cardiac side effects, accidental overdose, and build up in the body to potentially lethal levels. By drawing blood, levels of the TCA can be measured to determine whether these symptoms are a result of too much medication in the body or other factors related to the child's illness.

Antihypertensives

Antihypertensive agents such as clonidine (Catapres) and guanfacine (Tenex) have been found to be useful in the treatment of ADHD children, especially those who are extremely hyperactive, excitable, impulsive, and defiant. They have less effectiveness in improving attention. These drugs are also frequently used in to treat Tourette's disorder and other tic disorders and they help control aggression in children with autism and pervasive developmental disorder. Clonidine is also prescribed to help children who have difficulty falling asleep. It can be a great benefit to children with sleep onset difficulties whether the cause is ADHD overarousal, stimulant medication rebound, or unwillingness to fall asleep. Clonidine works on the adrenergic chemical system in the brain and affects the release of norepinephrine.

Clonidine is a relatively short-acting drug as it works for about four hours in children so multiple doses are needed. It comes in a tablet form or in a skin patch. The skin patch may be useful to improve compliance and provide more even absorption in the body. Sudden discontinuation of this medication can cause increased hyperactivity, headache, agitation, elevated blood pressure and pulse, and an increase in tics in patients with Tourette's syndrome. Sleepiness, which is the most common side effect of clonidine, gradually decreases after a few weeks. Other side effects may include dry mouth, dizziness, nausea, irritability, and light sensitivity. The skin patch can cause a rash.

Clonidine may be combined with stimulants for children with severe hyperactivity and aggression, for children with tic disorders and ADHD, or sleep problems in children with ADHD.

Guanfacine is a long-acting noradrenergic agonist similar to clonidine in effect, but it has a longer duration of action and less side-effects. It is used with children who cannot tolerate the sedative effects of clonidine or with children for whom the effects of clonidine were too short.

Antidepressants

Selective serotonin reuptake inhibitors (SSRIs) are the most commonly used antidepressants for children. These include fluoxetine (Prozac), paroxetine (Paxil), citalopram (Celexa), sertraline (Zoloft), escitalopram (Lexapro), and fluvoxamine (Luvox). These drugs have not been well studied in the treatment of ADHD. SSRIs have, however, gained considerable recognition for treatment of depression, anxiety, and obsessive-compulsive disorders. They are considered the first line of medication treatment for these conditions. They have fewer sedative, cardiovascular, and weight-gain side effects than other antidepressants. The SSRIs are similar in their overall effect of making serotonin available in certain regions of the brain, but they vary somewhat from one another in their chemical makeup. Therefore, when one SSRI proves ineffective for a child, another may be more effective. Parents should be cautious however, about the use of antidepressants in general (including the SSRIs) in children. In October 2003 the FDA issued a health advisory warning doctors to exercise caution in prescribing the SSRIs for children and adolescents and to closely monitor those who take these medications. There are concerns that the SSRIs may increase suicidal ideation or suicide attempts in children and adolescents.

Bupropion (Wellbutrin) is a novel antidepressant drug that has been used successfully for a number of years to treat ADHD. It has not been well studied in this regard, but clinicians using this medication find that it has a place in treating ADHD, especially in children who do not tolerate stimulants or who may have co-existing problems with mood. Bupropion appears to possess both indirect dopamine and noradrenergic effects. It works rapidly, peaking in the blood after two hours and lasting up to fourteen hours. The usual dose range in children is from 37.5 to 300 mg per day in two or three divided doses. There is a sustained-release preparation (100, 150, and 200 mg) that can be given once or twice daily. An extended-release form (150 mg and 300 mg) can be given once in the morning. The major side-effects in children are irritability, decreased appetite, insomnia, and worsening of tics. Irritability can be reduced with decreased dosing. Bupropion may worsen tics and should not be used when a seizure disorder is suspected.

Venlafaxine (Effexor) is an antidepressant that, like SSRIs, enhances serotonin in certain areas of the brain by blocking its reuptake, but it also possesses some noradrenergic properties. For this reason, it is known as an SNRI (serotonin-norepinephrine reuptake inhibitor). It can improve symptoms of ADHD and is also helpful for depression in children. The usual dose range is 12.5 mg up to a total of 225 mg daily in twice-a-day split dosing. An extended-release (XR) tablet is available allowing once-a-day dosing.

Side effects can include nausea, agitation, stomachaches, headaches, and, at higher doses, blood pressure elevation. As with other anti-depressants, there may be a greater risk of suicidally in children and therefore, careful observation of your child while starting this treatment and during the earlier phases of treatment is very important.

Buspirone, an anxiolitic medication, has been used in children and adolescents with anxiety disorders and researchers have reported significant improvement with it. It has not been well studied in the treatment of ADHD in children

Fenfluramine, benzodiazepines, or lithium are of benefit in other psychiatric disorders, but there is no support to their use in the treatment of ADHD.

Antipsychotics

The group of medications called antipsychotics are commonly used to treat disorders other than psychosis and have been found to be very helpful in children who have severe mood lability. They include haloperidol (Haldol), pimozide (Orap), thioridazine (Mellaril), chlorpromazine (Thorazine), and others. They are frequently prescribed to children with severe mood disorders when other medications have failed. Because they have serious side effects, they are reserved for children who show severe problems and who don't respond to other medications. Common short-term, reversible side effects are drowsiness, increased appetite and weight gain, dizziness, dry mouth, congestion, and blurred vision. Some of the anti-psychotic drugs can produce side effects that affect various muscle groups (extrapyramidal effects) leading to muscle tightness and spasm, rolling eyes, and restlessness. Some of these severe side effects may be reduced by using the newer, atypical antipsychotics.

Atypical Antipsychotics

This class of medication includes ziprasidone (Geodon), aripiprazole (Abilify), risperidone (Risperdal), clozapine (Clozaril), olanzapine (Zyprexa), and quetiapine (Seroquel). They are increasingly being used as first-line drugs for children with severe mood disorders, disruptive disorders, self-injurious behavior, bipolar disorder, and psychosis. These drugs affect the dopamine system and have less severe side-effects than the traditional antipsychotics. Side effects of Risperdal, Zyprexa, and Seroquel appear similar to those of the traditional antipsychotics, but the rate of side effects and the risk of long-term tardive dyskinesia (irreversible motor writing/twitches/spasms) seem to be much lower. One of the most problematic long-term effects of some of the atypical antipsychotics (particularly Zyprexa and to a lesser extent, Risperdal), is weight gain and potential effects on metabolism. It is unclear whether Seroquel or Geodon have these problems. Abilify does not appear to cause increased weight, but may cause motor spasms that may result in a greater risk for tardive dyskinesia with prolonged use.

Sticking with Medication

ADHD is a chronic condition with symptoms that persist throughout childhood and adolescence. Therefore, children receiving medical treatment may have to continue such treatment for years depending on the severity of their symptoms. The presence of co-morbid conditions such as oppositional defiant disorder, conduct disorder, or anxiety and mood disorders make it even more important that medical treatments be adhered to. However, parents may worry about the long-term effects of continuously dispensing ADHD medication to their child. Anxious children may also worry about taking the medication. Children with oppositional defiant disorder often refuse to take medication. And older children and adolescence tend to dislike taking

DRUG	FORM	DOSING	SIDE EFFECTS	DURATION	PROS	PRECAUTIONS
METHYLPHENIDATE						
RITALIN METADATE Generic MPH METHYLIN	Short Acting Tablet 5 mg 10 mg 20 mg Chewable Tablet 2.5 mg, 5 mg, 10 mg Oral Solution 5mg/5ml & 10mg/5ml	Starting dose for children is 5 mg twice daily, 3-4 hours apart. Add third dose about 4 hours after second. Adjust timing based on duration of action. Increase by 5-10 mg increments. Daily dosage above 60 mg not recommended. Estimated dose range .3-.6 mg/kg/dose	Insomnia, decreased appetite, weight loss, headache, irritability, stomachache, and rebound agitation or exaggeration of pre-medication symptoms as it is wearing off.	About 3-4 hours. Most helpful when need rapid onset and short duration	Works quickly (within 30-60 minutes). Effective in over 70% of patients.	Use cautiously in patients with marked anxiety, motor tics or with family history of Tourette syndrome, or history of substance abuse. Don't use if glaucoma or on MAOI.
FOCALIN (with isolated dextroisomer)	Short Acting Tablet 2.5 mg 5 mg 10 mg	For short-acting, start with half the dose recommended for normal short acting methylphenidate above. Dose may be adjusted in 2.5 to 5 mg increments to a maximum of 20 mg per day (10 mg twice daily). As above.	There is suggestion that Focalin (dextro-isomer) may be more prone to causing sleep or appetite disturbance.	About 3-4 hours. Most helpful when need rapid onset and short duration. For Focalin XR duration supposed to be about 6-8 hours.	Only formulation with isolated dextro-isomer. Works quickly (within 30-60 minutes). Possibly better for use for evening needs when day's long acting dose is wearing off. As above.	Similar to other short and longer acting preparations.
FOCALIN XR (with isolated dextroisomer) 50% immediate release beads and 50% delayed release beads	Mid Acting Capsule 5 mg 10mg 20mg					
RITALIN SR METHYLIN ER METADATE ER	Mid Acting Tablet 20mg Mid Acting Tablet 10 mg 20mg	Start with 20 mg daily. May combine with short acting for quicker onset and/or coverage after this wears off.	Insomnia, decreased appetite, weight loss, headache, irritability, stomachache.	Onset delayed for 60-90 minutes. Duration supposed to be 6-8 hours, but can be quite individual and unreliable.	Wears off more gradually than short acting so less risk of rebound. Lower abuse risk.	As above. Note: If crushed or cut, full dose may be released at once, giving twice the intended dose in first 4 hours, none in the second 4 hours.
RITALIN LA 50% immediate release beads and 50% delayed release beads	Mid Acting Capsule 20 mg 30 mg 40 mg	Starting dose is 10-20 mg once daily. May be adjusted weekly in 10 mg increments to maximum of 60 mg taken once daily. May add short acting dose in AM or 8 hours later in PM if needed.	Insomnia, decreased appetite, weight loss, headache, irritability, stomachache, and rebound potential.	Onset in 30-60 minutes. Duration about 8 hours.	May swallow whole or sprinkle ALL contents on a spoonful of applesauce. Starts quickly, avoids mid-day gap unless student metabolizes medicine very rapidly.	Same cautions as for immediate release. If beads are chewed, may release full dose at once, giving entire contents in first 4 hours.
METADATE CD 30% immediate release and 70% delayed release beads	Mid Acting Capsule 10 mg 20 mg 30 mg					
CONCERTA 22% immediate release and 78% gradual release	Long Acting Tablet 18 mg 27 mg 36 mg 54 mg	Starting dose is 18 mg or 36 mg once daily. Option to increase to 72 mg daily.	Insomnia, decreased appetite, weight loss, headache, irritability, stomachache.	Onset in 30-60 minutes. Duration about 10-14 hours.	Works quickly (within 30-60 minutes). Given only once a day. Longest duration of MPH forms. Doesn't risk mid-day gap or rebound since medication is released gradually throughout the day. Wears off more gradually than short acting, so less rebound. Lower abuse risk.	Same cautions as for immediate release. Do not cut or crush.

This chart was updated 9/10/05. Consult with your physician before making any decision regarding medication usage.

DRUG	FORM	DOSING	SIDE EFFECTS	DURATION	PROS	PRECAUTIONS
DEXTROAMPHETAMINE						
DEXTROSTAT DEXEDRINE PDR does not list short acting Dexedrine tablets	Short Acting Tablet 5 mg 10 mg Short Acting Tablet 5 mg	For ages 3 -5 years: starting dose is 2.5 mg of tablet. Increase by 2.5 mg at weekly intervals, increasing first dose or adding/increasing a noon dose, until effective. For 6 years and over, start with 5 mg once or twice daily. May increase total daily dose by 5 mg per week until reach optimal level. Tablet is given on awakening. Over 6 years, one or two additional doses may be given at 4-6 hour intervals. Usually not need more than 40 mg/day.	Insomnia, decreased appetite, weight loss, headache, irritability, stomachache. Rebound agitation or exaggeration of pre-medication symptoms as it is wearing off.	Onset in 30-60 minutes. Duration about 4-5 hours.	Approved for children under 6. Good safety record. Somewhat longer action than short acting methylphenidate.	Use cautiously in patients with marked anxiety, motor tics or with family history of Tourette syndrome, or history of substance abuse. Don't use if glaucoma or on MAOI. High abuse potential particularly in tablet form.
DEXEDRINE SPANSULE dextroamphetamine sulfate ER	Long Acting Spansule 5 mg 10 mg 15 mg 5mg 10 mg 15 mg	In chidren 6 and older who can swallow whole capsule, morning dose of capsule equal to sum of morning and noon short acting. Increase total daily dose by 5 mg per week until reach optimal dose to maximum of 40 mg/day.	Same as above.	Onset in 30-60 minutes. Duration about 5-10 hours.	May avoid need for noon dose. Rapid onset. Good safety record.	As above. Less likely to be abused intranasal or IV than short acting. Must use whole capsule.
MIXED AMPHETAMINE						
ADDERALL	Short Acting Tablet 5 mg 7.5 mg 10 mg 12.5 mg 15 mg 20 mg 30 mg	Starting dose is 5 or 10 mg each morning (age 6 and older). May be adjusted in 5-10 mg increments up to 30 mg per day.	Same as above.	Onset in 30-60 minutes. Duration about 4-5 hours.	Only stimulant approved for children, adolescents, and adults. Wears off more gradually than dextroamphetamine alone, so rebound is less likely and more mild.	Same as for Dexedrine tablets.
ADDERALL XR 50% immediate release beads and 50% delayed release beads	Long Acting Capsule 5 mg 10 mg 15 mg 20 mg 25 mg 30 mg	Starting dose is 5 or 10 mg each morning (age 6 and older). May be adjusted in 5-10 mg increments up to 30 mg per day.	Same as above.	Onset in 60-90 minutes (possibly sooner). Duration 10-12 hours.	May swallow whole or sprinkle ALL contents on a spoonful of applesauce. May last longer than most other sustained release stimulants. Less likely rebound than with long acting dextroamphetamine.	Same as for Dexedrine Spansules except that it has documented efficacy when sprinkled on applesauce.
ATOMOXETINE						
STRATTERA	Long Acting Capsule 10 mg 18 mg 25 mg 40 mg 60 mg	Starting dose is 0.5 mg/kg. The targeted clinical dose is approximately 1.2 mg/kg. Increase at weekly intervals. Medication must be used each day. Usually started in the morning, but may be changed to evening. It may be divided into a morning and an evening dose, particularly if need higher doses.	In children: decreased appetite, GI upset (can be reduced if medication taken with food), sedation (can be reduced by dosing in evening), lightheadedness. In adults: insomnia, sexual side effects, increased blood pressure.	Starts working within a few days to one week, but full effect may not be evident for a month or more. Duration all day (24/7) so long as taken daily as directed.	Avoids problems of rebound and gaps in coverage. Doesn't cause a "high," thus it does not lead to abuse, and so a) it is not a controlled drug and b) may use with history of substance abuse.	Use cautiously in patients with hypertension, tachycardia, or cardiovascular or cerebrovascular disease because it can increase blood pressure and heart rate. Has some drug interactions. While extensively tested, short duration of population use.

.This chart was updated 9/10/05. Consult with your physician before making any decision regarding medication usage

DRUG	FORM	DOSING	SIDE EFFECTS	DURATION	PROS	PRECAUTIONS
BUPROPION						
WELLBUTRIN IR	Short Acting Tablet IR-75 mg 100 mg	Starting dose is 37.5 mg increasing gradually (wait at least 3 days) to maximum of 2-3 doses, no more than 150 mg/dose.	Irritability, decreased appetite, and insomnia.	About 4-6 hours.	Helpful for ADHD patients with comorbid depression or anxiety. May help after school until home.	Not indicated in patients with a seizure disorder or with a current or previous diagnosis of bulimia or anorexia. May worsen tics. May cause mood deterioration at the time it wears off.
WELLBUTRIN SR	Long Acting Tablet SR-100 mg 150mg 200 mg	Starting dose is 100 mg/day increasing gradually to a maximum of 2 doses, no more than 200 mg/dose.	Same as Wellbutrin IR	About 10-14 hours.	Same for Wellbutrin IR. Lower seizure risk than immediate release form. Avoids noon dose.	Same as Wellbutrin IR. If a second dose is not given, may get mood deterioration at around 10-14 hours.
WELLBUTRIN XL	Long Acting Tablet 150mg 300mg	Starting dose is 150 mg /day increasing gradually to a maximum of 2 doses, no more than 300 mg/day.	Same as Wellbutrin IR	About 24 + hours.	Same for Wellbutrin IR. Single daily dose. Smooth 24 hour coverage. Lower seizure risk than immediate release form.	Same as Wellbutrin IR.
ALPHA-2 AGONISTS						
CATAPRES (clonidine)	Tablet 0.1 mg 0.2 mg 0.3 mg	Starting dose is .025 - .05 mg/ day in evening. Increase by similar dose every 7 days, adding to morning, mid-day, possibly afternoon, and again evening doses in sequence. Total dose of 0.1 - .3mg/day divided into 3-4 doses. Do not skip days.	Sleepiness, hypotension, headache, dizziness, stomachache, nausea, dry mouth, depression, nightmares.	Onset in 30-60 minutes. Duration about 3 - 6 hours.	Helpful for ADHD patients with comorbid tic disorder or insomnia. Good for severe impulsivity, hyperactivity and/or aggression. Stimulates appetite. Especially helpful in younger children (under 6) with ADHD symptoms associated with prenatal insult or syndrome such as Fragile X.	Sudden discontinuation could result in rebound hypertension. Minimize daytime tiredness by starting with evening dose and increasing slowly. Avoid brand and generic formulations with red dye, which may cause hyperarousal in sensitive children.
CLONIDINE	Tablet 0.1 mg 0.2 mg 0.3 mg					
CATAPRES Patch	TTS-1 TTS-2 TTS-3	Corresponds to doses of 0.1 mg, 0.2 mg and 0.3 mg per patch. (If using .1 mg tid tablets, try TTS 2 but likely need TTS 3).	Same as Catapres tablet but with skin patch there may be localized skin reactions.	Duration 4-5 days, so avoids the vacillations in drug effect seen in tablets.	Same as above.	Same as above. May get rebound hypertension and return of symptoms if it isn't recognized that a patch has come off or becomes loose. An immature student may get excessive dose from chewing on the patch.
TENEX (guanfacine)	1 mg 2 mg 3 mg	Starting dose is 0.5 mg/day in evening and increase by similar dose every 7 days as indicated. Given in divided doses 2-4 times per day. Daily dose range 0.5 - 4mg/day. DO NOT skip days	Compared to clonidine, lower severity of side effects, especially fatigue and depression, less headache, stomache, nausea, dry mouth. Minimal problem of rebound hypertension if doses are missed.	Duration about 6 - 12 hours.	Can provide for 24/7 modulation of impulsivity, hyperactivity, aggression and sensory hypersensitivity. This covers most out of school problems, so stiumlant use can be limited to school and homework hours. Improves appetite. Less sedating than clonidine.	Avoid formulations with red dye as above. Hypotension is the primary dose-limiting problem. As with clonidine, important to check blood pressures with dose increases and if symptoms suggest hypotension, such as light-headedness.
guanfacine tablets	1 mg 2 mg 3 mg					

This chart was updated 9/10/05. Consult with your physician before making any decision regarding medication usage.

medication. Because of these factors, adherence to medication treatment is an ongoing process. Children may discontinue medication over time, but children may also restart medication after varying lengths of time. It is important to maintain an open mind about the risks and benefits of medication over the course of the child's development.

Summary

Medications are commonly used to treat people of all ages who have ADHD. We used to think ADHD medications were a treatment of last resort, only to be used after other treatments have been tried and failed, or in children and adolescents who are most severely affected. This is no longer the case. The use of medication is common, generally safe, and very effective for the treatment of ADHD. Results of many controlled studies indicated that medication alone can be very effective to reduce core symptoms of ADHD if dosing is carefully adjusted and monitored.

There are several classes of medications used in the treatment of ADHD. Stimulants are the most frequently used, and antidepressants and anti-hypertensives are less often prescribed. There have been many controlled studies of stimulants in the treatment of ADHD. These studies confirm their effectiveness in more than seventy percent of children with improvements noted in attention, activity level, impulsivity, work completion in school, and compliant behavior. New, long-acting stimulants, which can last for ten to twelve hours, will eliminate the need for mid-day dosing and may reduce rebound effects.

Antidepressants have been less well studied, but are useful in treating adolescents who do not respond well to the stimulants or who are suffering from depression or low self-esteem in addition to ADHD. The antihypertensive medications have also been less well studied than stimulants and are used to treat those with ADHD who may be very hyperactive, who are aggressive, or who have an accompanying tic disorder. New medications are being tested for treatment of ADHD with some promising results.

When medications are used in treatment, their effects should be monitored. Adjustments in dosage, time taken, or changes in medication type may be made by the physician if problems arise. Parents, teachers, and the adolescent taking the medication should each be responsible for communicating medication effects.

Medication will rarely be the only treatment a child, adolescent, or adult with ADHD receives. A multi-modal treatment program should be considered including counseling, education about ADHD, and school-based or work-based accommodations and interventions.

Chapter 12
Addressing Academic Skill Problems

Students with ADHD have a greater risk of having academic skill problems. These problems could be the result of different factors. For example, difficulty with attention and focus will obviously cause the student to miss important instruction. Insufficient practice and review of material taught in class will reduce the chance to strengthen skills. Deficits in speech and language, or in perceptual processing (such as auditory or visual memory, association, or discrimination), may be more common in students with ADHD. Such deficits are often associated with problems in learning.

Unexpected difficulty in learning to read and spell is often called dyslexia. Unexpected means that there is no obvious reason for the difficulty, such as inadequate schooling, auditory or visual sensory problems, acquired brain damage, or low overall IQ. Dyslexia is a prevalent disorder, affecting as many as twenty percent of the population.

Both genetic and environmental factors can cause dyslexia. Current evidence supports the view that dyslexia is a familial disorder (about one third of first degree relatives are affected). It also has a high degree of heritability (about fifty percent). Environmental factors such as large family size and low socioeconomic status (SES) may contribute to reading problems. Some lower SES families read less to their children, play fewer language games with them, and children in such families may lack sufficient preschool experiences to accelerate growth in reading and language development. Early exposure to language enrichment activities may be a very important factor in developing later reading and language skills.

Below are strategies teachers and parents can use to help students who have problems in reading, written or oral language, and mathematics.

Strategies for Problems with Reading—Decoding and Comprehension

- In young children look for early signs that can be precursors to reading or spelling problems: speech delay, articulation difficulty, problems learning letter names or color names, word-finding problems, sequencing of syllables incorrectly ("aminals" for "animals," "donimoes" for "dominoes"), and problems remembering addresses, phone numbers, and other verbal sequences.

- Other signs to look for in a student with language or potential reading problems is difficulty following directions, reduced speech or difficulty expressing ones self, and problems with peer relations. Language problems can interfere with a child's ability to express emotions. The child may be more likely to act out his feelings physically or withdraw from social interaction.

- The single most important step to overcome a reading problem is for the child to receive tutoring in a phonics-based approach to reading. Being able to sound out words is so central to reading development that it cannot be bypassed even if the student has difficulty with this process. While whole language approaches to reading may work well with non-dyslexic youngsters, such approaches do not help dyslexic youngsters. They need much more sustained and systematic instruction in phonological coding. Some examples of programs that use a phonics approach and which teach letter-sound relations and blending are the Orton Gillingham, Slingerland, and DISTAR aproaches.

- It is also quite important to teach students skills involved in reading comprehension. An important reading comprehension skill is learning the meaning of words and how to use them correctly. Building an extensive reading vocabulary should be the goal of every teacher and parent for every student across all grades. The most effective way to increase a student's vocabulary is to introduce new words. Par-

ents tend to do this naturally. When a child hears a new word he will often ask its meaning. Provide definitions and use the new word in a sentence. Continue to use the new word in the days to follow so the child has continued exposure to it.

- Teachers and parents can build vocabulary by using visual imagery. For example, if you were trying to teach the meaning of the word "apex" you might create an index card with an image of an ape standing on the top of a mountain or on the top of the letter "X".

APEX
Definition:
highest point

Sentence:
An ape climbed to the
apex of the mountain.

Note: from Leslie Davis, Sandi Sirotowitz, and Harvey C. Parker (1996). *Study Strategies Made Easy.* Florida: Specialty Press, Inc. Reprinted with permission.

- We can increase the size and depth of a student's vocabulary by teaching the meanings of the most common prefixes and suffixes.

- Reduce over-reliance on common words by teaching synonyms and antonyms.

- Provide additional reading time. Use "previewing" strategies. Select text with less on a page. Shorten amount of required reading. Avoid oral reading. Allow use of "Cliff Notes" to gain an understanding of subject matter prior to reading the complete document. Use books on tape to assist in comprehension of book. Use highlighters to emphasize important information in a reading selection.

• Students with reading problems may prefer to subvocalize when reading silently. Recitation of the reading selection aloud (but quietly) may enable them to better attend to and recall information read. If you observe students doing this, allow them to continue as the additional auditory input may be helping them.

• Poor readers often focus on decoding more than comprehension. They may not be actively focusing on the meaning of what they are reading. Teachers can help by introducing main concepts of the reading selection beforehand, thereby providing contextual clues to the poor reader.

• Even students with ADHD who have excellent decoding skills and who can read fluently will have trouble maintaining their concentration while reading. They often report having to reread material due to lapses in concentration. Focus may be improved by shortening the length of reading assignments; pausing and asking questions of the student; encouraging the student to take short notes while reading; or listing questions the student should try to answer while reading before the reading begins. Note, that these strategies are geared to encourage the student to be an "active" reader as opposed to a "passive" reader. Active reading may help the student keep focused on the task at hand.

• Introduce new vocabulary words or difficult concepts found in a reading selection ahead of time so the student will be better able to read the material with fluency and understanding.

• Make sure the material being read by the student is at the student's independent reading level—material the student is capable of reading successfully on his own.

• A student who has trouble with visual tracking may lose his place easily while reading. Use of a tracking device such as the Reading Helper which contains a clear window that goes over a line of type can help the student maintain his place while reading.

• If a reading selection is too long or too difficult for the student, have others in the class read the material out loud (either taking turns or as a whole class) to help ease the burden.

• The teacher could read the selection to the student as the student follows along. After reading a few paragraphs have the student read back what was covered.

• Assign a "reading partner" to a student who is weak in reading. The student and his partner can take turns reading paragraphs or pages. By partnering, students can help one another with decoding words, answering questions, and understanding the content of the material read.

• Provide time each day (fifteen to twenty minutes) for students to do free choice reading. Encourage building a class library of books students enjoy. Have students make recommendations of certain books to others. Start a reader's club and award points to students who read.

• Perhaps the most effective strategy to improve reading comprehension is previewing by the teacher. In previewing, the teacher summarizes key points of the material to be read in the same sequence as they appear in the reading selection. Unfamiliar words should also be previewed to reduce decoding and comprehension problems.

- Teachers can improve reading comprehension by asking students questions before reading rather than after reading. Pre-reading questions alert readers to what the writer wants them to know.

- Teach students how to find the main idea of paragraphs and to identify sub-ideas.

- Have the student paraphrase (describe in his own words) the main ideas and sub-ideas of a reading selection. The ability to paraphrase is critical for success in both reading and writing.

- Use the strategy of reciprocal teaching to improve reading comprehension. Pair children off in the classroom and have one teach the other what has been learned from reading a selection. Start by having each child read the material and make up a few questions about the content that could be asked to the other child.

- Teach outlining so the student can practice picking out the main idea and sub-ideas.

- Teach students how authors construct textbooks. Explain the purpose of chapters, headings, subheadings, print that is bolded, italicized, or underlined, side-boxes, illustrations, charts, captions, etc.

- Have the student highlight important ideas in the reading selection on a photocopied sample.

- Teach the SQ3R technique of reading comprehension. This involves the following steps (see chapter 13 for more details on reading comprehension strategies):
  1. **S**urvey—briefly review the reading selection. Scan the titles, headings, subheadings, and read the chapter summary.

  2. **Q**uestion—rephrase the headings and subheadings of a selection into questions.

  3. **R**ead—read the material and ask yourself questions about the selection, (i.e., What is the main idea of this paragraph?).

  4. **R**ecite—paraphrase the meaning of what you have read.

  5. **R**eview—after reading, review the selection once again by scanning and checking to see how much you remember and understood.

- Parents have important roles to play in the treatment of their dyslexic child. They serve as advocates and sources of emotional support. Although parents may serve the role as tutor for children who do not have serious reading and language problems it may be inadvisable for them to assume such a role if their child is significantly dyslexic. For one, they do not have the proper training. Secondly, the parent-child tutoring relationship can negatively affect the normal relationship the parent and child should have in the course of their family life.

- Reading is a fundamental skill that is learned and practiced both inside and outside the classroom. Parents play an important role in the development of reading and language skills. Parents should make sure that their child sees them read often and write letters, messages, and instructions. Showing their child they read and write often, sends a powerful message to the child.

- Parents should be encouraged to help their child find reading material that is of interest to the child. This makes the reading process easier. If the child is a sports fan, for instance, locate books, magazines, or articles in the newspaper that fit this interest. If fashion is what catches your child's eye, find books on this topic. Parents and teachers should encourage recreational reading.

- Among the unproven treatments for dyslexia or reading problems are the visual therapies: convergence training, eye movement exercises, colored lenses, and devices to induce "peripheral" reading. Medications intended to affect vestibular system functioning have not proved to be helpful. Chiropractic, megavitamins, and dietary treatments have also not been shown to be helpful.

Strategies for Problems with Spelling and Written or Oral Expression

- In the past twenty years the approach to instruction in written language has changed. Today there is more emphasis on the use of writing to express and communicate ideas than on the mechanics of writing—handwriting, punctuation, spelling, etc. Writing involves a process of thinking, planning, composing, revising, editing, and sharing ideas. Teach these five steps for writing papers.

1. Teach pre-writing as the first step in writing. The purpose of this step is to think about ideas to write about. Help the student select a topic and talk about the topic with the student. Encourage the student to brainstorm ideas and make note of them on paper. Use these notes to form a list of what he wants to write about in some sequential order.

2. The second step of the writing process involves writing a first draft. Stress content rather than spelling, penmanship, or grammar.

3. The third step is revising. Acknowledge the student's efforts in the first draft and build on these efforts together by discussing additional ideas or changes that could be made to the work product.

4. The fourth step is editing. The teacher directs attention to grammar, spelling, punctuation, capitalization, and word usage. Encourage the student to use the COPS method to check his work. COPS stands for:
   C Capitalization—check for capitalization of the first words in sentences and proper nouns.
   O Overall appearance of work—check for neatness, margins, paragraph indentation, complete sentences.
   P Punctuation—check for commas and appropriate punctuation at end of sentences.
   S Spelling—check to see all words are spelled correctly.

5. The fifth step is publishing. The student should make a final copy of the work to share with others.

- For some children writing can be such a grueling chore the teacher should be willing to accept non-written forms for reports (i.e. displays, oral, projects). Accept use of a typewriter, a word processor, or a tape recorder. Do not assign large quantity of written work. When possible, test with multiple choice or fill-in questions.

- Students with ADHD may have more difficulty with spelling. They may not pay attention to detail when writing or may be careless. This can cause spelling errors. Some students may have weaknesses in auditory or visual memory which can also contribute to problems with spelling.

- If spelling is weak: allow use of Franklin Spellers (headphone if speller talks), a dictionary, or other spell check tools.

- Encourage the student to play games such as Scrabble™, Hangman™, and Boggle™ to encourage focus on how words are spelled.

- Teach a phonetic approach to word analysis. Although many words are not spelled as they sound, a good understanding of phonics can be a powerful aid to weak spellers. Help the student find little words within the word and show the student how to break words into syllables.

- Encourage the student to keep track of his most often misspelled words. These words can be collected on a list or on index cards and put in a card file. The word should be written on the front of the card and the meaning on the back for new words.

- Overlook spelling errors when appropriate on assignments where spelling is not the focus of the assignment.

- If spelling is a diagnosed disability, disregard misspellings when grading.

- Students with ADHD often have difficulty with fine-motor control. This can affect their handwriting. For some, written work becomes so laborious they avoid it. Writing assignments that may take other students a few minutes, may take the student with fine-motor problems hours to complete.

- Encourage the student to use a sharp pencil and have an eraser available.

- Teach appropriate posture and how to position the paper correctly.

- Experiment with pencil grip, special papers, etc.

- Allow student to use laminated handwriting cards, containing samples of properly formed letters.

- Explain to the student that he will have a better chance of getting good grades if his work is done neatly. Help the student improve the legibility of his work by teaching him to evaluate the quality of his handwriting. In their book, *Overcoming Underachieving*, Sam Goldstein and Nancy Mather encourage students to use the acronym PRINT to check their work:
  P Proper letter formation?
  R Right amount of spacing between letters and words?

I   Indented paragraphs?

N   Neatness?

T   Tall letters above the middle line, short letters below?

- Permit the student in the upper grades to print rather than use cursive writing if this is a struggle for him.

- Stress the importance of neatness and organization in written assignments. Provide guidelines of how you expect papers to be written. Encourage the use of headings on papers, use of specific formats, etc.

- Permit the student to tape record assignments as opposed to writing.

- Reduce the amount of written work required. Stress accuracy rather than amount.

- Although it is very important to continue to help students with motor coordination problems to write legibly, many can benefit from learning keyboarding skills so they can use a word processor.

- For secondary students who take classes which require a great deal of note taking, have another student make a photocopy of his notes.

- Allow the student to dictate an assignment to another student or a parent or sibling at home.

- If oral expression is weak: accept all oral responses, substitute display for oral report, encourage expression of new ideas or experiences, pick topics that are easy for the student to talk about.

Strategies for Problems with Mathematics

Over the past decade schools have changed the focus of the math curriculum. There has been a shift from paper and pencil computation to activities which require mathematical reasoning and problem solving. To teach these skills, math teachers must stimulate students to learn in a different way. Students are encouraged to observe and experience their world and use these observations and experiences to solve problems involving mathematical concepts. Although it remains important for students to learn to add, subtract, multiply, and divide, they will also need to learn to use calculators, computers, and thinking skills to problem solve.

- For young children, provide instruction in telling time. Begin by making sure the child can recognize numbers from one to twelve on the face of a clock or watch. The child must be able to count by ones and fives to sixty and to differentiate the hour hand from the minute hand on a clock or watch. Move from the simple to the complex by first teaching how to tell time on the hour, then the half hour, then the quarter hour, and then by minutes. Teach the different ways that people express times before and after certain hours. For example, 9:30 can be described as "nine-thirty," "half past nine," or "thirty minutes to the hour." Go over other phrases which describe time such as "almost ten," "five past nine," "a quarter past four," etc.

- Teach or reinforce concepts associated with money. Counting money and making change correctly are important life skills. Children need to be able to estimate costs. Children with math weaknesses often have trouble in this area.

Begin by teaching the value of coins and bills. Use play money from a Monopoly™ game or real currency. Encourage counting money out loud and adding to amounts to come up with new totals. Give the child the opportunity to make change, make purchases in stores, etc.

- Children need to learn concepts of measurement. This involves measuring objects, liquids, solids, and being able to read fractional parts of an inch on a ruler. To help the child with measurement of liquids or solids encourage the child to follow recipes that include measurement terms. Have the child work with a ruler to measure length and to read temperatures from a thermometer.

- Understanding the concept of directions and the vocabulary associated with describing different directions is an important concept for children to learn.

- Review math vocabulary frequently.

- Give sample problems and provide clear explanations on how to solve them. Permit use of these during tests.

- Encourage student to estimate answers prior to calculating problems.

- Allow use of calculators when appropriate.

- Some students will make careless math errors when calculating because they are not able to line up figures correctly on paper. Encourage these students to use graph paper to space numbers evenly.

- Provide additional time to complete assignments for students who are weak in math. By reducing time pressure the student may have more time to check work.

- Provide immediate feedback and instruction via modeling of the correct computational procedure. Teach the steps needed to solve a particular type of math problem. Give clues to the process needed to solve problems and encourage use of "self-talk" to proceed through problem-solving.

- Reduce the number of math problems assigned.

- Reduce the amount of copying needed to work math problems from a text book by supplying photocopied work sheets.

- Provide models of sample problems.

- Teach signal words in a math problem that tell the process to be used to solve the problem. For example, words such as "plus," "sum," and "together" indicate addition; words such as "product," "times," and " doubled" indicate multiplication; words such as "quotient," " parts," " average," and " sharing" all indicate division.

Summary

Academic skill problems in areas related to reading, spelling, handwriting, and mathematics can be found in students with ADHD. Reading comprehension deficits may be due to problems with decoding, poor language comprehension, short attention span, rushing through reading selections, forgetfulness, or other difficulties. Strategies for decoding words through a phonics-linguistic approach, previewing, peer partnering, outlining, vocabulary building, and many others can be very helpful with dyslexic students.

Students with ADHD may also have problems with handwriting, spelling, and organization of written work. Accommodations can be very helpful, but strategies should also be taught to improve legibility of the student's writing.

Problems in learning mathematical concepts and in doing math work neatly and accurately can be a significant factor for students with ADHD. Lack of close attention to detail, carelessness in writing and solving problems, and other problems in mathematics can be helped through the use of appropriate strategies described in this chapter.

Chapter 13
Teaching Study Strategies

"True education is to learn *how* to think, not *what* to think."… J. Krishnamurti

Study skills refer to those things that individuals do when they have to locate, organize, and remember information. As I mentioned earlier, helping students learn to use study strategies is not the responsibility of only the reading or language arts teacher; it is something that needs to be done school-wide. Literacy learning focuses on helping students to become independent in their ability to learn. By using study strategies we can help students understand how to learn, not just what to learn. Study strategies can be taught to students in elementary as well as secondary schools.

This chapter reviews several study strategies that can help children understand *how* to learn more effectively in school. Study strategies included are in areas of organization, time-management, reading comprehension, vocabulary development, note-taking, and test-taking. I have only included a few samples of strategies in each area. Some are appropriate for elementary students and others for secondary school students. The forms included in this book may be repro-

duced for use in the classroom. See the appendix. For more detailed information and a large collection of worksheets and study strategy exercises for children in grades three to six see *Study Strategies for Early School Success* and for secondary school students see *Study Strategies Made Easy* both by Leslie Davis, Sandi Sirotowitz, and Harvey C. Parker.

Organizational Strategies

Students who organize their materials, their time, and their school assignments often do well in school. Unfortunately, a common characteristic of students with ADHD is chronic disorganization. As one fifteen year old recently said, "I start off the year great with a new notebook, clean backpack, all new pens and pencils, but by the end of the second week it's all a mess and I can never get it back together."

Disorganization is often cited by teachers as the biggest problem their students face. It pays to spend time each day reminding students how to get themselves organized so they can develop good organization habits.

Encourage students to use the following strategies to stay organized:

- use a homework assignment book
- write down all assignments when they are given
- prioritize assignments
- use a calendar to keep track of long term projects, appointments, tests, and due dates of assignments
- refer to assignment book and calendar often
- regularly sort through desk and locker at school to maintain neatness
- draw a diagram of the inside of the student's desk and/or locker indicating exact placement of books and materials. Tape the diagram to the inside so student can refer to it as often as necessary.
- pass out a list of school supplies you expect your students to have on hand either in class or at home for homework. These items may be included on the list:
  - 3-ring notebook
  - spiral notebooks
  - dividers with pockets
  - pen/pencil holder
  - assignment planbook
  - appointment book
  - calendar to schedule work
  - electronic organizer
  - dictionary
  - thesaurus
  - atlas
  - encyclopedia
  - Internet access
  - index cards and box
  - folders to store papers
  - writing tools
  - pencil sharpener
  - ruler, compass, protractor
  - markers and highlighters
  - glue stick, tape
  - scissors, hole punch
  - stapler and staples
  - paper clips
  - rubber bands
  - Post-It® notes
  - reinforcers for notebook
  - "accordion" files
  - clear plastic bins
  - bulletin board and
  - stopwatch or timer

Many students have trouble managing time. For students with ADHD, time management seems impossible. Students with the inattentive type of ADHD may have difficulty getting started on tasks. They procrastinate and often need frequent prompts to get them going. The hyperactive-impulsive ADHD students have trouble stopping enjoyable tasks and starting ones that are less attractive. They both have difficulty planning how to spend their time. Teach time management strategies such as: daily, weekly, monthly planning; prioritizing; and using "Do Lists" (see pages 157-159).

- Have the student make a weekly planner to map out time commitments for the week. This could include class time, time set aside for homework and studying, work time, or time for recreation and appointments.
- Monthly planning can be done using a calendar with daily squares large enough to write notes. Students could keep track of assignments, study times, appointments, after school activities, long term projects, etc.
- Explain how much time is wasted each day by people waiting for something to happen and how we could make better use of time. Suggest that students carry a book, class notes, make calls, or catch up on assignments while waiting.
- Teach lessons on how to overcome procrastination. Ask students to give examples of times they have procrastinated and elicit solutions from students about times they have overcome procrastina-

Organize Your School Papers You Need Now

You can use a 3-ring binder or folders to keep your papers organized. Read the suggestions below to help you organize the papers you need now.

<u>3-Ring Binder</u>
Use a 3-ring binder, with dividers, one per subject. Label each divider by subject name.

<u>Folders with Pockets</u>
Use pocket folders. Use a different color for each subject, and write the subject on the outside.

- Use a separate pocket folder with 3-hole clasps for homework (see the illustration below). Label the inside left pocket, "TO DO" for homework papers that need to be done. Use the inside right pocket to keep an assignment agenda page or homework calendar.

- Also buy a plastic sleeve with 3-holes to put into the folder. You will put your completed homework into the sleeve to keep it neat and clean and ready to turn in.

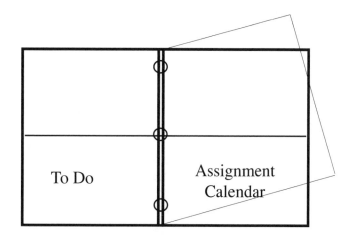

Homework Folder
2 Pockets-3 hole punched

Note: From Sandi Sirotowitz, Leslie Davis and Harvey C. Parker (2004). Study Strategies for Early School Success. Florida: Specialty Press, Inc. Copyright 2004 by Leslie Davis and Sandi Sirotowitz. Reprinted with permission.

Organize Your Old School Papers You Will Need Later

There are some papers, like old tests, you will want to save to use later and some papers that you can throw away. Follow these six steps:

1. Separate your papers into two piles—TRASH and SAVE.
2. To Trash: doodlings, notes from friends, old homework papers, etc.
3. To Save: old tests with questions and answers written on them, class notes, important hand-outs.
4. Get manila file folders. Label them by subject and store them in a file drawer or plastic crate.
5. Write the subject, date, and page or chapter number on the top of each paper you file. When you are ready to study for a test, you will have an easy time reviewing old, but still important notes and tests.
6. It is important to get into the habit of filing your saved work every day.

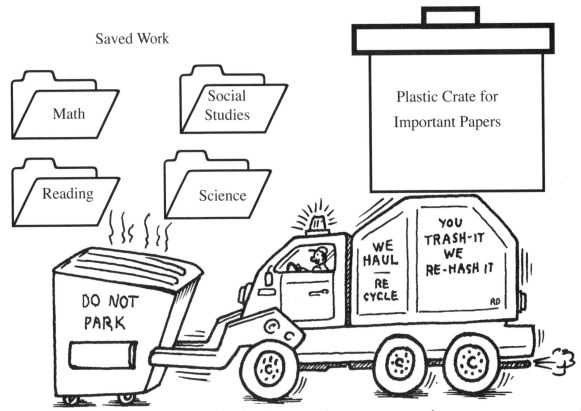

Garbage truck to haul away unimportant papers!

Do List

Use this "Do List" to help you organize assignments (jobs) that need to be done and to plan your time. Each day (or the night before), fill in the Do List with things that you need to complete the next day. Add items to the list each day such as specific homework assignments. Give each item on the list a priority number from 1 to 3. One is highest for the most important tasks. Do the assignments with the highest priority first. Put a check on the right when the assignment has been completed.

Date: _____

Priority	Assignment	Check below when completed
___	_____	___
___	_____	___
___	_____	___
___	_____	___
___	_____	___
___	_____	___
___	_____	___
___	_____	___
___	_____	___

What is Your Time Schedule Like?

Find a study place at home that works best for you, but first answer these questions.

HOW do I like to do my homework or study?

___ alone

___ with a friend or classmate

___ with my parents nearby

WHEN do I like to do my homework?

___ right after school

___ after I've had a snack

___ after I've had time to play or watch TV

___ after dinner

___ after my parents get home from work

WHERE do I like to do my homework or study?

___ in my room

___ in another room in my house where my family is

___ in a room near where my family hangs out

___ at a desk or table

___ on my bed

___ on the floor

___ wherever_____

Now that you know how, when and where to study, it is time to get down to work.

Note: from Sandi Sirotowitz, Leslie Davis and Harvey C. Parker (2004). Study Strategies for Early School Success. Florida: Specialty Press, Inc. Copyright 2004 by Leslie Davis and Sandi Sirotowitz. Reprinted with permission

Weekly Planning

Use this weekly planner to schedule how you want to use your time this week. Block out times for after school activities, homework, and time to relax. Write the times of your favorite TV shows so you can plan to watch them.

Time	Monday	Tuesday	Wednesday	Thursday	Friday
2:00	_____	_____	_____	_____	_____
2:30	_____	_____	_____	_____	_____
3:00	_____	_____	_____	_____	_____
3:30	_____	_____	_____	_____	_____
4:00	_____	_____	_____	_____	_____
4:30	_____	_____	_____	_____	_____
5:00	_____	_____	_____	_____	_____
5:30	_____	_____	_____	_____	_____
6:00	_____	_____	_____	_____	_____
6:30	_____	_____	_____	_____	_____
7:00	_____	_____	_____	_____	_____
7:30	_____	_____	_____	_____	_____
8:00	_____	_____	_____	_____	_____
8:30	_____	_____	_____	_____	_____
9:00	_____	_____	_____	_____	_____
9:30	_____	_____	_____	_____	_____
10:00	_____	_____	_____	_____	_____

tion.

- Help students prepare "Do Lists" to prioritize their work. When something is written on the list the student gives it a number from 1 to 3 to indicate the priority. Items on the list marked "1" should be done first. See earlier pages for a sample Do List and other time management planning forms.

Note-taking Strategies

Taking good notes in class or from material read from a textbook or other sources can be important for successful learning. Note-taking becomes more important as students proceed through middle school and high school. Note-taking provides a means by which students can maintain and organize information. Good information management will be a big advantage to students when they are preparing for class, studying for exams, or writing research papers.

Study Strategies Made Easy (Davis, et al.,1996) describes several types of notes and skills students should learn about to be effective note takers (see worksheets pages 161-165).

- simple outlining
- mind mapping
- combo notes
- using abbreviations
- using recall questions to study
- improving listening skills
- taking notes from lectures
- adding textbook notes to lecture notes

Simple Outlining

Outlining provides a way for students to organize information in notes and a means by which to identify the main ideas and supporting details of lectures or reading selections. Students should be taught how to construct an outline.

- When outlining a reading selection such as a book chapter, the section or chapter title will be the title of the outline.

- Roman numerals designate the headings or topics of a chapter.
- Capital letters designate the subheadings or subtopics of a chapter.
- Arabic numerals designate supporting details.
- Lower case letters designate subdetails within supporting details.

Mind Mapping

Mind mapping is another strategy students can use to organize and manage information acquired through lectures or reading selections. Mind maps are less formal than simple outlines and allow the student to create their own pattern by which to organize information. Davis, et al. point out several steps students should use in making a mind map.

1. Identify the main ideas and supporting details of a reading selection.
2. Write the subject or topic in the center of the page and draw a box or circle around it.
3. Write the main ideas that have to do with the topic.
4. Connect a line from the topic to each main idea and list the main ideas.
5. List all details that connect to the main ideas they support.

Combo Notes

Combo notes is a method of organizing information which combines simple outlining and mind mapping. Instead of using roman numerals and letters, the student might use circles, boxes, stars, and other signs to designate main ideas, supporting details, and subdetails.

Some General Rules for Note-taking

- Instruct students to keep notes well organized. All notes for a particular class should be maintained in a spiral notebook or section of a looseleaf binder dedicated

Simple Outlining

There is so much information included in textbooks or lectures that you must have a way to include only the most important. This strategy teaches you how to arrange information in your notes in an organized way and quickly identify the main ideas and supporting details of a lecture or reading selection.

Directions:

1. Refer to the sample outline below.
2. The section or chapter title will be the title of your outline.
3. The headings/topics of a chapter are the headings of your outline and are   designated by Roman numerals.
4. The subheadings/subtopics of a chapter are the main ideas and are designated by capital letters.
5. The supporting details within main ideas are designated by Arabic numerals
6. The subdetails within the supporting details are designated by lower   case letters.

Sample Outline

TITLE
I. Heading/Topic
   A. Main idea
      1. Supporting detail
      2. Supporting detail
        a. Subdetail
        b. Subdetail
   B. Main idea
      1. Supporting detail
      2. Supporting detail

Note: From Leslie Davis, Sandi Sirotowitz, and Harvey C. Parker (1996). Study Strategies Made Easy. Florida: Specialty Press, Inc. Copyright 1996. Reprinted with permission.

Mind Mapping

Mind mapping is another way to take notes that you may find fun. It is a visual "map" of how supporting details relate to main ideas. Mind maps are less formal than simple outlines and allow you to use any pattern that works best for you.

Directions: The look of your mind map is up to you, but these basic directions will make using a mind map easy.

1. First, identify the main ideas and supporting details of what you are reading.
2. Write the subject or topic in the middle of the page. Then draw a circle or box around it.
3. Find the main ideas that relate to the topic.
4. Draw one line from the topic to each main idea and write the main ideas.
5. Write all relevant details on lines that connect to the main ideas they support.
6. Practice mind mapping by following the above directions for the information in your school textbooks.

The figure below is only one of several basic patterns. You will find more on the next pages. These are our maps, but use your imagination to draw your own maps that will help you "see" the relationships and understand the concepts. Have fun.

Sample Mind Map

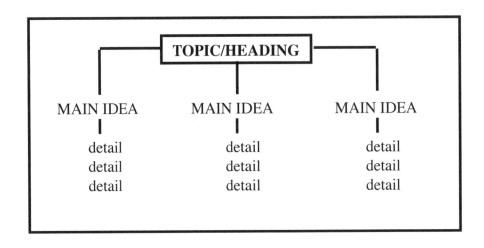

Mind Mapping

Directions: Read and this article and complete the Mind Map on the following page.

The Brain

What Does Brain Size Actually Mean?

When it comes to the brain, bigger doesn't necessarily mean better. Though an elephant's brain or whale's brain weighs much more than a human brain, scientists say size doesn't count. Instead, scientists compare how much space the brain takes up in comparison to the size of the body it inhabits. For example, an elephant's brain takes up 1/1000 of its body weight, and a whale's brain takes up only 1/10,000 of its body weight. On the other hand, the human brain takes up a sizable 1/50 of a person's body weight. The human brain takes up much more space; therefore, scientists concluded that the proportion of a brain to the amount of space it takes up, rather than mere size, is really what tells how intelligent we are.

What Is the Structure of the Human Brain?

The brain looks like a large gray mushroom with many folds, called convolutions, on its surface. The brain consists of three main parts: the cerebrum, the cerebellum, and the medulla oblongata.

The cerebrum is the largest part of the brain. It lies in the upper region of the skull. Its surface has many deep convolutions and the deepest furrow actually divides the cerebrum into two halves. These halves are called the right and left brain hemispheres. The cerebellum lies in the rear of the skull, just behind the cerebrum. The medulla oblongata, at the top of the spinal cord, connects the brain with the spinal cord that runs down the back of the human skeleton.

What Are the Brain's Basic Functions?

Our brain controls all of our bodily functions. It is the transmission and receipt of messages by the various parts of the brain that allow us to perform these amazing skills.

The cerebrum controls our five senses, determining whether and how we see, hear, taste, smell, or feel. The hemispheres of the cerebrum are truly remarkable because the right hemisphere controls the left side of the body while the left side controls the right side. This means that if you are right-handed, it is the left hemisphere of the brain that is more dominant for you. Many people believe that left-brained people are highly verbal with better math and logic skills while right-brained people have great imaginative and creative abilities. Thus, the cerebrum plays a major role in our lives.

The cerebellum has important functions, as well. It allows us to move smoothly instead of in jerky spurts. It also controls our balance. A dancer's or an athlete's coordination and agility can be attributed to the intact functioning of the cerebellum.

The medulla oblongata controls our basic life functions, such as the involuntary movements of breathing or heartbeats. It also controls our reflexes like sneezing or a quick response to avert an accident. If the cerebrum and cerebellum stop working, a human may survive strictly due to the continued functioning of the medulla.

How Else Is the Brain Important to Our Lives?

Each region of the brain serves a specific purpose and affects specific functions. Damage to the brain, such as from a head injury, results in loss of the skill the damaged area controlled. However, research has proven that if one area is damaged, another area often takes over the job.

It used to be thought that as a person aged, the brain diminished until it barely functioned, often referred to as senility. Today, it has been proven that the brain does shrink in size as we age. However, it has also been proven that we can exercise our brains by using mnemonics, continuing to learn new skills and having new experiences. Even reading and doing crossword puzzles seem to keep our aging memories sharp.

The brain controls every aspect of our thinking, feeling, and behavior. A computer may beat the human brain in speed or the total amount of information it can retain, but it is the brain that is the most intricate and amazing creation known to man.

Exercise
Mind Mapping
The Brain

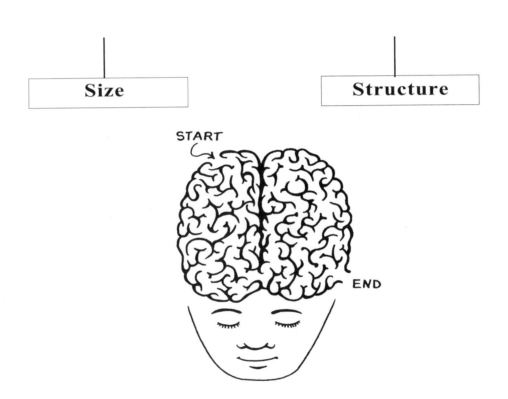

HOW DOES THE BRAIN CONTROL BEHAVIOR?

Taking Combo Notes

Since you need to take notes in most classes, using this method will allow you to organize your notes quickly and easily. You can use combo notes when you take notes from your textbooks. A terrific advantage of this style is that you can use it as you listen to lectures with no need to re-write and reorganize later. What a time saver! As you become more proficient taking combo notes, you will create your own symbols, patterns and general style.

Directions: As with outlining and mind mapping, you will first identify the main concepts and supporting details. Below is a sample of combo notes.
1. Topic or title is written in the middle of a line and circled.
2. The first main idea is written at the margin and boxed.
3. Supporting detail is indented and designated by a symbol..
4. The subdetail is indented further and designated by a different symbol.
5. For clear organization margins are kept consistent.

Sample Combo Notes

```
┌─────────────────────────────────────────────────┐
│   ┌─────────────────────────────────────────┐    │
│   │ Combines outline organization w/ mind map visuals │
│   └─────────────────────────────────────────┘    │
│       •  Advantages                              │
│           ••  can be used for textbooks and during lectures │
│           ••  no need to rewrite - reorganize    │
│       •  Similarities to outlines & mindmaps     │
│           ••  identify main idea & supporting details │
│           ••  organizes ideas                    │
│   ┌──────────────┐                                │
│   │ How to do    │                                │
│   └──────────────┘                                │
│       •  Write topic                             │
│           ••  middle of line                     │
│           ••  box or circle                      │
│       •  Write main idea                         │
│           ••  box or circle                      │
│       •  Indent and write supporting details     │
│           ••  use symbol to identify             │
│       •  keep margins consistent                 │
│                                                   │
└─────────────────────────────────────────────────┘
```

to that class only.

- Notes should be further organized by main topics and supporting ideas and details.
- Write only information that is important in notes.
- Instruct students to highlight or underline any new vocabulary words or terms.
- Emphasize that students should review notes as soon after class as possible. Fill in any gaps and look over notes each day and again before the next class session.
- If the student has poor note taking skills consider these strategies:
  - review instructions on how to outline or mind map, allow use of a note taker
  - instruct how to make an outline or mind-mapping
  - teacher supplies copy of notes
  - portable computers
  - supply copy of another student's notes
  - allow use of a tape recorder

Using Abbreviations

Note-taking is made faster and easier by using common abbreviations such as ones listed below:

Symbols		A Few Letters Only	
#	number	amt	amount
%	percent	assoc	association, associate
$	money, dollars	b/c	because
+	plus, and, more	bio	biology, biography
-	negative, not, no	cont	continue(d)
=	equal	def	definition
≠	unequal, does not equal	eg, ex	for example
>	greater than	etc.	etcetera, also, so forth

<	less than	govt	government
≥	equal to or greater than	info	information
≤	equal to or less than	intro	introduce, introduction
re	regarding, about	pp	pages
\	therefore	s/t	something, sometimes
±	about, more or less	w/	with
@	at, per, each	w/o	without

Note: from Leslie Davis, Sandi Sirotowitz, and Harvey C. Parker (1996). Study Strategies Made Easy. Florida: Specialty Press, Inc. Copyright 1996 by Leslie Davis and Sandi Sirotowitz. Reprinted with permission

- use key words, not complete sentences
- omit unimportant words such as: "a," "the," "to," etc.
- develop own system of abbreviating

Listening Strategies

Good note taking requires good listening skills. Listening in class can often be improved by providing the textbook chapter the night before the lecture so the student has an idea of what to listen for and what to write down. Taking notes will also help students focus on the lecture. In this way, students become active participants instead of passive observers. Students should also pay attention to the lecturer's verbal, presentation and body language cues to determine if a piece of information is important.

Using Recall Questions to Improve Studying

By using recall questions a student can turn notes into study sheets. Recall questions ask who, what, where, when, why, and how and should be written in the margins of notes. They can be valuable aids in studying and can help the student remember factual information.

Making up a recall questions is a powerful way for students to check their understanding of information found in textbooks and notes.

Explain to students that the easiest way to understand what recall questions are is to think

Improving Your Listening Power

When a teacher talks, it pays to listen. Why? Because when a teacher is lecturing, you are getting the information that is considered the most important to learn. Therefore, it will probably be included on future tests. This strategy will help you to identify clues that lecturers give you when they think some information is particularly important.

Lecturers use three types of cues to let you know which facts are important. Therefore, pay close attention to the information that follows these cues.

1. VERBAL CUES

    Review the signals listed on pages 38 and 39 because the same signal words that are used in textbooks are used in lectures to indicate important information.

2. PRESENTATION CUES

    While a textbook uses presentation cues such as bold type to indicate important information, the lecturer may:
    • say certain words or phrases slower, faster, louder, or softer.
    • repeat key phrases.
    • spell important words.
    • write key concepts on the board.

3. BODY LANGUAGE CUES

    Pay attention if the lecturer changes the usual movement of hands, head or body. Since body language cues are often subtle, become aware of each teacher's unique and unusual use of body language. You may be surprised at how often a change of routine can cue what the teacher thinks is important.

Directions:

1. Pay careful attention to all of these cues, and note the information they signal.

2. Preview your textbook chapter the night before the lecture so that you have an idea of what to listen for. This will help you decide what to include in your notes.

3. Do the exercise on the following page to improve your listening power.

Note: From Leslie Davis, Sandi Sirotowitz, and Harvey C. Parker (1996). Study Strategies Made Easy. Florida: Specialty Press, Inc. Copyright 1996. Reprinted with permission.

Improving Your Listening Power

Exercise 1: Listen to a television newscast. As you listen, write any verbal or presentation cues the speaker is using. As you watch, write any body language cues the speaker is using.

Newscast channel and/or speaker: _____Date:_____
CUES:
Verbal: _____
          _____
          _____
          _____

Presentation: _____
          _____
          _____
          _____

Body language: _____
          _____
          _____

Exercise 2: For one day, choose a class to watch for the teacher's lecture cues. As you listen, write any verbal or presentation cues the speaker is using. As you watch, write any body language cues the speaker is using.

Class or teacher: _____

CUES:
Verbal: _____
          _____
          _____
          _____

Presentation:
          _____
          _____
          _____
          _____

Body language:
          _____
          _____
          _____
          _____

Roadblocks to Concentration

There are a lot of things that can block us from concentrating. Below is a list of these "roadblocks to concentration". Circle the ones that make it hard for you to concentrate. Then, write down what you can do about it.

Roadblocks to Concentration   What I can do about it!

1.   Music playing   _____

2.   Computer games   _____

3.   Other people   _____

4.   Kids playing outside   _____

5.   Pets   _____

6.   Television   _____

7.   Toys   _____

8.   Telephone conversations   _____

9.   People talking   _____

10.   Brother or sister   _____

11.   Tired   _____

12.   Bored   _____

13.   Hungry   _____

14.   Restless   _____

15.   Nervous   _____

16.   Frustrated   _____

17.   Confused   _____

of the game, *Jeopardy*. In this game, you are given an answer and then must figure out the question.

After reading, highlighting, and/or taking notes on a section or chapter of their textbook, have the students think of the main idea and its supporting details of that section. That is their answer. Next, encourage them to come up with as many questions as possible for that answer: who, what, where, when, why, and how.

Memory Strategies

Learning requires both understanding and memory. Without either it is impossible to fully benefit from education. There are essentially three types of memory: immediate memory, short-term memory, and long-term memory. Immediate memory enables us to recall information we were recently exposed to (i.e., when a telephone number is given to you). Short-term memory enables us to briefly retain information from a few hours or a few days. Long-term memory enables us to retain information for weeks, months, or years. There are strategies students can use to improve the storage of information into memory. In their book, *Study Strategies Made Easy*, Davis, et al. (1996) describe nine different memory techniques to improve recall: acrostics, acronyms, charting, visual emphasis, visualization, association, word linking, story linking, and rehearsal. These techniques can be taught in school.

- Acrostics. Teach the student to use mnemonics to improve recall. A mnemonic is a trick that helps you remember something. For example, the mnemonic to remember the planets is order is: My Very Educated Mother Just Served Us Nine Pickles—Mercury, Venus, Earth, Mars, Jupiter, Saturn, Uranus, Neptune, and Pluto.

- Acronyms. An acronym is a short version of an acrostic. An acronym uses the first letter of each concept to be learned to form one word. For example, to remember the Great Lakes—**H**uron, **O**ntario, **M**ichigan, **E**rie, **S**uperior—**HOMES**.

- Encourage students to use visualization to improve recall. By visualizing (forming mental pictures) of facts or concepts we can strengthen our recall. For example, to remember a new vocabulary word try to form a picture in your mind that conveys the meaning.

- Visualization can also be used to remember math facts, such as liquid measurement. For example, if you want to remember how many cups, pints and quarts are in a gallon, you can use the visual image below to remember that there are four quarts, eight pints, and sixteen cups to a gallon. Teach students how to form visual associations between facts or concepts to improve recall.

Note: from Leslie Davis, Sandi Sirotowitz, and Harvey C. Parker (1996). Study Strategies Made Easy. Florida: Specialty Press, Inc. Reprinted with permission.

Steps in Writing a Research Paper

1. Select an appropriate topic. Help the student understand that choosing a topic that is too broad or too narrow could make it difficult to write about.
2. Do preliminary research to find out if there is enough information about the topic to fulfill the assignment.
3. Collect sources such as encyclopedias, on-line sources, books, periodicals, etc.
4. Narrow the topic to your specific area of interest.
5. Write a thesis statement—a sentence that states the central theme of the paper.
6. List the main ideas that should be included in the paper and organize the sequence in which they will be included in the paper.
7. List details for each of the main ideas and put in outline form and on note cards.
8. Put the main ideas and details in sentence form in a rough draft.
9. Check spelling, capitalization, and punctuation.
10. Have someone proofread the rough draft.
11. Make certain the rough draft proves the point of the paper and backs it up with facts in a logical order.
12. Rewrite the paper in final form and ask someone to proofread once again.
13. Prepare final copy.

Reading Comprehension Strategies

From elementary grades on, students must be able to read and understand and recall what information they read. Reading comprehension strategies emphasizes the importance of picking out the topic, main idea, and supporting details of a reading passage. By organizing this information, the reader will be able to answer questions of where, when, why, and how about the passage and write the topic, main idea, and supporting details down for note-taking.

Picturing an umbrella is a good way for children to understand what they have read.

Topic or Title Main Idea

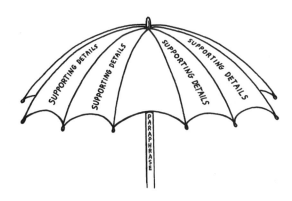

1. Picture an umbrella. The topic is the center of the top. You should be able to tell the topic in only one or two words.
2. The main idea covers the whole umbrella, just as it covers the whole paragraph.
3. The important details are the ribs that support the umbrella just as they support the main idea. Without support, both the umbrella and the main idea fall apart.
4. Finally, *get a handle* on the whole paragraph by paraphrasing what you have read.

SQ3R for Reading Comprehension

Many educators like to use the reading and studying method called SQ3R. Reading research indicates that it is an extremely effective method for both comprehension and memory retention because it requires active reader involvement.

Step 1. "S"= Survey

In this step the student is encouraged to preview the chapter by scanning or surveying the contents for a few minutes before reading it thoroughly. While surveying, the student checks headings and subheadings in order to understand how information is organized. All visual material is scanned. Introductory and summary paragraphs are read. This preview will enable the student to anticipate what the chapter is about.

Step 2. "Q"= Question

In this step the student asks questions about the material that was surveyed. What is the main points of this section? What is the author trying to get across? What information is important to remember? The student should keep these questions in mind while reading. This can give the student a clearly defined purpose for reading and can help maintain interest in the chapter.

Step 3. "R"= Read

Now the student reads the chapter actively for meaning and underlines key words and phrases to help recall the main points. The student should summarize main concepts in his own words in the margins. The more active the student is in the reading process, the more he will retain.

Step 4. "R"= Recite

After reading a few pages the student can close the book and recite aloud the main points to the questions posed in step 2.   Answers can be checked in the text. This is a time when the student can test himself to see if he has learned the main points.

Step 5. "R"= Review

Finally, the student should review the chapter every so often to fix the material in his mind. Re-reading notes written in margins and underlined sentences will reinforce them. Verbalizing the sequence of main ideas and supporting facts can aid retention. Reviewing once right after having finished reading and then every couple of days is better than cramming the night before a test.

3 Sweeps Method to Really Read a Textbook

To help students read a chapter in a textbook and understand what they read, Leslie Davis and Sandi Sirotowitz suggest your teach their 3 Sweeps Method (see next page).

1. Preview the chapter
2. Read the study questions
3. Read the chapter carefully

Test Taking Strategies

Students in all grades take tests and could benefit from learning strategies that may improve their test performance.

- The most common mistake students make when taking tests is they don't read instructions carefully. Show students how they can benefit by underlining key words in instructions and by taking their time to fully understand what they are supposed to do before they proceed.

- Encourage students to take an inventory of the study strategies they use to prepare for tests. Does the student:
  - start studying well in advance of the test
  - look over the chapter each night
  - read the class notes each night
  - use recall questions to review for a test
  - have someone quiz them to see how well the information is learned
  - make notes of the study material that is to be best remembered
  - read the content over and over
  - wait until the last minute to study and then cram
  - get very nervous before a test and can they relax
  - look over previous tests the teacher has given to get some idea of the types of questions that may be asked next time
  - review how they answered questions on previous tests to get some idea of what types of answers the teacher may be looking for
  - save old tests
  - write answers to possible essay ques-

3 Sweeps or How to Really Read a Textbook

To really read a chapter in a textbook and understand what you've read, it is best to use a method of reading comprehension which we call "3 Sweeps." — PREVIEW THE CHAPTER; READ THE STUDY QUESTIONS; and REALLY READ THE CHAPTER. Read the details of each step described below to help you learn the "3 Sweeps" method to read and comprehend any of the chapters in your textbooks.

I.   SWEEP 1:   Preview the Chapter

Previewing gives you an overview of what is included in the chapter.

A. **Title**: Read the title and ask yourself what you already know about the title and how it fits in with what you previously studied.

B. **Introduction**: Read the introduction to the chapter and ask yourself what it is about (paraphrase aloud).

C. **Headings/Topics; Subheadings/Subtopics**: Read each to gain a general idea of the content to be covered.

D. **Pictures, Maps, Charts**: Look at each to gain additional information concerning the chapter.

II. SWEEP 2:   Read the Study Questions

Reading the questions gives you the purpose for reading and provides clues about what details the author thinks are important.

A. Read the study questions at the end of each section, one section at a time.

B. The study questions that begin with these words ask for details:

Who? ———	asks for people
What? ———	asks for events
Where? ———	asks for places
When? ———	asks for time
How? ———	asks for process
Why? ———	asks for reasons

Note: From Leslie Davis, Sandi Sirotowitz, and Harvey C. Parker (1996). Study Strategies Made Easy. Florida: Specialty Press, Inc. Copyright 1996. Reprinted with permission.

III. SWEEP 3:   *Really* Read the Chapter

Use your reading comprehension strategies to read the chapter for the main ideas, details and meanings.

A. Read the first heading/topic to understand the central theme of the section.

B. Read the first paragraph to identify the main idea.

C. After you have read one paragraph, highlight the main ideas and supporting details in yellow. Use the author's signals to help you identify the details that are important. Remember, though, important ideas will not always be introduced by signals.

D. Highlight the vocabulary words and their meanings in a second color. If a definition is not given, look it up and write it in the margin.

E. After each section, paraphrase the main idea and details in your own words. If a section is long or filled with details, paraphrase after each paragraph.

F. Since you have already read the questions at the end of a section, as you come to their answers, write the question numbers next to the line of text.

G. Use the margin of the book to jot notes, definitions, or key words.

If you cannot mark in the textbook, either photocopy necessary pages or, in a notebook, take notes of the main ideas, supporting details, and vocabulary.

Remember: The more active your reading is, the easier it will be to learn and remember the content.

Studying for Mid-Terms and Final Exams

Mid-term and final exams are given to test your ability to organize, understand, and recall information that has been taught over a period of weeks or even months. Since these tests are usually given for more than one subject and at around the same time, it is easy to feel overloaded with studying. To help, you need a method of preparation that will allow you to accomplish as much as possible without wasting valuable time.

The good news is that since you have been highlighting, taking notes, writing and reviewing recall questions, and learning information for chapter tests, you are better prepared than you may think. Now it's time for you to put all of those strategies together and show how well you have really been able to learn. So, enter those tests with confidence!

I. Get a Head Start Two Weeks Before the Exam.
   A. Find out all that you can about the exam.
   1. In class, listen for the teacher's clues and signals as to which material might be included on the tests.
   2. What type format will the test be?

      a. If objective only, review and memorize important details.

      b. If subjective also, learn overall concepts, but memorize enough facts to back them up in an essay.

   3. Can you bring notes into the exam? (Find out any limits as to how many pages, etc.)

   4. Will any chapters or material not be included on the test? (Unless the teacher tells you exactly what won't be included, study every chapter and all material.)

B. Start the preparation

   1. Get out your filed notes, old tests, etc., and organize them now.

   2. Make sure that all chapters have been highlighted and recall questions written.

   3. Make up a study schedule to follow for the next two weeks.

C. Organize your study session.
1. Follow the study schedule and pace yourself so that you can study a little each day.
    a. Divide the number of chapters or pages to cover by the number of days you have set aside to study.
    b. Study each subject for one-half hour before breaking and beginning the next.
2. As you review the textbook, also review the lecture notes and clues from the teacher.
3. Review old tests since the same questions (possibly worded differently) may show up again.
4. For each chapter, concentrate on highlighted material and recall questions. Also, read and answer end of chapter study questions.

D. Remember to use your strongest learning style and preferences.
1. Auditory learners may want to read the highlighted information aloud, or tape record recall questions that you can then listen to and answer later.
2. Visual learners may want to picture the look of a page or associations.
3. Kinesthetic learners may want to rewrite information (e.g.,brief summary outlines or charts).
4. Study during the times and in the environments that will help you focus best.

II. Cramming
A. If you have consistently followed the strategies from *Study Strategies Made Easy*, you should not have to cram. However, just in case …

B. What is cramming and how can you use it?
1. Cramming is really stuffing as much information into your head as possible just before you'll need to use it, such as the night before or morning of a test!
2. Unfortunately, cramming only works for very brief periods and for very small amounts of information, so it is not an efficient study strategy.
3. If you find that you absolutely must cram, don't try to read and remember every bit of information from the chapters and notes. Rely upon your highlighted information, vocabulary, and recall questions. This will be the most important information, and you can cram it into your memory in the shortest amount of time.

III. Final Words About Final Exams.
Successful test takers relax before exams. They go to sleep early, wake up early to eat a nutritious breakfast, listen to some soothing music, and pump themselves up with confident attitudes. Take advice from the successful test takers and be a successful test taker yourself!

tions in advance
- use a highlighter to highlight important information in books or class notes
- study with other students in a small group

Making Old Tests Work for You

One of the most valuable study aids students have is a returned test. By analyzing their errors, they can learn from their mistakes and actually plan ways to score higher on future tests. Also, if information was important enough to be included on the test, it may show up again on a midterm or final exam. Encourage students to look over old tests carefully and to study from them for mid-terms and final exams when it is practical to do so.

Summary

Students of all ages can benefit from learning study strategies. Study strategies can greatly enhance a student's ability to stay organized, manage time, take notes in class from lectures and from books, listen attentively, memorize and recall information, write papers, and prepare for tests. Teaching study strategies should be part of the curriculum at every grade level. Students with ADHD, in particular, could benefit from strategies aimed at improving organizational skills, planning, and time management. All of the strategies in this chapter are considered by teachers to be essential for school success.

Chapter 14
Teaching Social Skills

Jody is a nine-year-old fourth grader. She is extremely timid. Her parents feel she is missing out socially because of her shyness. Her teachers would tell her parents she was the perfect student, but too quiet. Jody rarely speaks to other children and stays to herself most of the time.

David is anything but quiet. He is loud and boisterous and can get on your nerves if you're with him for more than ten minutes. He never seems to notice when others are irritated with him. His parents say he was born with a megaphone in his mouth. They often go to another room when David is home just to get some peace and quiet. David usually finds them and keeps right on talking. His parents hoped that when he got into high school he'd become more aware of his behavior and would quiet down. No such luck!

Frank's biggest problem is his temper. He can't ever seem to control his anger. When he gets mad, his younger brother and sister run for cover. In elementary school he frequently visited the principal's office. In high school he was disciplined twice for fighting. Now he has a job at a service station after school, and he's on probation for arguing with a customer.

Jody, David, and Frank have ADHD and they are having problems with social skills. They might benefit from social skills training. Social skills training involves educating people about social skills and teaching them to use learned skills in their social interactions. Through social skills training, kids can learn to advocate for themselves in different situations, deal with authority figures appropriately, maintain control over their behavior, initiate and carry on conversations, and show empathy and compassion for others to make friends.

Social skills training may be particularly important for children and adolescents with disabilities such as ADHD. People with ADHD may have more trouble holding conversations because they may not be able to listen attentively to a speaker or they may interrupt others. They have difficulty waiting their turn in games or in organized activities which require giving others a chance at equal participation. They may not be able to control their temper when they feel they have been wronged, causing them to lash out inappropriately. Social skills training can help them recognize when their behavior is inappropriate. The first step in teaching social skills is to do a social skills assessment.

Assessing Social Skills

The Tough Kid Social Skills Book by Susan M. Sheridan is an excellent resource for materials to help teachers assess students' social skills. Sheridan discusses three steps in the assessment process.

Step 1—Do a General Screening to Identify Students with Social Problems

The objective of this step is to identify students who teachers and peers recognize as having social problems.

Teacher nomination forms can be completed by teachers to identify students who: have few friends, frequently fight or argue with classmates, blame others for problems, do not show ability to solve problems cooperatively, fail to exhibit self-control, or are not well liked.

Sociograms can be completed by classmates. Similar to teacher nominations, sociograms are easy to administer. Each child in a classroom is asked to nominate three peers with whom they like to play or work and three peers with whom they would not like to play or work. Below are directions to make a sociogram of the students in a class.

1. Ask students to list the names of three classmates with whom they like to play.
2. Ask students to list the names of three classmates with whom they do *not* like to play.
3. Ask students to list the names of three classmates whom they would like to invite to a party or activity.
4. Ask students to list the names of three classmates whom they would like to *not* invite to a party or activity.

Count the number of times each student was listed in each of the activity categories. Based on the students' responses to the sociogram you could classify students in your class as either popular, rejected, neglected, or controversial.

Step 2—Use Rating Scales to Collect More In-Depth Information About a Student's Social Skills

There are several rating scales published to evaluate social skills. Rating scales are helpful because they can pinpoint a students' social skills strengths and weaknesses. Some examples of rating scales or books which contain such scales are:

- Walker-McConnell Scale of Social Competence (Elementary and Adolescent Versions) by Hill Walker and Scott R. McConnell
- Social Skills Rating Scale (SSRS) by Frank Gresham and Stephen Elliott
- Skillstreaming in Early Childhood, Skillstreaming the Elementary School Child, and Skillstreaming the Adolescent by Arnold P. Goldstein and Ellen McGinnis contain social skills inventories
- The Tough Kid Social Skills Book by Susan Sheridan contains social skills inventories

The Skills Survey (Sheridan, 1995) is an abbreviated rating scale for teachers. This brief scale can be used to identify social skills that could be targeted for training in a social skills training group. The items in the scale are rated from 1 to 4 (never a problem to almost always a problem). Sample items are listed below:

- Noticing and talking about feelings
- Starting a conversation
- Joining in

- Playing cooperatively
- Keeping a conversation going
- Solving problems
- Solving arguments
- Dealing with teasing
- Dealing with being left out
- Using self-control
- Accepting "No"

Self-ratings by students can provide useful information about how students perceive their own social skills. However, many students with social difficulties attribute social problems to others and often deny or minimize social problems in themselves. Therefore, self-rating scales should be interpreted cautiously.

The *Skillstreaming* programs (Goldstein and McGinnis, 1997) have student manuals for elementary-age and adolescent students that contain very helpful self-rating scales. Below are examples of questions students are asked:

- Do I listen to someone who is talking to me?
- Do I start conversations with other people?
- Do I talk with other people about things that interest both of us?
- Do I introduce myself to new people?
- Do I ask for help when I am having difficulty?
- Do I help others who might need or want help?
- Do I pay full attention to whatever I am working on?
- Do I handle complaints made against me in a fair way?
- Do I deal positively with being left out of some activity?
- Do I stay in control when someone teases me?
- Do I control my temper when I feel upset?

Step 3—Interviewing Others and Observing Students

This step in the assessment process is the most costly and time consuming to do, but it often provides the most useful information about a child's social functioning. There are two procedures used in direct assessment: social skills interviews and direct observations of the student in the classroom, playground, cafeteria, and hallways at school.

Social skills interviews are conducted with parents, teachers, students, and peers. Parents may be asked about the specific concerns they have about their child's social skills, which concerns trouble them the most, what types of situations trigger problem behavior, etc. Students may be asked about the types of problems they have with peers, whether they are happy with their friendships, what areas they would like to improve, etc.

Through direct observation of the student in school, we can objectively measure the frequency with which students exhibit certain behavior. Direct observation of the student gives us first-hand data that cannot be collected through teacher nominations, sociograms, rating scales, or interviews. Some useful direct observation instruments are:

- ADHD School Observation Code by Kenneth Gadow, Joyce Sprafkin, and Edith Nolan (1996)
- Social Skills Direct Observation Form by Susan Sheridan (in *The Tough Kid Social Skills Book*)

When doing direct observation the observer watches the student and counts the number of times the student displays behavior described on the observation system. Observations are typically made during fifteen second intervals and then recorded on a data sheet. For example, when using the Social Skills Direct Observation Form the following social skills are rated:

<u>Positive Social Behaviors</u>
- Social Entry—student initiates social interaction
- Playing Cooperatively—student appropriately keeps an interaction going
- Solving Problems—student tries to manage conflict in an appropriate manner

<u>Negative Social Behaviors</u>
- Verbal Aggression—student makes threatening, negative remark or gesture
- Physical Aggression—student displays an overt, physical behavior that can inflict physical harm or damage
- Social Noncompliance—student displays behavior indicating defiance or intention of breaking a rule
- Isolated—student does not participate with others

Training Social Skills

For many years social skills were not taught in school in a systematic way. Teaching social skills was regarded as the parents' job rather than the teachers'. However, with the increase in child and adolescent aggression and violent behavior in our nation's schools and communities, programs were developed for educators to work with youth to improve self-control, social behavior, and build character. Youth now can receive group training to help them learn social skills. There are a number of social skills training programs commercially available.

Hill Walker and his colleagues developed a social skills program called *ACCESS* or the *Adolescent Curriculum for Communication and Effective Social Skills*. It was designed to teach thirty-one social skills in three areas: relating to peers, relating to adults, and relating to yourself. Specific skills across these areas include listening, greeting, offering assistance, getting an adult's attention, disagreeing with adults, following classroom rules, taking pride in your appearance, being organized, and using self-control.

One of the pioneers in the area of social skills training is Arnold P. Goldstein, who developed the *Prepare Curriculum* to teach children how to act and react in different social situations. With Ellen McGinnis, he developed the *Skillstreaming* program for early childhood, elementary, and adolescent age groups. *Skillstreaming the Adolescent* identifies fifty social skills within six different groups.

Social Skills in the *Skillstreaming the Adolescent* Program

<u>Group 1: Beginning Social Skills</u>
1. Listening
2. Starting a conversation
3. Having a conversation
4. Asking a question
5. Saying thank you
6. Introducing yourself
7. Introducing other people
8. Giving a compliment

<u>Group II: Advanced Social Skills</u>
9. Asking for help
10. Joining in
11. Giving instructions
12. Following instructions
13. Apologizing
14. Convincing others

<u>Group III: Skills for Dealing with Feelings</u>
15. Knowing your feelings
16. Expressing your feelings
17. Understanding feelings of others
18. Dealing with someone else's anger
19. Expressing affection
20. Dealing with fear
21. Rewarding yourself

<u>Group IV: Skill Alternatives to Aggression</u>
22. Asking permission
23. Sharing something
24. Helping others

25. Negotiating
26. Using self-control
27. Standing up for your rights
28. Responding to teasing
29. Avoiding trouble with others
30. Keeping out of fights

Group V: Skills for Dealing with Stress
31. Making a complaint
32. Answering a complaint
33. Being a good sport
34. Dealing with embarrassment
35. Dealing with being left out
36. Standing up for a friend
37. Responding to persuasion
38. Responding to failure
39. Dealing with conflicting messages
40. Dealing with an accusation
41. Getting ready for a difficult
42. Dealing with group pressure

Group VI: Planning Skills
43. Deciding on something to do
44. Deciding what caused a problem
45. Setting a goal
46. Deciding on your abilities
47. Gathering information
48. Prioritizing problems
49. Making a decision
50. Concentrating on a task

The core training procedures involved in the *Skillstreaming* program are modeling, role-playing, performance feedback, and generalization training. Trainers lead individuals in the group through nine steps to learn a skill, practice using it, and receive feedback from group members during role-play exercises.

A program called *Job-related Social Skills (JRSS)* by Marjorie Montague and Kathryn Lund covers a number of skills: prioritizing job responsibilities, understanding directions, giving instructions, asking questions, asking permission, asking for help, accepting help, offering help, re-questing information, taking messages, engaging in a conversation, giving compliments, convincing others, apologizing, accepting criticism, and responding to complaints. Skills are taught using direct instruction, rehearsal, modeling, and role playing.

Berthold Berg has developed a series of games and workbooks that are designed to train social skills in older children and adolescents. His programs can be used with the guidance of a health care professional, educator, or parent. Berg identifies specific social skills and provides an inventory to assess the individual's current use of these skills in social interactions.

These are introduced to the child or adolescent in a game-like format and reinforced with a workbook the student can write in to strengthen skill knowledge. Through playing the game and completing the exercises in the workbook, children learn to identify the things they say to themselves during social interactions. They identify what Berg refers to as "negative self-talk," which he believes mediates behavior and causes us to act in negative ways to others or to ourselves. The games and exercises encourage children to replace negative self-talk with "positive self-talk," which is more constructive and likely to lead to self-confidence, better self-control, and positive interactions with others. His games and workbooks also focus on teaching children to say things to themselves that make them feel competent, expect success in what they try to do, not worry, accept making mistakes, give themselves credit, and compliment themselves.

In the *Social Skills Game* and the *Social Skills Workbook*, Berg lists four categories of skills containing specific behaviors under each:
Making friends
Asking a question
Giving a compliment
Introducing yourself
Listening
Starting a conversation

Responding positively to peers
Accepting a compliment
Helping peers in trouble
Offering help
Showing concern for peer
Standing up for peers

Cooperating with peers
Following rules
Joining in
Sharing
Suggesting an activity
Taking turns

Communicating needs
Asking for help
Asking to borrow another's property
Expressing negative feelings
Expressing positive feelings
Getting attention appropriately

Generalization of Skill Training to the Real World

Teaching children and adolescents social skills is not difficult. Getting them to apply what they have learned and to use these skills in the real world is another matter. The results have been disappointing.

To be socially competent, a person must be able to determine when a social skill would be appropriate to use in a given social situation *and* must be motivated to use it. Social skill problems can be the result of an acquisition deficit or a performance deficit. An acquisition deficit is a problem which is the result of a person not knowing what to do within a social situation. A performance deficit is a problem which is the result of a person not doing what he knows.

After receiving social skills training, a child may know what skill to use and how to use it within a given social situation, but may fail to use the skill correctly, if at all. If they have ADHD, they may not be able to regulate their behavior sufficiently to use the social skill—even if they know what it is.

For example, a child with ADHD may know the appropriate negotiation skill to use to ask his parent for permission to stay out past his curfew. He may not, however, be capable of controlling his frustration if his parent doesn't grant permission. At the slightest sign of a negative response, the ADHD adolescent's emotions may erupt into an aggressive attack. The parent may respond aggressively, and the conversation erupts into an argument. Instead of giving permission to stay out later, the parent may punish the teen by grounding him that night.

Many social skills training programs contains strategies designed to increase the likelihood that a trainee will use the social skill in daily life. In the *Skillstreaming* program, Arnold Goldstein and Ellen McGinnis provide training to parents as well as the kids. Parent training groups meet separately from the kid's group. Parents are instructed to use the trained social skill in the presence of their son or daughter. They strengthen the skill for their child by modeling. Parents are also trained to give praise when they observe a social skill being used properly.

How Parents Can Promote Positive Social Skills

- Serve as good role models and behave in socially appropriate ways. Children and adolescents learn what they live. Parents who model appropriate social behavior are more likely to promote appropriate social behavior in their children. This is particularly true when a specific social skill is targeted for learning. Make an effort to model use of the social skill as much as possible.

- Recognize when the child is using a social skill well and provide positive reinforcement to the child. This will strengthen the use of the social skill in the future.

- Calmly and constructively point out inappropriate social behavior and suggest a more appropriate replacement behavior. It is important to couch reminders in a positive, non-condescending way.
- Encourage the child to use problem-solving strategies. Through use of the problem-solving strategies children could learn to successfully resolve potential conflicts with peers in an appropriate manner.

How Teachers Can Promote Positive Social Skills

- Students with ADHD often are not aware of how their behavior affects others. Some will talk incessantly about a favorite topic, not realizing others are no longer interested. Some will overreact to situations and become oblivious to how foolish they appear to others. Teachers may be able to strengthen pro-social behavior by pointing out examples of positive interaction and praising.
- Monitor social interactions to gain clearer sense of student's behavior with others.
- Set up social behavior goals with student and implement a social skills program.
- Prompt appropriate social behavior either verbally or with a private signal.
- Encourage student to observe a classmate who exhibits appropriate social skills.
- Avoid placing student in competitive activities where there is a greater likelihood of stress leading to negative social behavior.
- Encourage cooperative learning tasks.
- Provide small group social skills training in-class or through related services using a systematic program.
- Praise student to increase esteem to others.
- Assign special responsibilities to student

in presence of peers to elevate status in class.
- Pair students instead of letting students choose.
- Encourage participation in after school "clubs" and activities.

Helping Students Develop Empathy, Self-control, and Cooperativeness

Empathy toward others, self-control, and cooperativeness are core social skills. Many ingredients that go into forming good friendships involve the ability of a person to show empathy and self-control and to display a cooperative attitude towards others. Below is a questionnaire that will help students identify their strengths or weaknesses in these areas (Davis, et al. 1996).

Read each of the statements below and rate whether the statement describes you:

Yes   No   Empathy
____ ____   1. I show sympathy for others.
____ ____   2. I am considerate of others.
____ ____   3. I am a good listener.
____ ____   4. I go out of my way to show a helpful attitude to others.

Self-control
____ ____   5. I show self-control in difficult situations.
____ ____   6. I can accept constructive criticism from others.
____ ____   7. I stay calm when things don't go my way.
____ ____   8. It takes a lot for me to get angry.

Cooperativeness
____ ____   9. I make friends easily.
____ ____   10. I can keep a conversation going.
____ ____   11. I invite others to participate in activities.
____ ____   12. I compliment others on their work, appearance, etc.

If the student had three or more "Yes" answers in each category he probably communicates well with other students. If the student had less than three "Yes" answers in any of the categories, improvement in that area is needed. I have included exercises on the following pages to help students increase empathy, self-control, and cooperativeness.

Exercise—Increasing Empathy Toward Others

Empathy is the act of showing consideration, sympathy, and sensitivity to the needs of others. Empathy towards someone else can be shown by our words, facial expressions, body language, and our behavior towards others. When we show empathy towards others, we are saying to someone else, "I understand what you're going through and I care about you." We usually show empathy towards others to provide support when someone is going through a difficult time. Needless to say, showing consideration to others and being sensitive to their feelings help build strong relationships.

Directions: Follow these steps to improve your ability to show empathy to others:

1. Figure out how the person is feeling, i.e., sad, angry, nervous, worried, etc. Watch the other person when they are describing their situation. Notice facial expressions, tone of voice, and body movements. They all give you clues about how this person is feeling.
2. Listen carefully to what the person is saying. Try to follow the content of what they are saying.
3. Decide on ways to show that you understand what the person is feeling such as through a gentle touch or a concerned look or gesture.
4. Review the examples below of statements and actions that do or do not show empathy.

Examples of statements that show empathy:
- "You seem upset."
- "I understand how you feel."
- "I can imagine how that must be for you."
- "It sounds like you're going through a rough time."
- "I see what you're saying."
- "I understand."
- "I know what you mean."

Actions that do not show empathy:
- offering unsolicited advice
- showing disapproval or disrespect
- responding in a judgmental way
- being long-winded
- taking sides
- changing the topic
- looking away while the person is talking
- showing disinterest in the other person
- "If you think you've had it rough, listen to me. My story is worse."

Role Play and Discussion
- A good way to practice showing empathy is to role play a conversation. Two or more students can play different parts and be involved in the role playing while other students try to identify statements or behaviors which show empathy.
- Example: A student was counting on getting a job in the mall this summer. His application was turned down and he's worried he won't be able to find another job.
- Discussing real-life situations when showing empathy helps form and strengthen a relationship

Exercise—Increasing Self-Control

Self-control is the ability to control one's behavior and emotions under stressful conditions. Self-control is shown by calmness in our voice and behavior as we react in an even-tempered way without emotional extremes of anger, sadness, or frustration.

Directions: Follow these steps when faced with a stressful situation.

1. Give yourself time to "cool off" before reacting.
2. Keep your thoughts and your body calm.
3. Think about your choices and make logical decisions.

Common statements people say to themselves to keep in control:

- I can work this out.
- I can handle this situation.
- Relax and think this through.
- Stay calm. Breathe easily. Just continue to relax.
- I'm not going to let this thing get the best of me.
- I can stay in control.
- Getting upset won't help anything.
- Don't worry. Things will work out for the best.
- There is no point in getting mad.

A good way to practice self-control is through role playing and modeling behavior. Two or more students can act out a stressful situation demonstrating different methods of showing self-control. Other students can identify other methods of self-control that can be used.

Discuss examples of real-life situations when self-control could have made for a better outcome in a situation.

Exercise—Increasing Cooperativeness

Cooperativeness is the act of showing cooperation to get along with others. Cooperativeness is shown by being helpful, waiting one's turn, sharing, trusting others, listening to others, and following instructions. When we show cooperativeness we are working or playing alongside others in a helpful, positive way.

Directions: Follow these steps to show cooperativeness:

1. Determine if the other person may need and want help before offering help. Use verbal, facial, and behavioral cues to judge whether someone needs help (person asks for help, looks puzzled, looks as if he is struggling).
2. When playing a game or sport, show respect for the other person. Follow the rules of the game or sport. Determine who starts and wait for your turn. Congratulate the other person if he won or tell the other person he did well, even if he lost.
3. When working on a project with others, show respect for them. Determine each person's part in the project and make certain to do your share as best you can. Offer help to others, wait your turn when speaking, and be considerate of others' feelings when making comments.

Summary

Many children with ADHD would benefit from learning and using appropriate social skills. Social behavior is often inappropriate in those with ADHD. Hyperactive-impulsive people tend to interrupt others, shift topics in conversations, intrude into other's "space," and have difficulty controlling behavior and emotions. Other people notice this behavior within a short time of meeting someone with ADHD and quickly form a negative impression. People with ADHD—inattentive type, tend to be more quiet and passive. They would benefit from learning and using social skills that would enable them to communicate more assertively.

There are a number of social skills training programs available. These programs are usually run in small social skills groups and are offered in schools or in counseling settings. Parents can reinforce the use of social skills by appropriately modeling skills to their child and by praising positive behavior.

Chapter 15
Teaching Students Who Have ADHD and Other Mental Health Disorders

A significant number of children with ADHD have other mental health disorders. Some exhibit oppositional behavior or more serious problems with conduct. Some suffer from anxiety and depression. Others may develop obsessive compulsive disorder, Tourette's syndrome, or motor tics. Many have significant social problems causing them to have few or no friends.

Students with mental health disorders often have certain patterns of behavior as listed below:

- difficulty making and keeping friends
- withdrawal from social activities
- somatic complaints (stomachaches, headaches, etc.)
- excessive lateness or absence from school
- statements or actions indicating lack of confidence or low self-esteem
- avoidance of difficult tasks
- feelings of sadness, discouragement, or hopelessness
- excessive worry
- irritability
- poor concentration due to worry or preoccupation
- lack of interest in school work
- easily frustrated
- aggressiveness
- defiance
- problems with self-control
- anger outbusts
- mood shifts
- excessive elation
- rapid speech, racing thoughts
- depression
- lethargy, low energy
- significant weight gain or loss
- recurrent obssessive thoughts
- suicidal thinking
- substance abuse
- low self-esteem
- problems with sleep (insomia or hypersomnia)

Symptoms of a mental health disorder can reach a level where there is significant impairment in a child's functioning at home, school, or in the community or work setting. As indicated earlier, many children do not have adequate access to mental health services. Schools play a vital role in identifying students at risk for mental disorder and schools also provide opportunities for prevention and treatment. Classroom teachers may be the first to spot signs of problems. Make a referral for an evaluation to better understand the nature, causes, and the severity of the student's problem. Below are descriptions of different mental disorders, all of which can co-occur with ADHD, and suggestions for classroom teachers and other school personnel to help the student function better in the classroom.

Oppositional Defiant Disorder and Conduct Disorder

Up to forty percent of children and as many as sixty-five percent of adolescents with ADHD exhibit such degrees of stubbornness and noncompliance they fall into a category of disruptive behavior disorder known as *oppositional defiant disorder*. Below is a list of characteristics of oppositional defiant disorder.

1. often loses temper
2. often argues with adults
3. often actively defies or refuses to comply with adults' requests or rules
4. often deliberately annoys people
5. often blames others for his or her mistakes or misbehavior
6. is often touchy or easily annoyed by others
7. is often angry and resentful
8. is often spiteful or vindictive

Conduct disorder co-occurs with ADHD in about thirty percent of children and adolescents referred for treatment. Adolescents with conduct disorder may exhibit behavior which is characterized by aggression to people and animals, destruction of property, deceitfulness or theft, and serious violation of rules. Below is a list of characteristics of conduct disorder.

Aggression to people and animals
1. often bullies, threatens, or intimidates others
2. often initiates physical fights
3. has used a weapon that can cause serious physical harm to others (e.g., a bat, brick, broken bottle, knife, gun)
4. has been physically cruel to people
5. has been physically cruel to animals
6. has stolen while confronting a victim (e.g., mugging, purse snatching, extortion, armed robbery
7. has forced someone into sexual activity

Destruction of property
8. has deliberately engaged in fire setting with the intention of causing serious damage
9. has deliberately destroyed others' property (other than by fire setting)

Deceitfulness or theft
10. has broken into someone else's house, building, or car
11. often lies to obtain goods or favors or to avoid obligations (i.e., "cons" others)
12. has stolen items of nontrivial value without confronting a victim (e.g., shoplifting, but without breaking and entering; forgery)
Serious violations of rules
13. often stays out at night despite parental prohibition, beginning before age thirteen
14. has run away from home overnight at least twice while living in paren-

tal or parental surrogate home (or once without returning for a lengthy period)
15. often truant from school, beginning before age thirteen

The severity of conduct disorder ranges from mild to severe based on the number of symptoms demonstrated and the degree of harm rendered to person or property. There are two broad groups of adolescents with conduct disorder. In one group are adolescents who had an early onset of symptoms of conduct disorder. Those in this group developed symptoms before age ten. They are more likely to have antisocial behavior problems throughout life. In the second group are adolescents who had a later onset of symptoms of conduct disorder. Those in this group developed symptoms after the age of ten. Their antisocial problems are not as chronic and persistent and are not likely to continue beyond adolescence.

As with oppositional defiant disorder, when ADHD and conduct disorder co-occur, problems can multiply. Early intervention is extremely important to prevent serious antisocial behavior, substance abuse, and potential delinquency. Parents will benefit from learning behavior management strategies. Treatment with medication can improve symptoms of aggression, defiance, and irritability as well as targeting ADHD symptoms. Educational interventions can reduce stress on the student and may make school a more positive experience.

Teachers can use the following strategies to help students with behavioral problems such as oppositional disorder or conduct disorder.

- Model appropriate social behavior. State commands and instructions in a respectful manner.

- Post clear rules of classroom behav-

ior. Review these rules frequently. Point out positive instances where students followed these rules and offer praise and reward when indicated.

- Provide structure to students who are likely to act out. Closely monitor their behavior, especially during transitions or during stress times of the day.

- Use proximity control to project authority and to easily cue students to behave. Standing by the student with a stern look may encourage the student to obey.

- Prior to a new activity, review how you expect the students in your class to behave.

- Quickly intervene if a student's behavior or emotions are getting out of control. Move closer to the student, redirect the focus of attention, and remind the student to behave appropriately.

- Use "prudent" reprimands for misbehavior. A prudent reprimand is one which directs the student to stop inappropriate behavior without causing shame, embarrassment, or unnecessary attention. Imprudent reprimands contain unnecessary lectures, threats, belittling remarks, etc.

- Examine antecedents of a student's misbehavior to determine if factors in the environment may be precipitating the unwanted reactions.

- Seat student near quiet students who may have a positive impact.

- Use a nonverbal signal with the disruptive student (a look, gesture, etc.) to help the student realize his or her behavior needs to be modified.

- Use humor to defuse a potential problem situation.

- Keep student occupied with work or appropriate activities to prevent opportunities for acting out.

- Plan ahead and try to foresee potential problem situations.

- Increase the frequency and the immediacy of rewards and praise.

- For oppositional children, do not overreact to minor disruption. It may be more helpful to ignore a minor outburst than to confront the student, especially if confrontation generally leads to escalation of the behavior.

- Give the student who loses his or her temper some time to cool off. Give the student an opportunity to walk somewhere else in the room, run a quick errand, or get some water. This break can prevent an aggressive outburst and defuse an otherwise volatile situation.

- Have an intervention plan ready in case a student's behavior escalates out of control. Call for help from an administrator. Ask the student to leave the room and visit another teacher or a guidance counselor who could help the student quiet down. Try not to get into a power struggle with the student as this typically escalates negative situations.

- Use behavioral contracts, token programs, a home-school daily report card to set goals and provide the student with the opportunity to earn privileges for appropriate behavior.

Depression and Bipolar Disorder

Children and teens with ADHD may be at greater risk for developing depressive disorders. It is estimated that as many as thirty percent develop symptoms of depression.

One type of depression is known as *dysthymia*. Children and adolescents with dysthymia have low mood most of the day, more often than not, for at least one year. Their low mood may take the form of irritability. In addition, they may have symptoms of poor appetite or overeating, insomnia or hypersomnia, low energy, low self-esteem, poor concentration, and feelings of hopelessness.

Another type of depression children and adolescents may develop is known as *major depression*. Those with major depression have depressed mood most of the day nearly every day for at least two weeks. Other symptoms include: deriving little or no pleasure from activities; significant weight loss when not dieting or less weight gain than expected; insomnia or hypersomnia nearly every day; low energy; feelings of worthlessness or inappropriate guilt nearly every day; diminished ability to think, concentrate, or make decisions; and recurrent thoughts of death.

Children and adolescents with ADHD are also at greater risk to develop *bipolar disorder.* People with bipolar disorder have frequent and rapid dramatic shifts of mood including elation, depression, irritability, and anger. At times they may have an exaggerated positive view of themselves, believing they are right and others wrong. Their speech may become "pressured" marked by intense rapid talking and accompanied by "racing thoughts" they cannot control. In addition to the symptoms noted above, a family history of bipolar disorder, severe symptoms of ADHD, oppositional disorder, and conduct disorder are markers that could signal the presence of bipolar disorder.

Teachers can use the following strategies to help students who suffer from dysthymia or depression.

- Ease negative mood by complimenting positive behavior and bring the student's focus to positive things.

- Look for signs of stress and provide encouragement or reduced work load.

- Spend more time talking to students who seem pent up.

- Train anger control. Encourage student to walk away and use calming strategies.

- If the student seems unhappy with school, talks about dropping out, or seems unhappy in general try these additional strategies:
  - emphasize student's strengths and abilities

- find ways the student can succeed
- praise in public; reprimand in private
- mark correct responses on tests/assignments, not errors
- prohibit any humiliation or teasing from other students
- arrange for meeting with parents and other teachers to find ways to help student feel better about school and/or self
- consider referral to child study team for help

Teachers can use the following strategies to help students with bipolar disorder.

- Some children with bipolar disorder may be easily distracted. Seat the student in a low-distraction area of the classroom.

- Have the student sit near the teacher.

- Bipolar students may have severe mood swings. The teacher should avoid arguing with the student. Set firm boundaries with appropriate consequences. Schedule frequent breaks to give the student a chance to relax. Use a private signal to alert the student if he needs to calm down.

- Give the student an extra minute or two to process instructions when asked to do something or to make a decision.

- If the student has difficulty with transitions allow her to finish a task before moving on to another one.

Give warnings and prompts to the next task.

- Reassure and be supportive, especially if you sense the student is getting tense or anxious about something that is coming up. Allow the student to explain his feelings to you.

- Maintain a calm demeanor. Be flexible, emotionally sensitive to the student, and understanding.

Anxiety Disorders

Children and adolescents with ADHD are more likely to have anxiety related disorders. Two of the more common types of anxiety disorders that occur are *separation anxiety disorder* and *overanxious disorder*. Below is a list of characteristics of children who suffer from separation anxiety disorder.

1. recurrent, excessive distress when separation from home or a major attachment figure (i.e., parent or other relative) occurs or is anticipated
2. persistent and excessive worry about losing, or about possible harm befalling, major attachment figures
3. persistent and excessive worry that an untoward event will lead to separation from a major attachment figure (e.g., getting lost or being kidnapped)
4. persistent reluctance or refusal to go to school or elsewhere because of fear of separation
5. persistently and excessively fearful or reluctant to be alone without major attachment figures at home or without significant adults in other settings
6. persistent reluctance or refusal to go to sleep without being near a major

attachment figure or to sleep away from home
7. repeated nightmares involving the theme of separation
8. repeated complaints of physical symptoms (such as headaches, stomachaches, nausea, or vomiting) when separation from major attachment figures occurs or is anticipated

Overanxious disorder of childhood may exist if there is excessive anxiety and worry about a number of events or activities (such as school) occurring more days than not for at least six months. The child or adolescent with this type of anxiety disorder finds it difficult to control worrying and may have some of the following additional symptoms: restlessness or feeling keyed up or on edge; becoming easily fatigued; difficulty concentrating or their mind going blank; irritability; muscle tension; and a sleep disturbance that can cause difficulty falling asleep, staying asleep, or having a restful sleep.

Teachers can use the following strategies to help students with anxiety disorders.

- Provide reassurance and encouragement. Children suffering from anxiety or depression often have low self-esteem, they worry excessively, and often withdraw from others. A support relationship with a meaningful adult can make a very big difference to these children.

- Try to understand factors that may be causing the student to become upset. By helping the student sort out his or her feelings the teacher may help the child feel better.

- Speak softly in a non-threatening manner if student shows nervousness.

- Review instructions when giving new assignments to make sure student comprehends. If you notice a student is confused or nervous, provide additional attention to help her understand instructions and to reassure.

- Look for opportunities for student to display leadership role in class.

- Focus on student's talents and accomplishments. Psychologist, Dr. Robert Brooks, encourages teachers to find each child's special talent or "island of competence" and build on it.

- Conference frequently with parents to learn about student's interests and achievements.

- Assign student to be a peer teacher. Peer teaching can be a great help to students who need additional instruction to boost confidence.

- Make time to talk alone with student.

- Encourage social interactions with classmates if student is withdrawn or excessively shy.

- Reinforce frequently when signs of frustration are noticed.

Obsessive Compulsive Disorder (OCD)

Approximately twenty-five percent of people with *obsessive-compulsive disorder* (OCD) have ADHD. OCD is characterized by the following behavior patterns:

1. intrusive, forceful, and repetitive thoughts, images, or sounds that are lodged in one's mind and cannot be willfully eliminated
2. compulsions to perform motor or mental acts
3. excessive and recurrent doubting about matters of either major or minor importance

The obsessions or compulsions cause marked distress, are time consuming, and significantly interfere with normal functioning. Many children with OCD are secretive about their condition so it may be difficult for teachers to identify symptoms.

Examples of obsessive or compulsive behavior in children and adolescents may include: fear of contamination and overconcern with cleanliness; repeated hand washing; fear of harm, illness, or death; unusual or overly rigid eating habits; excessive concern about the tidyness of their room and their belongings; compulsion to place items around the house in a particular way; repeated checking if something is on or off, locked or unlocked; ritualistic counting; repetition of a series of acts before moving on to something else; obsessions revolving around a need for symmetry, fear of sharp objects, etc.

Treatment for OCD usually involves a combination of medication and cognitive-behavior therapy. When ADHD is also present, the treatment can become much more complicated. Multiple medications may be prescribed to treat both disorders.

Teachers can use the following strategies to help students with OCD.

- Do not punish the student for situations or behaviors over which he has no control (i.e., the student may be tardy or absent because of adherence to rituals, the student may not be able to finish a writing assignment on time because of numerous cross-outs/erasures/checking, etc.).

- If the student with OCD has difficulty taking notes or writing due to writing compulsions, consider accommodations such as use of a tape recorder, a student scribe, or reduce amount of written work required.

- Do not allow other students to tease the child with OCD because of rituals or fears.

- Provide support and understanding to parents. Understand that the child's disorder can put a great deal of stress on the family.

- If the OCD student has reading compulsions the teacher may tape-record chapters in texts, allow others to read to the student, or assign shorter reading assignments.

- Allow accommodations for test-taking if the OCD student has difficulty taking tests. Allow extra time, provide a different location, permit the student to write directly on the test booklet rather than filling out computer test forms, allow the student to take the test orally.

- While most students with OCD try their best, some may try to use OCD as a crutch to avoid schoolwork or homework. If you suspect this is occurring coordinate your teaching strategies with the parents and with the child's counselor or therapist if one is available.

Asperger's Disorder

Asperger's Disorder is an impairment in social interaction, which was first described in the 1940s. Children and adolescents with Asperger's also have unusual patterns of communication and behavior.

When communicating, they exhibit some of the following symptoms:

1. a marked impairment in nonverbal behaviors used to communicate with others such as eye contact, facial expression, body postures, and gestures
2. failure to develop friendships appropriate to one's age and development
3. failure to seek out others to communicate
4. lack of social reciprocity when interacting with others.

Those affected by Asperger's seem uninterested in social interaction. They have difficulty predicting other people's behavior, leading to a fear or avoidance of others. They may not understand the intentions of others or the motives behind other people's behavior. They often do not clearly understand their own emotions and have trouble explaining their behavior. They lack empathy.

Those with Asperger's also exhibit unusual behavior patterns including preoccupation with a specific interest; inflexible adherence to specific routines or rituals; repetitive motor mannerisms (such as hand or finger flapping or twisting or whole body movements); preoccupation with parts of objects.

Asperger's disorder is rare and is not frequently seen in those with ADHD. However, some people with Asperger's also have problems with hyperactivity, impulsivity, and inattention. For some, this may be caused by the Asperger's itself, while others may have a co-diagnosis of

ADHD.

Teachers can use the following strategies to help students with Asperger's disorder.

- Be explicit when giving instructions. Don't assume that the student understands what you have said.

- Draw the child's attention to the use of gesture, facial expression, eye direction, and closeness of social interactions to convey meaning to what is being said.

- Help the student understand the meaning behind what others say.

- Explain "pretending" and help the student discriminate between pretend and reality.

- Explain the child's role in certain tasks, situations and event.

- Avoid ambiguity. Use a visual model when possible to clarify what you mean.

- Maintain a calm classroom environment with structure and clear rules.

- Understand the student's limited ability to interpret social cues. Help in teaching appropriate social interaction skills, such as taking turns, cooperating, sharing, etc.

- Guide other students to help them understand the social differences in the Asperger student.

- Support the student in physical activities if clumsiness is a problem.

- Simplify your communications with the student. Give one instruction at a time. Keep your facial expressions and gestures simple and clear. Give the child a chance to respond.

- Be aware that the student may prefer to be alone rather than in close contact with other students. Give the student time to get to know others. Move slowly, but positively in introducing new people.

Tics and Tourette's Syndrome

Tics are sudden, repetitive, and involuntary movements of muscles. Vocal tics involve muscles that control speech and cause involuntary sounds such as coughing, throat clearing, sniffing, making loud sounds, grunting, or calling out words. Motor tics involve other muscles and can occur in any part of the body.

Some examples of motor tics are eye blinking, shoulder shrugging, facial grimacing, head jerking, and a variety of hand movements. Tics that are less common involve self-injurious behavior such as hitting or biting oneself and coprolalia (involuntary use of profane words or gestures). When these types of tics occur many times a day, nearly every day for at least four weeks, but for no longer than twelve consecutive months, the child may have a transient tic disorder.

It is estimated that ten percent of children and adolescents with ADHD will develop a transient tic disorder. Others may develop a tic disorder that is associated with the use of stimulant medication.

A child who has either a motor or a vocal tic (but not both), which occurs many times a day, nearly every day, for a period of at least one year (without stopping for more than three months), may be diagnosed as having a chronic tic disorder. *Tourette's syndrome* is a chronic tic disorder characterized by both multiple motor tics and one or more vocal tics, although not necessarily concurrent. These tics are more severe than the simple, transient motor tics described earlier. They occur many times a day, nearly every day or intermittently throughout a period of more than one year. They involve the head and frequently other parts of the body such as the torso, arms, and legs. Vocal tics may include the production of sounds like clucking, grunting, yelping, barking, snorting, and coughing. Utterances of obscenities, coprolalia, are rare and occur in about ten percent of children with Tourette's.

Dr. David Comings and Dr. Brenda Comings, of the City of Hope Medical Center in Duarte California, studied 130 patients with Tourette's. They found that more than half of them had ADHD. Stimulants should be used cautiously with children who have chronic tic disorder or Tourette's syndrome and ADHD.

Teachers can use the following strategies to help students with tic disorders or Tourette's syndrome.

- Ignore the tics. The teacher's reaction to the student's tics can make a critical difference in the student's life. Teachers should understand that tics are the result of a brain-based condition and are performed in response to insistent sensory urges (something like an itch). Do not express frustration, annoyance, or anger at the student for exhibiting a tic.

- Tics tend to worsen when the student is under stress. Students with Tourette's syndrome perform best when they are in a calm, supportive environment.

- Most children with tics or Tourette's are embarrassed and frustrated by

their tics. Help the child develop strategies for coping with tics in the classroom.

- Help other children in the classroom be sensitive to the student with tics. Teach them to ignore the student's tics.

- Extend time limits on tests. Tics occur in bouts and these bouts can occur at inopportune times.

- The student may be able to suppress a tic for awhile and may need to leave the room for a short time to release or let out tics.

Summary

Students with ADHD often have other mental health disorders that can affect their behavior and academic performance. Access to mental health services in the United States is often poor, especially for minority groups and impoverished families. Many children with mental health disorders go are undiagnosed and untreated.

Schools play a vital role in identifying students at risk for mental health disorder and schools also have programs for prevention and treatment. If you notice the student has difficulty making and keeping friends, is withdrawn, has frequent somatic complaints, is excessively late or absent from school, has low self-esteem, worries excessively, appears sad and depressed, or is irritable, becomes aggressive and defiant, has suicidal thoughts, is involved in substance abuse the student may have a mental disorder and may be in need of assessment and treatment.

Refer the student to guidance or to the child study team for an evaluation. Teachers can help students with mental disorders by providing understanding and using specific classroom strategies to help the student adjust. Classroom teachers also play an important role in working with health care professionals and mental health specialists on behalf of the student with a mental health disorder.

Chapter 16
Helping Parents Find the Right Help

Every parent would like to raise their child to be a happy, healthy and productive member of society. Even when their kids are on the right track toward reaching that goal, it is hard for parents to relax and not worry about what could go wrong. Fortunately, most children do okay. They usually start off on an even footing with everyone else and with a decent education, proper support from their families, and with a little persistence and effort, they make it through their child and adolescent years ready to handle adult responsibilities.

Some children, however, have trouble right from the start. Parents of children with hidden handicaps such as learning disabilities, emotional problems, or ADHD often sense a problem with their child at a young age, but can't quite put their finger on what is wrong. They wait for the child to develop and hope that problems will improve with time. Sometimes they get lucky and mother nature does the trick. The child matures and the problems resolve. For other children, problems become even more pronounced when the child enters school.

Teachers play an extremely important role in helping parents identify problems in their child's development. Being familiar with normative behavior and the characteristics of similar aged children, teachers have a good basis of comparison. In many instances the teacher is the first person to document a problem with the child. While some parents become defensive when told by the teacher that their child has a problem, most are relieved to find that someone else notices what they may have sensed for years. Although often frightened by the thought of something being wrong, most parents are eager to look for answers and to seek help.

The first step is to get a comprehensive assessment of the child. As indicated in chapter five, ADHD assessments usually involve getting information from a variety of sources. Often the child's medical doctor, teachers, and parents will be involved in the process. For many children, this process will start with a referral to a child study team that may recommend a psychoeducational evaluation be done to determine the needs of the child. Clinical or school psychologists will frequently be called upon to administer tests of intellectual functioning, information processing, achievement, and emotionality. A medical examination may rule out any medical problems that could contribute to the child's difficulties. Teachers and parents will complete rating scales designed to objectively measure the child's behavior in school and at home. When it is finished, a comprehensive evaluation should result in accurate diagnosis and should provide parents with a greater understanding of the nature and severity of their child's problems.

If the assessment reveals that the child has ADHD, parents should be given material to read so they can become more familiar with how to help their child. Parent education becomes an integral part of the treatment process. Typical questions parents ask upon hearing the ADHD diagnosis center around causes, outcomes, and concerns about what the future will hold for their child. Those parents whose children are advised to take medication, for example, can become anxious about the process of giving their child medicine and often need time to become educated, to digest the concept, and to become comfortable with it before taking that step. To assist in the process of parent education, we have included a listing of suggested readings that teachers can give to parents. These are located in the references and resources section.

Through education about the disorder, parents of ADHD children learn to make adjustments for their child's welfare. Given the special needs that ADHD children have for structure and consistency in the home, many parents have to face the fact that they may have to make considerable changes in the way their households operate. Parents whose ADHD children require a great deal of supervision in school will often rearrange priorities to make time to assist their child with school work. For some, this may mean setting aside more time, while others may have to pay for tutors or special private schools. Medical expenses and bills for counseling can strain the family's budget. Helping siblings understand the special needs of their ADHD brother or sister, as well as educating grandparents, cousins, and other relatives about ADHD, can be an important step in building family teamwork to help the child succeed.

Teachers, knowing well the challenges that the child poses in the classroom, should be able to relate to the difficulties that parents face at home. Parents appreciate teachers who are willing to listen compassionately and who offer assistance to their child without any hint of judgement or disapproval. Unfortunately, some teachers are quick to judge the child and the parent without fully understanding what ADHD is all about. Such teachers may still believe that ADHD comes from improper parenting, abuse, or neglect. They think the solution to the child's problems will come in the form of tighter rules and harsher discipline. They blame the parent for allowing the child to get out of control. Parents of ADHD children did not cause their child to have ADHD as a result of their parenting methods. In general, these parents are no different than parents of normal children.

Proven and Unproven/Disproven Therapies

Teachers may be asked to provide some direction to parents who are looking for sources of help. There are a number of therapies that have been used to treat children and adolescents with ADHD. Unfortunately, they are not all helpful. Therapies can be divided into two groups; those that have been proven to be effective treatments and those that are unproven or have been disproven as effective.

Proven Therapies for ADHD

Generally, therapies that have been shown to be effective in the treatment of ADD include:
- Parent counseling and education about ADHD
- Parent training in child and adolescent management

- Parent support groups
- Family communication training
- Pharmacological therapies
- Teacher training for classroom management
- Classroom accommodations and interventions

Many of these treatments were discussed in previous chapters. Not all of them will be used for every child. Use of any one or more specific therapies will depend upon the unique needs of the child.

Unproven or Disproven Therapies for ADHD

A number of therapies have not been proven to be effective in the treatment of ADHD or have been disproven as effective. A brief description follows of some of the more common therapies which are sometimes provided to ADHD children, but which have not been scientifically proven to be effective for the treatment of this disorder.

Dietary Management (Elimination Diets)

Those who advocate the use of elimination diets for the treatment of learning and attentional disorders applaud the results they have seen with the use of such dietary restrictions. The most popular elimination diet, the Feingold Diet (also called the K-P diet) is based on Dr. Benjamin Feingold's work with hyperactive children. Dr. Feingold estimated that in forty to fifty percent of cases, food additives cause hyperactivity. The diet seeks to eliminate artificial colors and flavors and a number of food preservatives along with naturally occurring chemicals known as salicylates. Although some parents report very positive results when they adjust their child's diet to meet Feingold's specifications these results have not been able to stand up to scientific scrutiny in double-blind research studies.

Despite the lack of research support for the efficacy of dietary management in the treatment of ADHD, many parents and teachers continue to hold on to the misconception that dietary factors strongly influence student behavior. Dietary management remains a controversial and a still unproven therapy for ADHD.

Megavitamin/Orthomolecular (Supplement Diets)

Orthomolecular therapy is based on the premise that certain disorders result from a deficiency of specific chemical substances in the brain which can be resupplied through the ingestion of large quantities of vitamins, usually vitamins C, B_3, and B_6. Initially having gained popularity several years ago as a treatment for severe mental disorders, for which it has also been disproven as an effective treatment, interest in orthomolecular therapy as a treatment for learning and behavior disorders surfaced. To date there is no conclusive evidence that this approach is an effective treatment for ADHD.

Sensory Integration Therapy

Based upon the research of A. Jean Ayres, some occupational therapists will use sensory integration therapy to help ADHD children by reducing the child's tactile defensiveness or sensitivity to touch. In sensory integration therapy, the child is exposed to physical stimulation in carefully selected and controlled doses. The therapist adjusts the amount of tactile stimulation over time as a way of conditioning the child to tolerate such stimulation more easily. To do this the therapist may stimulate touch sensations by using cloths or brushes rubbed against the skin. Graded stimulation is believed to enhance the capacity of the brain for intersensory integration. Although sensory integration therapy may have some limited benefit for children suffering from developmental disabilities such as pervasive developmental disorder (autism) or mental retardation, as a treatment for attention deficit disorder its effectiveness has not been proven.

Chiropractic Manipulation

Chiropractors believe that a number of diseases, some mental illnesses, behavior and learning disorders included, are caused by misaligned vertebrae which disrupt normal nerve function. They attempt to restore normal functioning through spinal manipulation. While widely accepted as an effective treatment for a number of disorders of the joints and muscles, the efficacy of chiropractic manipulation in the treatment of attention deficit disorder has not been proven.

Optometric Training

Some optometrists believe that problems with visual perception can have serious implications for learning, and especially for reading. Through sensory-motor-perceptual training techniques, optometrists who do such training suggest that visual perceptual problems can be corrected, thereby rendering the child more accessible for learning. Several professional associations, including the AAP, the American Academy of Ophthamology and Otolaryngology, and the American Association of Ophthamology issued a joint statement which was critical of a sensory-motor-perceptual training approach to treating learning disabilities.

Cerebellar-Vestibular Dysfunction

Initially, Dr. Harold Levinson's approach to treating learning disabilities and hyperactivity by correcting vestibular dysfunction gained popularity when it was first presented in his 1981 book on the subject. Dr. Levinson advocated that some forms of learning problems are caused by dysfunction of the body's balance system, the vestibular system. He suggested that this dysfunction could be corrected by using medications such as those used for motion sickness. Dr. Levinson's successes using this method are described in his

books, but the information is purely anecdotal in nature and his theories have not been scientifically proven.

Play Therapy

Play therapy is a nondirective type of psychotherapy which is used with children who display certain types of emotional difficulties. While play therapy may be of some benefit in the treatment of some of the secondary emotional problems that are sometimes found in children suffering from ADHD, there is no scientific evidence that such therapy is effective in reducing rates of inattention, impulsivity, or hyperactivity in children.

Relaxation Therapy/Biofeedback Training

Relaxation therapy was initially developed as a treatment for stress-related disorders. In relaxation therapy, the person is given instructions on how to relax, either through use of; guided imagery, progressive muscle tensing and relaxing, or through autogenic training. Certain types of biofeedback training can assist people in learning the relaxation response by providing feedback regarding the body's physiologic state. Different types of physiologic feedback are helpful for different conditions. Temperature feedback has been shown to be effective for migraine sufferers, for example, while muscle potential may be useful feedback in the treatment of stress-related problems. EEG brain waves feedback has been publicized as an effective treatment for ADHD children. The premise behind such treatment is that children can be taught to control their level of neurological arousal, thereby, learning to better control behavior and attention. The use of EEG biofeedback remains an unproven treatment for ADHD.

Parent Support Groups

Support groups can be immensely beneficial to parents. By meeting other parents who share similar problems in raising their children with ADHD, parents develop a sense of comraderie with one another and find support. Usually groups of parents meet on a monthly or twice-monthly basis. Guest speakers lead discussions on various topics and provide expert information on medical management, child rearing issues, educational interventions, self-esteem building, family dynamics, etc. Most groups leave time for both formal and informal "rap" sessions among the parents, giving parents the opportunity to share experiences and to learn from one another. Teachers are encouraged to attend and parents welcome the opportunity to share ADHD information with them.

Support groups have become a valuable resource for parents who are looking for information and help. Parents network to help each other find professionals in the community who are most knowledgeable about the disorder and to locate schools which work well with ADHD students. As advocates, parent groups can influence local school districts to provide inservice training for teachers and can encourage local libraries to have ADHD information available to the community. Local and regional conferences, sponsored by parent support groups, provide a source of continuing education for professionals from all related disciplines, as well as the opportunity for parents to learn side-by-side with educators and health care professionals.

CHADD, Children and Adults with Attention Deficit Hyperactivity Disorder, is a national support group. With more than 250 chapters nationally, and international affiliates in progress, CHADD provides information and services to thousands of members throughout the United States. CHADD members receive monthly newsletters on attention deficit disorders which contain valuable tips for raising and teaching children with ADHD and help for adults sufferers and their families. CHADD members also receive conference discounts, ADHD fact sheets,

and a guide for educators. Conferences held annually attract ADHD researchers, educators, clinicians, and parents who can offer practical information to other parents and professionals. For more information about CHADD and to locate the CHADD chapter nearest you visit www.chadd.org.

ADDA, the Attention Deficit Disorder Association, is a national organization which has been active in addressing the needs of adults with ADHD. Through its annual conference on adult issues, ADDA has succeeded in bringing important information to the forefront. For more information, visit www.add.org.

LDAA, the Learning Disabilities Association of America, is a national support group for parents of children with learning disabilities. In existence for more than twenty-five years, LDA is well known for the support and information it provides to parents of learning disabled children world over. For more information, visit www.ldanatl.org.

Summary

Teachers are often at the forefront in helping parents of children with ADHD find help. Often the first step is getting a comprehensive assessment either within the school via the convening of a child study team meeting or through referral to community resources. If a diagnosis of ADHD is made, the parent will likely need information about the disorder and possible treatment options. Decisions about school placement, accommodations, eligibility for special education, etc. will be based on the needs of the child and the severity of impairment in learning and socialization. Schools can provide parents with quite a bit of information about services that are available.

Parent training in child management, parent support groups, family communication training, medication therapies, and classroom accommodations and interventions are effective and proven treatments for ADHD. Parents should be cautious about trying unproven or disproven treatments.

There are support groups in many cities throughout the country. Parents could contact Children with Attention-Deficit/Hyperactivity Disorder (CHADD) at www.chadd.org or seek help from the Attention Deficit Disorder Association at www.add.org or the Learning Disability Association of America at www.ldanatl.org.

Chapter 17
Helping Children with ADHD Understand Themselves Better

In the past few years, many books have been written for children and teens to help them understand what ADHD is all about. Parents and teachers are often uncertain about how to explain this sensitive issue to children. The following books and videos will be helpful in assisting teachers who would like to acquaint their students with ADHD about this disorder.

A Bird's-Eye View of Life with ADD and ADHD: Advice from Young Survivors
by Chris A. Zeigler Dendy and Alex Zeigler

This book for teenagers and preteens is filled with great advice from young people who are living with ADHD. Through humor and personal examples, these young survivors give advice on disorganization, sleep problems, forgetfulness, medication, and much more that affects teens.

A Boy and a Bear: The Children's Relaxation Book
by Lori Lite

This book teachers young children ages three to ten years of age how to relax and calm themselves. The book tells the story of a young boy who encounters a polar bear while they are both climbing a snow-covered mountain. The boy and bear become friends and learn an important lesson in relaxation together. Children will enjoy the story and will also benefit by learning a self-calming technique to reduce stress, prepare for sleep, and improve self-confidence.

A Walk in the Rain with a Brain
by Edward M. Hallowell, MD

Filled with charming illustrations and a funny whimsical story this book will teach children to play and learn in order to find the strengths they have. Includes a discussion for parents and educators that will help them teach children about learning differences and appreciation for each child's uniqueness. For children ages 6-10.

Adolescents and ADHD: Gaining the Advantage
by Patricia O. Quinn, MD

This book was written for teens who have been diagnosed with ADHD. It helps them understand what ADHD is, offers tips on getting organized, on dating, driving, how to achieve greater success in school, and how to stand up for your rights.

Eagle Eyes: A Child's View of Attention Deficit Disorder
by Jeanne Gehret, M.A.

Clumsy and impulsive on a nature walk, Ben drives away the birds he admires. Over time, however, he learns to focus his attention like an eagle on the things that really count. By the end of this sympathetic story, Ben successfully helps his father when an emergency arises. *Eagle Eyes* helps readers of all ages understand ADHD and gives practical suggestions for organization, social cues and self-calming. Expressive illustrations with a nature theme enhance this tale for reluctant readers.

Eukee the Jumpy Jumpy Elephant
by Cliff Corman, M.D. and
Esther Trevino, M.F.C.C.

Eukee moves through the jungle like a tornado, unable to pay attention like the other elephants. He begins to feel sad, but gets help after a visit to the doctor who explains why Eukee is so jumpy and hyperactive. With love, support and help, Eukee learns ways to help himself and gains renewed self-confidence. Ideal for ages 3-8.

Help 4 ADD @High School
Kathleen Nadeau, Ph.D.

This book is designed like a web site that you can surf. It has short, easy-to-read, information-packed sections that tells teens what they need to know about how to get their life together—for themselves, not for their parents or teachers. It includes tips on studying, ways their high school can help them succeed, tips on getting along better at home, on dating, exercise, and much more.

How to Take the Grrrr Out of Anger
by Elizabeth Verdick and
Marjorie Lisovskis

Everyone gets angry sometimes, but if you are angry a lot...or stay angry for a long time...or get in trouble for getting angry....you can take the Grrrr out of anger. This book will help kids lean to cool down their hot temper. For children ages 7-15.

I Would if I Could
by Michael Gordon, Ph.D.

This book provides straight-forward information for teenagers about ADHD and explores its impact on family relationships, self-esteem, and friendships. The author's unique style and sense of humor makes this enjoyable for teens to read.

It's Just Attention Disorder: A Video Guide for Kids
by Sam Goldstein, Ph.D. and
Michael Goldstein, M.D.

Accurate diagnosis for ADD has become a reality and now the next step becomes treatment. To be helped, children and adolescents with ADHD must want help. *It's Just Attention Disorder* was created to help parents, teachers, and counselors assist the child and adolescent with ADHD to become an active participant in the treatment process. Filmed in an "MTV" format, this video will hold the attention of even the most inattentive. It has been designed to acquaint the ADHD child and adolescent with basic information concerning the nature and treatment of ADHD. Included with the video are a User's Manual and Study Guide.

Jumpin' Johnny Get Back To Work! A Child's Guide to ADHD/Hyperactivity
by Michael Gordon, Ph.D.

This entertaining and informative book will help children understand the essential concepts involved in the evaluation and treatment of ADHD. *Jumpin' Johnny* tells what it's like to be inattentive and impulsive, and how his family and school work with him to make life easier. Children find this book to be amusing, educational and accurate in its depiction of the challenges that confront them daily. Dr. Gordon's humor and extensive clinical experience with ADHD children shine through every page of this charming but realistic story.

Keeping A Head In School: A Student's Book About Learning Abilities and Learning Disorders
by Mel Levine, M.D.

This book, written especially for students by Dr. Mel Levine, a pediatrician and well known authority on learning problems, demystifies learning disorders for young people affected by them. *Keeping A Head In School*, helps nine to fifteen year old students with learning disorders gain a better understanding of their personal strengths and weaknesses. They see that learning styles vary greatly and find specific ways to approach work and manage the struggles that may beset them in school. Dr. Levine's helpful book is intended to convince students that the struggle is worth the effort and will ultimately be rewarding.

Learning To Slow Down and Pay Attention: Third Edition
by Kathleen Nadeau, Ph.D. and Ellen Dixon, Ph.D.

Written for children to read, and illustrated with delightful cartoons and activity pages to engage the child's interest, *Learning To Slow Down and Pay Attention* helps children to identify problems and explains how their parents, their doctor and their teacher can help. In an easy-to-understand language the book describes how an ADHD child can learn to pay better attention in class, manage feelings, get more organized, and learn to problem solve.

Making the Grade: An Adolescent's Struggle with ADD
by Roberta N. Parker and Harvey C. Parker, Ph.D.

Making the Grade is the heartwarming story of seventh-grader Jim Jerome's struggle to succeed in school. Eager to make a good showing in junior high, Jim soon finds his problems with self-control and inattention threaten his chances of success scholastically and athletically. With the help of his parents, teachers, and concerned healthcare professionals, Jim learns about ADHD and ways to help himself.

Although a fictional account of how ADHD can affect pre-teen and young teenage students, *Making the Grade* is, nonetheless, a very relatable story for eleven- to fourteen-year old adolescents who have attention deficit disorder.

Following the story is a section entitled *Facts About ADD: Commonly Asked Questions* which offers more direct information to young readers. Dr. Parker explains the symptoms, causes, treatments, and outcomes of ADHD in a frank and positive way.

My Brother's A World-Class Pain: A Sibling's Guide to ADHD
by Michael Gordon, Ph.D.

This is the first book written for the oft-forgotten group of those affected by ADD: the brothers and sisters of ADD children. While they frequently bear the brunt of the ADD child's impulsiveness and distractibility, siblings usually are not afforded opportunities to understand the nature of the problem and to have their own feelings and thoughts addressed. This story about an older sister's efforts to deal with her active and impulsive brother sends the clear message to siblings of the child with ADHD that they can play an important role in a family's quest for change.

Otto Leans About His Medication
by Mathew Galvin, M.D.

Dr. Galvin wrote a wonderful book explaining attention deficit disorder in story format. It is intended to be read to and by the child. Otto, a fidgety young car that has trouble paying attention in school, visits a special mechanic who prescribes a medicine to control his hyperactive behavior.

Putting On the Brakes
by Patricia O. Quinn, M.D. and Judith Stern, M.A.

An honest, accessible overview of attention deficit hyperactivity disorder for children ages 8 to 12. Written for children to read, *Putting On The Brakes* focuses on the feelings and emotions of children with ADD and suggests specific techniques for gaining control of the situation, becoming better organized, and functioning better at school, home, and with friends. Children with ADHD will find the acknowledgment and explanation of their problems a relief, and the coping strategies a great help. The book addresses such topics as the physiology and symptoms of ADD, medication used in treatment, and various types of family and community support that are available.

Shelly, The Hyperactive Turtle
by Deborah Moss

Shelly moves like a rocket and is unable to sit still for even the shortest periods of time. Because he and the other turtles are unable to understand why he is so wiggly and squirmy, Shelly begins to feel out-of-place. But after a visit to the doctor, Shelly learns what "hyperactive" means and gets the right kind of help.

Sometimes I Drive My Mom Crazy, But I Know She's Crazy About Me
Lawrence R. Shapiro, Ph.D.

This warm and humorous story of a young boy with ADHD addresses the difficult and frustrating issues—from sitting still in the classroom, to remaining calm, to feeling "different" from other children. For children ages 6-12.

Survival Guide for College Students with ADD or LD
by Kathleen G. Nadeau, Ph.D.

This is a useful guide for high school or college students diagnosed with ADHD or learning disabilities. It provides the information needed to survive and thrive in a college setting. It is full of practical suggestions and tips from an expert experienced in the field and from college students who also suffer from these difficulties.

The Buzz & Pixie Activity Coloring Book
by Bruce A. Brunger and
Cathy Reimers, Ph.D.

This is a wonderful companion to *ADHD in the Young Child* by the same authors. It uses over seventy-five cartoon illustrations and activities. Through these cartoons, young children can learn to distinguish appropriate from inappropriate behavior in a variety of situations at home, in school, and elsewhere. For children ages 3 -6.

The Girls' Guide to AD/HD
by Beth Walker

This book is guaranteed not to be boring. It is full of interactive quizzes, helpful tips, fun facts, whimsical illustrations, and more. Plus, throughout the book, the reader will get to eavesdrop on the very interesting conversations of three friends—Maddy, Helen, and Bo—who have AD/HD.

The Sibling Slam Book
Edited by Don Meyer

This book helps teens who have siblings with a disability. Readers will view the comments of other teenagers who have a brother or sister with a disability and will understand that there are common feelings to be shared. Readers will get an honest look at their own lives and experiences as they hear from eighty sibs from around the world who have contributed to this unique book.

Zipper, the Kid with ADHD
by Caroline Janover

Zipper (a.k.a. Zachary Winson) is always analyzing somebody. Underneath it all, Zipper is a bright fifth grader who has ADHD. This book encourages other kids to find ways to manage their behavior and understand what it is like to have ADHD through Zipper's story. For children 8-13.

For more information about what resources are available to help ADHD children directly, contact a local support group in your area. Many of these groups run programs for children with ADHD that enhance self-awareness and greater understanding of ADHD. CHADD maintains chapters in every state and will gladly help you locate a support group in your community. Visit www.chadd.org.

Appendix

ADHD Symptom Checklist
Homework Contract
Behavior Contract
Classroom Token Economy
Daily Report Cards
Weekly Progress Report
Self-Monitoring Forms
Study Strategy Forms

ADHD Symptom Checklist

Student_____ Date_____ Rater_____

Below is a checklist containing the eighteen symptoms of ADHD. Items 1-9 describe characteristics of inattention. Items 10-15 describe characteristics of hyperactivity. Items 16-18 describe characteristics of impulsivity. In the space before each statement, put the number that best describes the child's behavior (0=never or rarely; 1 = sometimes; 2 = often; 3 = very often).

Inattention Symptoms

____ 1. Fails to give close attention to details or makes careless mistakes in schoolwork, work, or other activities.

____ 2. Has difficulty sustaining attention in tasks or play activities.

____ 3. Does not seem to listen when spoken to directly.

____ 4. Does not follow through on instructions and fails to finish schoolwork, chores, or duties in the workplace (not due to oppositional behavior or failure to understand instructions).

____ 5. Has difficulty organizing tasks and activities.

____ 6. Avoids, dislikes, or is reluctant to engage in tasks that require sustained mental effort (such as schoolwork or homework).

____ 7. Loses things necessary for tasks or activities (e.g., toys, school assignments, pencils, books, or tools).

____ 8. Is easily distracted by extraneous stimuli.

____ 9. Is often forgetful in daily activities.

Hyperactive-Impulsive Symptoms

____ 10. Fidgets with hands or feet or squirms in seat.

____ 11. Leaves seat in classroom or in other situations in which remaining seated is expected.

____ 12. Runs about or climbs excessively in situations in which it is inappropriate (in adolescents or adults, may be limited to subjective feelings of restlessness).

____ 13. Has difficulty playing or engaging in leisure activities quietly.

____ 14. Is "on the go" or often acts as if "driven by a motor."

____ 15. Talks excessively.

____ 16. Blurts out answers before questions have been completed.

____ 17. Has difficulty awaiting his or her turn.

____ 18. Interrupts or intrudes on others (e.g., butts into conversations or games).

Count the number of items in each group (inattention items 1-9 and hyperactivity-impulsivity items 10-18) you marked "2" or "3." If six or more items are marked "2" or "3" in each group this could indicate serious problems in the groups marked.

Homework Contract

Name:_____ Date:_____

Use this homework contract to set goals for yourself and earn rewards and privileges.

I, _____ (child's name), do hereby declare that I will copy

all assignments that I am given in class and that I will do all my homework and turn it in

when it is due. Furthermore, I will only ask for help if and when I don't understand what

I am supposed to do. I will work as neatly as I can and I will check my work to make sure

it is done correctly. When I finish my homework I will put it away in a safe place to bring

to school the following day.

In WITNESS WHEREOF, we have subscribed our names on this date.

Date:_____

Child's signature:_____

Witness's signature_____

Behavior Contract

Name:_____ Date:_____

Use this behavior contract to set goals for yourself and earn rewards and privileges.

I, _____ (child's name), do hereby declare that I will:

_____

_____

I, _____ (teacher/parent), do hereby declare that in exchange

for _____(child's name) fulfilling his/her promise I will

_____.

In WITNESS WHEREOF, we have subscribed our names on this date.

Date:_____

Child's signature:_____

Teacher's/parent's signature:_____

Classroom Token Economy

START BEHAVIORS	Value	Mo	Tu	We	Th	Fr
Extra Credit!_____						
TOTAL TOKENS EARNED						

	Value					
Extra Loss!_____						
TOTAL TOKENS LOST						

TOTAL TOKENS AVAILABLE					

	Value					
TOTAL TOKENS REMAINING						

From: Parker, H. The ADHD Handbook for School. Specialty Press, Inc. 2005. This form may be reproduced for personal use.

Daily Report Card

Rating By Day

Instructions: Please use the report card for one week. Evaluate the student's daily performance on each behavior listed below. Using the guide below, write a number in each space that indicates the student's performance in that area for the day. Use the space at the bottom for comments.

Name_____   Grade_____

Teacher_____   Week of _____

	Days of the Week	MON	TUE	WED	THU	FRI
Behaviors:						
1. Paid attention in class		____	____	____	____	____
2. Completed work in class		____	____	____	____	____
3. Completed homework		____	____	____	____	____
4. Was well behaved		____	____	____	____	____
5. Desk and notebook neat		____	____	____	____	____
TOTALS		____	____	____	____	____

Teacher's Initials

5= Excellent
4= Good
3 = Fair
2 = Needs Improvement
1 = Poor
N/A = not applicable

Comments

Daily Report Card

Rating By Day

Instructions: Please use the report card for one week. Evaluate the student's daily performance on each behavior listed below (parent or teacher insert). Using the guide below, write a number in each space that indicates the student's performance in that area for the day. Use the space at the bottom for comments.

Name_____   Grade_____

Teacher_____   Week of _____

Days of the Week	MON	TUE	WED	THU	FRI
Behaviors					
1._____	____	____	____	____	____
2._____	____	____	____	____	____
3._____	____	____	____	____	____
4._____	____	____	____	____	____
5._____	____	____	____	____	____

TOTALS   ____ ____ ____ ____ ____

Teacher's Initials

5 = Excellent
4 = Good
3 = Fair
2 = Needs Improvement
1 = Poor
N/A = not applicable

Comments

Daily Report Card

Rating By Subject

Instructions: Please use the report card for one day. Evaluate the student's performance on each behavior listed below. Using the guide below, write a number in each space that indicates the student's performance in each subject for the day. Use the space at the bottom for comments.

Name_____ Grade_____

Teacher_____ Week of _____

Subject: ____ ____ ____ ____ ____

Behaviors:

1. Paid attention in class ____ ____ ____ ____ ____

2. Completed work in class ____ ____ ____ ____ ____

3. Completed homework ____ ____ ____ ____ ____

4. Was well behaved ____ ____ ____ ____ ____

5. Desk and notebook neat ____ ____ ____ ____ ____

TOTALS ____ ____ ____ ____ ____

Teacher's Initials
5= Excellent
4= Good
3 = Fair
2 = Needs Improvement
1 = Poor
N/A = not applicable

Comments

Daily Report Card

Rating By Subject

Instructions: Please use the report card for one day. Evaluate the student's performance on each behavior listed below (parent or teacher insert). Using the guide below, write a number in each space that indicates the student's performance in each subject for the day. Use the space at the bottom for comments.

Name_____   Grade_____

Teacher_____   Week of _____

Subject: ____ ____ ____ ____ ____

Behaviors

1._____   ____ ____ ____ ____ ____

2._____   ____ ____ ____ ____ ____

3._____   ____ ____ ____ ____ ____

4._____   ____ ____ ____ ____ ____

5._____   ____ ____ ____ ____ ____

TOTALS   ____ ____ ____ ____ ____

Teacher's Initials

5= Excellent

4= Good

3 = Fair

2 = Needs Improvement

1 = Poor

N/A = not applicable

Comments

Weekly Progess Report

Name: _____   Week of:_____

Teacher: _____   Subject: _____

Behavior

___ Positive
___ Satisfactory
___ Occasionally poor
___ Frequently poor

Effort

___ Good, working well
___ Satisfactory
___ Minimal
___ Declining

Progress

___ Satisfactory
___ Unsatisfactory
___ Improving
___ Declining

Homework

___ Thoroughly completed
___ Adequately completed
___ Sometimes unprepared
___ Often unprepared

Test Scores

___ Good
___ Average
___ Poor

Work Quality

___ Exceptional
___ Adequate
___ Poor

Attention Span

___ Good
___ Fair
___ Poor

Additional Comments

Note specific areas of improvement or problems with classwork/ homework or test scores.

Was I Paying Attention?

Name: _____   Date:_____

Instructions:
Listen to the beep tape * as you do your work. Whenever you hear a beep, stop working for a moment and ask yourself, "Was I paying attention?" Mark your answer (√) and go right back to work. Answer the questions on the bottom of the page when you finish.

Was I Paying Attention?

Start here

YES	NO

Was I Paying Attention?

YES	NO

Did I follow the directions?	Yes	No
Did I pay attention?	Yes	No
Did I finish my work?	Yes	No
Did I check my answers?	Yes	No

* Beep tape available in Listen, Look and Think Program by Harvey C. Parker, Ph.D. (800) ADD-WARE

I Can Do My Best In Class

Name: _____   Date:_____

Instructions:
Students who are well behaved, and organized often do well in school. Read each line and circle either "YES" or "NO" to describe how you did today in one of the subjects you underline below.

English   Math   Reading   Social Studies   Science   Other

I CAN PAY ATTENTION

1. I paid attention to the teacher today.   YES   NO

2. I concentrated on my work and not on

    other students.   YES   NO

3. I followed directions.   YES   NO

4. I finished all my work.   YES   NO

I CAN KEEP MY THINGS IN ORDER

5. My desk was neat.   YES   NO

6. My work was put away in its place.   YES   NO

7. My writing was neat.   YES   NO

I CAN CONTROL MY BEHAVIOR

8. I raised my hand.   YES   NO

9. I asked permission before getting up.   YES   NO

10. I cooperated with others.   YES   NO

Add up the number of times you circled "YES" _____

How did you do?   GREAT   PRETTY GOOD   ROOM FOR IMPROVEMENT
                          8-10   5-7   1-4

Just as with attention, you can improve your organization and behavior by working on one "NO" answer each week.

I Can Pay Attention TODAY

Name: _____   Date:_____

1.	I paid attention to the teacher today.	YES	NO
2.	I looked at the teacher while a lesson was being taught.	YES	NO
3.	I thought about what was important to remember while the teacher was teaching.	YES	NO
4.	I followed directions I was told.	YES	NO
5.	I read all the directions on written work.	YES	NO
6.	I asked questions if I didn't understand.	YES	NO
7.	I answered a question.	YES	NO
8.	I wrote all my homework in my assignment book.	YES	NO
9.	I remembered to take home what I needed.	YES	NO
10.	I reminded myself to pay attention if I got distracted.	YES	NO
11.	I finished all my work.	YES	NO

Add up the number of times you circled "YES" _____

How did you do today?   GREAT   PRETTY GOOD   ROOM FOR IMPROVEMENT
                          9-11   6-10   1-5

Now it is time to work on the ones you answered "NO." Each week select a new behavior to practice in class. Soon you'll see improvement in your attention and your grades as well.

Writing Reminders

Name: _____   Date:_____

> **Instructions:**
> Good posture, a proper grip on your pencil, and the paper placed correctly in front of you are important habits to get into for good handwriting. Take your time while writiing and pay attention to neatness. Use this list below to remind you to be careful with your handwriting.

Assignment: _____

1. Is my pencil sharp?	YES	NO
2. Am I holding the pencil correctly?	YES	NO
3. Am I sitting properly?	YES	NO
4. Is my paper on the desk where it should be?	YES	NO
5. Am I paying attention to neatness?	YES	NO
6. Am I taking my time when I write?	YES	NO

Self-Evaluation Form

Name: _____   Date: _____

Instructions:
Complete this form and evaluate yourself on how you worked in school today.

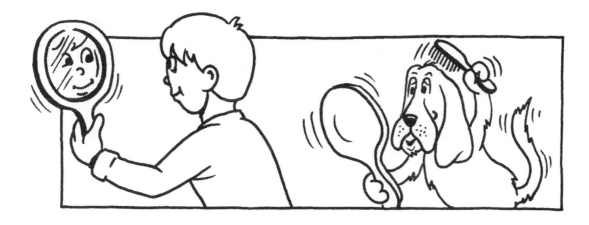

1. Did I pay attention and follow directions today?   YES   NO

2. Did I put my heading on my papers today?   YES   NO

3. Did I finish all my work on time today?   YES   NO

4. Were my papers and my desk organized today?   YES   NO

5. Did I compy my homework in my assignment planner?   YES   NO

6. Did I use my time wisely today?   YES   NO

7. Did I have all my homework completed from last night?   YES   NO

Getting Along

Name: _____   Date:_____

> **Instructions:**
> Choose one of the skills listed below to practice today or select one of your own and write it below.

I will practice: _____

Where (circle all areas):   In Class   At Lunch or Recess   After School

How did you get along with others today? _____ Great _____ Good _____ I could do better

Sample Social Skills

1. Giving others a turn.

2. Cooperating with others

3. Expressing my ideas and feelings.

4. Doing someone a favor.

5. Starting a conversation.

6. Telling the teacher when someone bothers me.

7. Leading a group.

8. Respecting the rights of others.

9. Saying I'm sorry.

10. Ignoring someone's behavior.

11. Being polite.

12. Controlling my temper.

Hand Raising Record Form

Name: _____   Date:_____

Instructions:
Find the hidden dog bone and fill it in each time you remember to RAISE YOUR HAND to ask permission to talk.

Proofreading Checklist

Name: _____   Date:_____

Instructions:
After you have finished your writing assignment, check your work for neatness, spelling and organization. Circle either YES or NO. Or, if you like, ask another student in your class to look over your work and complete this proofreading checklist.

Assignment: _____

1. Heading on paper?	YES	NO
2. Margins correct?	YES	NO
3. Proper spacing between words?	YES	NO
4. Handwriting neat?	YES	NO
5. Sentences start with capital letters?	YES	NO
6. Sentences end with correct punctuation?	YES	NO
7. Crossed out mistakes with only one line?	YES	NO
8. Spelling is correct?	YES	NO

Organize Your School Papers You Need Now

You can use a 3-ring binder or folders to keep your papers organized. Read the suggestions below to help you organize the papers you need now.

<u>3-Ring Binder</u>
Use a 3-ring binder, with dividers, one per subject. Label each divider by subject name.

<u>Folders with Pockets</u>
Use pocket folders. Use a different color for each subject, and write the subject on the outside.
- Use a separate pocket folder with 3-hole clasps for homework (see the illustration below). Label the inside left pocket, "TO DO" for homework papers that need to be done. Use the inside right pocket to keep an assignment agenda page or homework calendar.

- Also buy a plastic sleeve with 3-holes to put into the folder. You will put your completed homework into the sleeve to keep it neat and clean and ready to turn in.

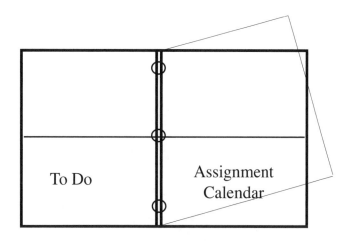

Homework Folder
2 Pockets-3 hole punched

Organize Your Old School Papers You Will Need Later

There are some papers, like old tests, you will want to save to use later and some papers that you can throw away. Follow these six steps:

1. Separate your papers into two piles—TRASH and SAVE.
2. To Trash: doodlings, notes from friends, old homework papers, etc.
3. To Save: old tests with questions and answers written on them, class notes, important handouts.
4. Get manila file folders. Label them by subject and store them in a file drawer or plastic crate.
5. Write the subject, date, and page or chapter number on the top of each paper you file. When you are ready to study for a test, you will have an easy time reviewing old, but still important notes and tests.
6. It is important to get into the habit of filing your saved work every day.

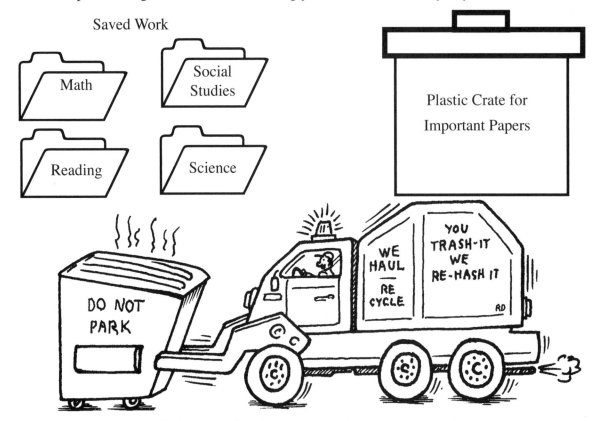

Garbage truck to haul away unimportant papers!

Do List

Use this "Do List" to help you organize assignments (jobs) that need to be done and to plan your time. Each day (or the night before), fill in the Do List with things that you need to complete the next day. Add items to the list each day such as specific homework assignments. Give each item on the list a priority number from 1 to 3. One is highest for the most important tasks. Do the assignments with the highest priority first. Put a check on the right when the assignment has been completed.

Date: _____

Priority	Assignment	Check below when completed
____	_____	____
____	_____	____
____	_____	____
____	_____	____
____	_____	____
____	_____	____
____	_____	____
____	_____	____
____	_____	____

What is Your Time Schedule Like?

Find a study place at home that works best for you, but first answer these questions.

HOW do I like to do my homework or study?

____   alone

____   with a friend or classmate

____   with my parents nearby

WHEN do I like to do my homework?

____   right after school

____   after I've had a snack

____   after I've had time to play or watch TV

____   after dinner

____   after my parents get home from work

WHERE do I like to do my homework or study?

____   in my room

____   in another room in my house where my family is

____   in a room near where my family hangs out

____   at a desk or table

____   on my bed

____   on the floor

____   wherever_____

Now that you know how, when and where to study, it is time to get down to work.

Reprinted with permission. Sandi Sirotowitz, Leslie Davis and Harvey C. Parker (2004). Study Strategies for Early School Success. Florida: Specialty Press, Inc. This form may be reproduced for personal use.

Weekly Planning

Use this weekly planner to schedule how you want to use your time this week. Block out times for after school activities, homework, and time to relax. Write the times of your favorite TV shows so you can plan to watch them.

Time	Monday	Tuesday	Wednesday	Thursday	Friday
2:00	_____	_____	_____	_____	_____
2:30	_____	_____	_____	_____	_____
3:00	_____	_____	_____	_____	_____
3:30	_____	_____	_____	_____	_____
4:00	_____	_____	_____	_____	_____
4:30	_____	_____	_____	_____	_____
5:00	_____	_____	_____	_____	_____
5:30	_____	_____	_____	_____	_____
6:00	_____	_____	_____	_____	_____
6:30	_____	_____	_____	_____	_____
7:00	_____	_____	_____	_____	_____
7:30	_____	_____	_____	_____	_____
8:00	_____	_____	_____	_____	_____
8:30	_____	_____	_____	_____	_____
9:00	_____	_____	_____	_____	_____
9:30	_____	_____	_____	_____	_____
10:00	_____	_____	_____	_____	_____

From: Parker, H. The ADHD Handbook for School. Specialty Press, Inc. 2005. This form may be reproduced for personal use.

Simple Outlining

There is so much information included in textbooks or lectures that you must have a way to include only the most important. This strategy teaches you how to arrange information in your notes in an organized way and quickly identify the main ideas and supporting details of a lecture or reading selection.

Directions:
1. Refer to the sample outline below.
2. The section or chapter title will be the title of your outline.
3. The headings/topics of a chapter are the headings of your outline and are   designated by Roman numerals.
4. The subheadings/subtopics of a chapter are the main ideas and are designated by capital letters.
5. The supporting details within main ideas are designated by Arabic numerals
6. The subdetails within the supporting details are designated by lower case letters.

Sample Outline

```
        TITLE
    I. Heading/Topic
        A. Main idea
            1. Supporting detail
            2. Supporting detail
                a. Subdetail
                b. Subdetail
        B. Main idea
            1. Supporting detail
            2. Supporting detail
```

Mind Mapping

Mind mapping is another way to take notes that you may find fun. It is a visual "map" of how supporting details relate to main ideas. Mind maps are less formal than simple outlines and allow you to use any pattern that works best for you.

Directions: The look of your mind map is up to you, but these basic directions will make using a mind map easy.

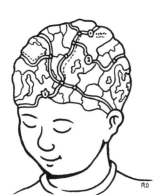

1. First, identify the main ideas and supporting details of are reading.
2. Write the subject or topic in the middle of the page. Then draw a circle or box around it.
3. Find the main ideas that relate to the topic.
4. Draw one line from the topic to each main idea and write the main ideas.
5. Write all relevant details on lines that connect to the main ideas they support.
6. Practice mind mapping by following the above directions for the information in your school textbooks.

The figure below is only one of several basic patterns. You will find more on the next pages. These are our maps, but use your imagination to draw your own maps that will help you "see" the relationships and understand the concepts. Have fun.

Sample Mind Map

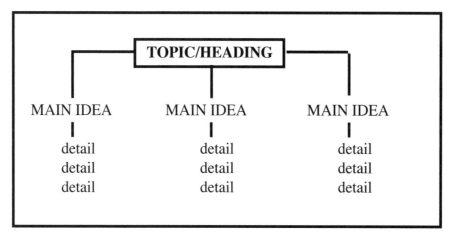

Reprinted with permission. Leslie Davis, Sandi Sirotowitz, and Harvey C. Parker (1996). Study Strategies Made Easy. Florida: Specialty Press, Inc.
This form may be reproduced for personal use.

Taking Combo Notes

Since you need to take notes in most classes, using this method will allow you to organize your notes quickly and easily. You can use combo notes when you take notes from your textbooks. A terrific advantage of this style is that you can use it as you listen to lectures with no need to rewrite and reorganize later. What a time saver! As you become more proficient taking combo notes, you will create your own symbols, patterns and general style.

Directions: As with outlining and mind mapping, you will first identify the main concepts and supporting details. Below is a sample of combo notes.

1. Topic or title is written in the middle of a line and circled.
2. The first main idea is written at the margin and boxed.
3. Supporting detail is indented and designated by a symbol..
4. The subdetail is indented further and designated by a different symbol.
5. For clear organization margins are kept consistent.

Sample Combo Notes

```
┌─────────────────────────────────────────────┐
│ Combines outline organization w/ mind map visuals │
└─────────────────────────────────────────────┘
    •  Advantages
        ••  can be used for textbooks and during lectures
        ••  no need to rewrite - reorganize
    •  Similarities to outlines & mindmaps
        ••  identify main idea & supporting details
        ••  organizes ideas
┌──────────────┐
│ How to do     │
└──────────────┘
    •  Write topic
        ••  middle of line
        ••  box or circle
    •  Write main idea
        ••  box or circle
    •  Indent and write supporting details
        ••  use symbol to identify
    •  keep margins consistent
```

Improving Your Listening Power

Exercise 1: Listen to a television newscast. As you listen, write any verbal or presentation cues the speaker is using. As you watch, write any body language cues the speaker is using.

Newscast channel and/or speaker: _____ Date: _____

CUES:

Verbal: _____
_____
_____

Presentation: _____
_____
_____

Body language: _____
_____
_____

Exercise 2: For one day, choose a class to watch for the teacher's lecture cues. As you listen, write any verbal or presentation cues the speaker is using. As you watch, write any body language cues the speaker is using.

Class or teacher: _____

CUES:

Verbal: _____
_____
_____

Presentation: _____
_____
_____

Body language: _____
_____
_____

Roadblocks to Concentration

There are a lot of things that can block us from concentrating. Below is a list of these "roadblocks to concentration". Circle the ones that make it hard for you to concentrate. Then, write down what you can do about it.

Roadblocks to Concentration	What I can do about it!
1. Music playing	_____
2. Computer games	_____
3. Other people	_____
4. Kids playing outside	_____
5. Pets	_____
6. Television	_____
7. Toys	_____
8. Telephone conversations	_____
9. People talking	_____
10. Brother or sister	_____
11. Tired	_____
12. Bored	_____
13. Hungry	_____
14. Restless	_____
15. Nervous	_____
16. Frustrated	_____
17. Confused	_____

3 Sweeps or How to Really Read a Textbook

To really read a chapter in a textbook and understand what you've read, it is best to use a method of reading comprehension which we call "3 Sweeps." — PREVIEW THE CHAPTER; READ THE STUDY QUESTIONS; and REALLY READ THE CHAPTER. Read the details of each step described below to help you learn the "3 Sweeps" method to read and comprehend any of the chapters in your textbooks.

I. SWEEP 1: Preview the Chapter

Previewing gives you an overview of what is included in the chapter.

A. **Title**: Read the title and ask yourself what you already know about the title and how it fits in with what you previously studied.

B. **Introduction**: Read the introduction to the chapter and ask yourself what it is about (paraphrase aloud).

C. **Headings/Topics; Subheadings/Subtopics**: Read each to gain a general idea of the content to be covered.

D. **Pictures, Maps, Charts**: Look at each to gain additional information concerning the chapter.

II. SWEEP 2: Read the Study Questions

Reading the questions gives you the purpose for reading and provides clues about what details the author thinks are important.

A. Read the study questions at the end of each section, one section at a time.

B. The study questions that begin with these words ask for details:

Who?	——	asks for people
What?	——	asks for events
Where?	——	asks for places
When?	——	asks for time
How?	——	asks for process
Why?	——	asks for reasons

III. SWEEP 3:   *Really* Read the Chapter

Use your reading comprehension strategies to read the chapter for the main ideas, details and meanings.

A. Read the first heading/topic to understand the central theme of the section.

B. Read the first paragraph to identify the main idea.

C. After you have read one paragraph, highlight the main ideas and supporting details in yellow. Use the author's signals to help you identify the details that are important. Remember, though, important ideas will not always be introduced by signals.

D. Highlight the vocabulary words and their meanings in a second color. If a definition is not given, look it up and write it in the margin.

E. After each section, paraphrase the main idea and details in your own words. If a section is long or filled with details, paraphrase after each paragraph.

F. Since you have already read the questions at the end of a section, as you come to their answers, write the question numbers next to the line of text.

G. Use the margin of the book to jot notes, definitions, or key words.

If you cannot mark in the textbook, either photocopy necessary pages or, in a notebook, take notes of the main ideas, supporting details, and vocabulary. The more active your reading is, the easier it will be to learn and remember the content.

Studying for Mid-Terms and Final Exams

Mid-term and final exams are given to test your ability to organize, understand, and recall information that has been taught over a period of weeks or even months. Since these tests are usually given for more than one subject and at around the same time, it is easy to feel overloaded with studying. To help, you need a method of preparation that will allow you to accomplish as much as possible without wasting valuable time.

The good news is that since you have been highlighting, taking notes, writing and reviewing recall questions, and learning information for chapter tests, you are better prepared than you may think. Now it's time for you to put all of those strategies together and show how well you have really been able to learn. So, enter those tests with confidence!

I. Get a Head Start Two Weeks Before the Exam.
   A. Find out all that you can about the exam.
   1.   In class, listen for the teacher's clues and signals as to which material might be included on the tests.
   2.   What type format will the test be?

   a. If objective only, review and memorize important details.

   b. If subjective also, learn overall concepts, but memorize enough facts to back them up in an essay.

   3.   Can you bring notes into the exam? (Find out any limits as to how many pages, etc.)

   4.   Will any chapters or material not be included on the test? (Unless the teacher tells you exactly what won't be included, study every chapter and all material.)

B. Start the preparation

   1.   Get out your filed notes, old tests, etc., and organize them now.

   2.   Make sure that all chapters have been highlighted and recall questions written.

   3.   Make up a study schedule to follow for the next two weeks.

Reprinted with permission. Leslie Davis, Sandi Sirotowitz, and Harvey C. Parker (1996). Study Strategies Made Easy. Florida: Specialty Press, Inc.
This form may be reproduced for personal use.

C. Organize your study session.

1. Follow the study schedule and pace yourself so that you can study a little each day.
   a. Divide the number of chapters or pages to cover by the number of days you have set aside to study.
   b. Study each subject for one-half hour before breaking and beginning the next.
2. As you review the textbook, also review the lecture notes and clues from the teacher.
3. Review old tests since the same questions (possibly worded differently) may show up again.
4. For each chapter, concentrate on highlighted material and recall questions. Also, read and answer end of chapter study questions.

D. Remember to use your strongest learning style and preferences.

1. Auditory learners may want to read the highlighted information aloud, or tape record recall questions that you can then listen to and answer later.
2. Visual learners may want to picture the look of a page or associations.
3. Kinesthetic learners may want to rewrite information (e.g.,brief summary outlines or charts).
4. Study during the times and in the environments that will help you focus best.

II. Cramming

A. If you have consistently followed the strategies from *Study Strategies Made Easy*, you should not have to cram. However, just in case …

B. What is cramming and how can you use it?

1. Cramming is really stuffing as much information into your head as possible just before you'll need to use it, such as the night before or morning of a test!
2. Unfortunately, cramming only works for very brief periods and for very small amounts of information, so it is not an efficient study strategy.
3. If you find that you absolutely must cram, don't try to read and remember every bit of information from the chapters and notes. Rely upon your highlighted information, vocabulary, and recall questions. This will be the most important information, and you can cram it into your memory in the shortest amount of time.

III. Final Words About Final Exams.

Successful test takers relax before exams. They go to sleep early, wake up early to eat a nutritious breakfast, listen to some soothing music, and pump themselves up with confident attitudes. Take advice from the successful test takers and be a successful test taker yourself!

References, Recommended Reading, and Resources

References

Achenbach, T.M., & Rescorla, L.A. (2001). *Manual for the ASEBA school age forms and profiles*. Burlington, VT: Research Center for Children, Youth and Families. University of Vermont.

Ambrosini, P.J. (2000). Historical development and present status of the schedule for affective disorders and schizophrenia for school-age children (K-SADS). *Journal of the American Academy of Child and Adolescent Psychiatry*, 39, 49-58.

American Academy of Pediatrics. (2001). Clinical practice guidelines: treatment of the school-aged child with attention-deficit/hyperactivity disorder. *Pediatrics*, 108 (4), 1033-1044

.
American Academy of Pediatrics. (2000). Clinical practice guidelines: diagnosis and evaluation of the child with attention-deficit/hyperactivity disorder. *Journal of the American Academy of Pediatrics*, 105 (5), 1158-1170.

American Psychiatric Association. (1994). *Diagnostic and statistical manual of mental disorders (4th ed.)*. Washington, DC: Author.

Angold, A., Erkanli, A., Egger, H.L., & Costello, E.J. (2000). Stimulant treatment for children: A community perspective. *Journal of the American Academy of Child and Adolescent Psychiatry*, 39, 975-984.

Barkley, R. A., & Murphy, K.R. (1998). *Attention-deficit hyperactivity disorder: A clinical workbook (2nd Ed.)* New York: Guilford Press.

Berg, B. (1990). *The social skills game*. Los Angeles, CA: Western Psychological Services.

Berg, E.A. (1948). A simple objective test for measuring flexibility in thinking. *Journal of General Psychology*, 39, 15-22.

Biederman, J., Faraone, S., Mick, E., Williamson, S., Wilens, T., Spencer, T., Weber, W., Jetton J., Draus, I., Pert, J., & Allen, B. (1999). Clinical correlates of ADHD in females: Findings from a large group of girls ascertained from pediatric and psychiatric referral sources. *Journal of the American Academy of Child and Adolescent Psychiatry*, 38, 966-975.

Brown, T.E. (2001). *Brown Attention-deficit Disorder Scales for Children and Adolescents manual*. San Antonio, TX: The Psychological Corporation.

Butcher, J.N., Williams, C.L., Graham, J.R. et al. (1992). *MMPI-A (Minnesota Multiphasic Personal-*

ity Inventory-Adolescent) manual for administration, scoring and interpretation. Minneapolis: University of Minnesota Press.

Campbell, S. B. (1990). *Behavior problems in preschool children*. New York: Guilford Press.

Casey, B.J., Castellanos, F.X., Giedd, J.N., Marsh, W.L., Hamburger, S.D., Schubert, A.B., Vauss, Y.C., Vaituzis, A.C., Dickstein, D.P., Sarfatti, S.E., & Castellanos, F.X. (1997). Toward a pathophysiology of attention-deficit/hyperactivity disorder. *Clinical Pediatrics,* 36, 381-393.

Chacko, A., Pelham, W.E., Gnagy, E.M., Greiner, A., Vallano, G., Bukstein, O.,& Rancurello, M. (2005). Stimulant medication effects ina summer treatment program among young children with attention-deficit/hyperactivity disorder. *Journal of the American Academy of Child and Adolescent Psychiatry*, 44, 249-257.

Conners, C.K. (1997). *Conners Rating Scales: Revised technical manual*. North Tonawanda, New York: Multi Health Systems, .

Cook, E. H., Jr., Stein, M.A., Krasowski, M.D., Cox, N.J., Olkon, D.M., Kieffer, J.E., & Leventhal, B. L. (1995). Association of attention-deficit disorder and the dopamine transporter gene. *American Journal of Human Genetics*, 56, 993-998.

Davila, R. R., Williams, M. L., & MacDonald, J. T. (1991, September 16). Clarification of policy to address the needs of children with attention deficit disorders within general and/or special education. Washington, DC: U.S. Department of Education, Office of Special Education and Rehabilitation.

Davis, L., Sirotowitz, S. & Parker, H. C. (1996). *Study strategies made easy: A practical plan for school success*. Plantation, FL: Specialty Press, Inc.,

DuPaul, G.J., McGoey, K.E., Eckert, T.L., & VanBrakle, J. (2001). Preschool children with attention-deficit/hyperactivity disorder: Impairments in behavioral, social, and school functioning. *Journal*

of the American Academy of Child and Adolescent Psychiatry, 40, 508-515.

DuPaul, G.J, Power, T.J., Anastopoulos, A.D., & Reid, R. (1998). *ADHD Rating Scale-IV: Checklists, norms, and clinical interpretations*. New York: Guilford Press.

Faraone, S.V., & Biederman, J. (1994). Is attention deficit hyperactivity disorder familial? *Harvard Review of Psychiatry*, 1, 271-287.

Faraone, S., Biederman, J., Keenan, K., & Tsuang, M. (1991). A family-genetic study of girls with DSM-III attention deficit disorder. *American Journal of Psychiatry,* 148 (1), 112-115.

Feingold, B. (1975). *Why your child is hyperactive?* New York: Random House.

Filipek, P.A., Semrud-Clikeman, M., Steingard, R.J., Renshaw, P.F., Kennedy, D.N., & Biederman, J. (1997). Volumetric MRI analysis comparing subjects having attention-deficit hyperactivity disorder with normal controls. *Neurology*, 48, 589-601.

Gadow, K.D., & Sprafkin, J. (1998). *Child Symptom Inventory 4: Screening manual*. Stony Brook, NY: Checkmate Plus.

Gadow, K.D., Sprafkin, J., & Nolan, E.E. (1996). ADHD School Observation Code (ADHD-SOC). Stony Brook, NY: Checkmate Plus.

Gioia, G.A., Isquith, P.K., Guy, S.C., & Kenworthy, L. (2000). *BRIEF: Behavior rating inventory of executive function. Professional manual*. Lutz, FL: Psychological Assessment Resources, Inc.

Goldstein, S. (2002). *Understanding, diagnosing, and treating ADHD through the lifespan*. Plantation, FL: Specialty Press, Inc.

Goldstein, A.P., & McGinnis, E. (1997). *Skillstreaming the elementary school child*. Champaign, IL: Research Press, Inc.

Goldstein, A.P. (2000). *The prepare curriculum: Teaching prosocial competencies.* Champaign, IL: Research Press, Inc.

Gordon, M., Anshel, K., Faraone, S., Barkley, R., Lewandowski, L., Hudziak, J., Biederman, J., & Cunningham, C. (2005). Symptoms versus impairment: The case for respecting DSM-IV's criterion D. *The ADHD Report,* 13(4), 1-9.

Gordon, M. (1989). *Attention training system.* DeWitt, NY: Gordon Systems.

Greene, Ross. (2001). *The explosive child: A new approach for understanding and parenting easily frustrated, chronically inflexible children.* New York: HarperCollins Publishers.

Gresham, F. M. & Elliot, S. N. (1990). Social skills rating scale. Circle Pines, MN: American Guidance Service.

Hinshaw, S., Carte, E., Sami, N., Treuting, J., & Zupan, B. (2002). Preadolescent girls with attention-deficit/hyperactivity disorder: II. Neuropsychological performance in relation to subtypes and individual classification. *Journal of Consulting & Clinical Psychology*, 70(5), 1099-1111.

Hodges, K., McKnew, D., Cytryn, L., Stern, L., & Kline, J. (1982). The Child Assessment Schedule (CAS) Diagnostic Interview: A report on reliability and validity. *Journal of the American Academy of Child and Adolescent Psychiatry*, 21, 468-473.

Hynd, G. W., Semrud-Clikeman, M., Lorys. A.R., Novey, E.S., Elopulos, D., & Lytinen, H. (1991). Corpus callosum morphology in attention deficit-hyperactivity disorder: Morphometric analysis of MRI. *Journal of Learning Disabilities,* 24, 141-146.

Ingersoll, B., & Goldstein, S. (1993). *Attention deficit disorder and learning disabilities: Realities, myths, and controversial treatments.* New York: Doubleday Publishing Group.

Kaufman, A.S. & Kaufman, N.L. (2004). *KABC-II:*

Kaufman assessment battery for children, (2nd Ed.) Circle Pines, MN: American Guidance Service,

Korkman, M., Kirk, U., & Kemp, S. (1997). *NEPSY.* San Antonio, TX: Psychological Corporation,

Kratochvil, C.J., Heiligenstein, J.H., Dittmann, R., et al. (2002). Atomoxetine and methylphenidate treatment in children with ADHD. A prospective, randomized, open-label trial. *Journal of the American Academy of Child and Adolescent Psychiatry*, 41, 776-84.

Lachar, D., & Gruber, C.P. (2001). Personality inventory for children (2nd Ed.) Los Angeles, CA: Western Psychological Services..

LaHoste, G.J., Swanson, J.M., Wigal, S.B., Glabe, C., Wigal, T., King, N., & Kennedy, J.L. (1996). Dopamine D4 receptor gene polymorphism is associated with attention deficit hyperactivity disorder. *Molecular Psychiatry*, 1, 121-124.

Lavigne J.V., Arend R., et al. (1998). Psychiatric disorders with onset in the preschool years: Stability of diagnosis. *Journal of the American Academy of Child and Adolescent Psychiatry,* 37,1246–1254

Levinson, H. N. (2000). *The discovery of cerebellar-vestibular syndromes and therapies: A solution to the riddle—dyslexia.* New York: Stonebridge Publishing.

Levy, F., Hay, D.A., McStephen, M.D., Wood, C. & Waldman, I. (1997). Attention-deficit hyperactivity disorder: a category or a continuum? Genetic analysis of a large-scale twin study. *Journal of the American Academy of Child and Adolescent Psychiatry*, 36, 737-744.

Levy, R., O'Hanlon, B., & Goode, T.N. (2001). *Try and make me! Simple strategies that turn off the tantrums and create cooperation.* Emmaus, PA: Rodale.

McMahon, R., & Forehand, R. (2003). *Helping the noncompliant child (2nd edition).* New York: Guilford Press.

Millon, T., Millon, C., & Davis, R. (1993). *The Millon*

Adolescent Clinical Inventory manual. NY: Pearson.

Montague, M. & Lund, K. (1995). *Job related social skills: A curriculum for students with special needs.* Exceptional Innovations.

MTA Cooperative Group. (1999). A fourteen month randomized clinical trial of treatment strategies for attention-deficit/hyperactivity disorder. *Archives of General Psychiatry*, 56, 1073-1086.

Murphy, K., & Barkley, R. A. (1996). Prevalence of DSM-IV symptoms of ADHD in adult licensed drivers: Implications for clinical diagnosis. *Journal of Attention Disorders*, 1, 147-161.

Nadeau, K., Littman, E., & Quinn, P. (2000). *Understanding girls with AD/HD.* Silver Spring, MD: Advantage Books.

Nagieri, J.A., & Das, J. P. (1997). *Cognitive Assessment System.* Itasca, IL: Riverside Publishing.

Needleman, H.L. (1998). Childhood lead poisoning: the promise and abandonment of primary prevention. *American Journal of Public Health*, 88, 1871-1877.

O'Leary, K.D., & Becker, W.C. (1967). Behavior modification of an adjustment class: A token reinforcement program. *Exceptional Children*, 33, 637-642.

Olbrich, S. (2002).Children's mental health: Currrent challenges and a future direction. The Center for Health and Health Care in Schools.Accessed at:www.healthinschools.org/cfk/annual02m.asp

Parker, H.C. (1992). *The ADAPT Program.* Plantation, FL: Specialty Press.

Pelham, W. E. (2002). Psychosocial Interventions for ADHD. In P.S. Jensen & J.R. Cooper (Ed.), *Attention deficit hyperactivity disorder: State of the science • best practices* (pp 12-1-12-24) New Jersey: Civic Research Institute, Inc.

Pelham, W.E., Greiner, A.R., & Gnagy, E.M. (1997). *Children's summer treatment program manual.* Buf-

falo, NY: Comprehensive Treatment for Attention Deficit Disorder.

Rabiner, D. (2001). New Support for the Use of QEEG Scanning in Diagnosing ADHD. *Attention Research Update*, Vol. 42.

Rabiner, D. (1999). *ADHD monitoring system: a systematic guide to monitoring school progress for children with ADHD.*Plantation, FL: Specialty Press.

Rapaport, J.L. (1997). Implications of right frontostriatal circuitry in response inhibition and attention deficit/hyperactivity disorder. *Journal of the American Academy of Child and Adolescent Psychiatry*, 36, 374-383.

Reich, W. (2000). Diagnostic interview for children and adolescents (DICA). *Journal of the American Academy of Child and Adolescent Psychiatry*, 39, 59-66.

Reynolds, C.R., & Kamphaus, R.M. (2002). *Manual for the Behavior Assessment System for Children (2nd Ed.).*Circle Pines, MN: American Guidance Service.

Rief, S. F. (2005). *How to reach and teach children with ADD/ADHD (2nd Edition).* New York: Jossey Bass.

Robin, A. L., & Foster, S.L. (2002). *Negotiating parent-adolescent conflict: A behavioral-family systems approach.* Guilford Press, NY.

Roid, G.H., & Miller, L. (1997). Leiter international performance scale-revised. Psychological Assessment Resources. Lutz, FL.

Rosvold, H.E., Mirsky,A.F., Sarason, L., Bransome, E.D., & Beck, L.H. (1956). A continuous performance test of brain damage. *Journal of Consulting Psychology*, 20, 3343-350.

Sanford, J.A. & Turner, A. (1992). *Integrated visual & auditory continuous performance test.* Richmond, VA: Braintrain

Searight, H. R., Burke, J. M., & Rottnek, F. (2000).

Adult ADHD: Evaluation and treatment in family medicine. *American Family Physician*, November.

Shallice, T. (1982). Specific impairments of planning. *Philosophical Transactions of the Royal Society of London*, B, 298, 199-209.

Sheridan, S.M (1995). *The tough kid social skills book*. Longmont, CO: Sopris West.

Sherrill, J.T. & Kovacs, M. (2000). Interview scheule for children and adolescents (ISCA). *Journal of the American Academy of Child and Adolescent Psychiatry*, 39, 67-75.

Simpson, G.A., Bloom, B., Cohen, R.A., Blumberg, S., & Bourdon, K.H. (2005). U.S. Children with Emotional and Behavioral Difficulties: Data from the 2001, 2002, and 2003 National Health Interview Surveys. Advance data from vital and health statistics; No. 360. Hyattsville, MD: National Center for Health Statistics.

Sirotowitz, S., Davis, L., & Parker, H.C. (2004). *Study strategies for early school success*. Plantation, FL: Specialty Press, Inc.

Sparrow, S.S., Balla, D.B., & Cicchetti, D.V. (1984). *The Vineland adaptive behavior scales*. Circle Pines, MN: American Guidance Service.

Still, G. (1902). Some abnormal psychical conditions in children. *Lancet*. 1: 1008-12, 1077-82, 1163-68.
Stroop, J.R. (1935). Studies of interference in serioal verbal reactions. *Journal of Experimental Psychology,* 18, 643-662.

Teeter, P.A. (1998). *Interventions for ADHD: Treatment in developmental context*. New York: Guilford Press.

Thorndike, R. I., Hagen, E. P., & Sattler, J.M. (1986). *Standford-Binet Intelligence Scale*, 4th ed. Chicago, IL: Riverside Publishing.

Tucker, J.A. (1985). Curriculum-based assessment: an introduction. *Exceptional Children*, 52, 199-204.

Ullman, R.K., Sleator, E.K., & Sprague, R.L. (1991). *ACTeRS manual*. Champaign, IL: MetriTech, Inc.

US DHHS. (1999). *Mental Health: A Report of the Surgeon General, Executive Summary*. Rockville, MD: U.S. Department of Health and Human Services, Substance Abuse and Mental Health Services Administration, Center for Mental Health Services, NIH, NIMH.

Visser, S.N., & Lesesne, C.A. (2005). Mental health in the United States: prevalence of diagnosis and medication treatment for Attention-Deficit/Hyperactivity Disorder — United States, 2003. *MMWR Weekly,* Sept. 2, 2005.

Walker, H.N, & McConnell, S.R. (1995) Walker-McConnell scale of social competence and school adjustment. Florence, KY: Thompson Learning.

Walker, H.,N., Todis, B., Holmes, D., & Horton, G. (1987). *The Walker social skills curriculum: ACCESS*. Austin, TX: Pro-Ed.

Wechsler, D. (2003). *WISC-IV: Wechsler Intelligence Scale for Children-Fourth Edition. Administration and scoring manual*. San Antonio, TX: The Psychological Corporation.

Wechsler, D. (2002). *WPPSI-III technical and interpretive manual*. San Antonio, TX: The Psychological Corporation.

Weiss, G., & Hechtman, L. T. (1993). *Hyperactive children grown up (2nd ed.)*. New York: Guilford Press.

Wilens, T. (2004). *Straight talk about psychiatric medications for kids*. New York: Guilford Press.

Yeates, K.O., Armstrong, K, Janusz, J, Taylor, H.G., Wade, S, Stancin, T., & Drotar, D. (2005). Long-term attention problems in children with traumatic brain Injury. *Journal of the American Academy of Child and Adolescent Psychiatry*, 44, 574-583.

Recommended Reading

Adamec, C. A. (2000). *Moms with ADHD: A self-help manual.* Maryland: Taylor Trade Publishing.

Barkley, R.A. (2005). *Attention-Deficit Hyperactivity Disorder: A handbook for diagnosis and treatment.* (3rd ed.) New York: Guilford Press

Barkley, R. A. (2005). *ADHD and the nature of self-control.* New York: Guilford Press.

Barkley, R. A. (2000) *Taking charge of ADHD: The complete authoritative guide for parents.* New York: Guilford Press.

Barkley, R.A., & Murphy, K. (2005). *Attention-Deficit Hyperactivity Disorder: A clinical workbook (3rd ed.).* New York: Guilford Press.

Bateman, B. D. & Golly, A. (2003). *Why Johnny doesn't behave: Twenty tips and measurable BIPs.* Verona, WI: IEP Resources.

Brown, T. E. (2005). *Attention deficit disorder: The unfocused mind in children and adults.* New Haven, CT: Yale University Press.

Crone, D. A., Horner, R.H., & Hawken, L.S. (2003). *Responding to problem behavior in schools.* New York: Guilford Press.

Davis, L., Sirotowitz, S., & Parker, H. (1996). *Study strategies made easy: A practical plan for school success.* Plantation, FL: Specialty Press, Inc.

Dendy, C.A. (2000). *Teaching teens with ADD and ADHD: A quick reference guide for teachers and parents.* Maryland: WoodbineHouse.

Dendy, C.A. (1995). *Teenagers with ADD: A parents' guide.* Maryland: Woodbine House.

Dornbush, M.P., & Pruitt, S.K. (1997). *Teaching the tiger.* Duarte, CA: Hope Press, Inc.

Dowd, T., & Tierney, J. (2005). *Teaching Social Skills to youth.* Boys, Town, NE: Boys Town Press.

DuPaul, G. J., & Stoner, G. (1994). *ADHD in the schools.* New York: Guilford Press.

Faraone, S.V. (2003). *Straight talk about your child's mental health.* New York: Guilford Press.

Flick, G. L. (1998). *ADD/ADHD Behavior-change resource kit*: West Nyack, NY: The Center for Applied Research in Education.

Goldstein, A.P., & McGinnis, E.(1997). *Skillstreaming the elementary school child.* Champaign, IL: Research Press, Inc.

Goldstein, S., & Goldstein, M. (1998). *Managing attention deficit hyperactivity disorder in children: a guide for practitioners (2nd ed.).* New York, NY: John Wiley.

Goldstein, S., & Mathers, N. (1998). *Overcoming underachievement: An action guide to helping your child succeed in school.* New York: John Wiley & Sons.

Gordon, M., & Keiser, S. (2000). *Accommodations in higher education under the Americans with Disabilities Act (ADA).* New York: Guilford Press.

Hallowell, E., & Ratey, J. (2005). *Delivered from distraction.* New York: Random House.

Hallowell, E., & Ratey, J. (1994). *Driven to distraction.* New York: Pantheon.

Ingersoll, B.D., & Goldstein, S. (2001). *Lonely, sad and angry: How to help your unhappy child.* Plantation, FL: Specialty Press, Inc.

Ingersoll, B., & Goldstein, M. (1993). *Attention deficit disorder and learning disabilities: Realities, myths, and controversial treatments.* New York: Doubleday.

Jensen, P. S. (2004). *Making the system work for your child with ADHD.* New York: Guilford Press.

Jensen, P.S., & Cooper, J.R. (2002). Attention Deficit Hyperactivity Disorder: State of science •best practice. New Jersey: Civic Research Institute.

John, K., Gammon, G.D., Prusoff, B.A., & Warner, V. (1987). The Social Adjustment Inventory for Children and Adolescents (SAICA): Testing of a new semistructured interview. *Journal of the American Academy of Child and Adolescent Psychiatry,* 26, 898-911.

Jones, C. B. (2003) *Practical suggestions for AD/HD.* East Moline, IL: Linguisystems, Inc.

Keller, M. H. (2001). *In control: A skill-building program for teaching yourng adolescents to manage anger.* Champaign, IL: Research Press, Inc.

Kilcarr, P. J., & Quinn, P. O. (1997). *Voices from fatherhood: Fathers, sons and ADHD.* Pennsylvania: Bruner/Mazel.

Koplewicz, H. S. (1996). *It's nobody's fault: New hope and help for difficult children and their parents.* New York: Random House.

Lavoie. R. (2005). *It's so much work to be your friend.* New York: Simon & Schuster.

Levy, R., O'Hanlon, B., & Goode, T.N. (2001). *Try and make me! Simple strategies that turn off the tantrums and create cooperation.* Emmaus, PA: Rodale.

Levy, R. and Smith, K. (2004). *I've had it with you.* Dallas, TX: Effective Behavior Solutions.

Matlen, T. (2005). *Survival tips for women with ADHD.* Plantation, FL: Specialty Press, Inc.

Mather, N., & Goldstein, S. (2001). *Learning disabilities and challenging behaviors: A guide to intervention and classroom management.* Baltimore, MD: Brookes Publishing Co.

McMahon, R., & Forehand, R. (2003). *Helping the noncompliant child (2nd edition).* New York: Guilford Press.

Nadeau, K. G., & Quinn, P. (2002). *Understanding women with AD/HD.* Silver Spring, MD: Advantage Books.

Nadeau, K. G., & Biggs, S. H. (1995). *School strategies for ADD teens.* Silver Spring, MD: Advantage Books.

Naglieri, J., & Pickering, E.G. (2003). *Helping children learn: Intervention handouts for use in school and at home.* Baltimore, MD: Paul H. Brookes Publishing.

Novotni, M. (1999). *What does everybody else know that I don't?* Plantation, FL: Specialty Press, Inc.

Papolos, D. F., & Papolos, J. (1999). *The bipolar child.* New York: Broadway Books.

Parker, H.C. (2005). *The ADHD workbook for parents.* Plantation, FL: Specialty Press, Inc.

Parker, H. C. (2002). *Problem solver guide for students with ADHD: Ready-to-use interventions for elementary and secondary students.* (2nd ed.). Plantation, FL: Specialty Press, Inc.

Parker, H. C. (1992). *Put yourself in their shoes. Understanding teenagers with attention deficit hyperactivity disorder.* Plantation, FL: Specialty Press, Inc.

Parker, H.C. (1992). *ADAPT: attention deficit accommodation plan for teaching.* Plantation, FL: Specialty Press, Inc.

Parker, H. C. (1990). *Listen, look, and think.* Plantation, FL: Specialty Press, Inc.

Pfiffner, L. J. (1996). *All about ADHD: The complete practical guide for classroom teachers.* New York: Scholastic, Inc.

Phelan, T. (2003). *1-2-3 magic: Effecitive discipline for children 2-12.* Illinois:Parentmagic, Inc.

Phelan, T., & Schonour, J.R., (2004) *1-2-3 magic. Effective classroom discipline pre-K through grade eight.* Illinois: Parentmagic, Inc.

Pliszka, S.R., Carlson, C.L., & Swnason, J.M. (2001). *ADHD with comorbid disorders: Clinical assessment and management.* New York: Guilford Press.

Rief, S. F. (2005). *How to reach and teach children with ADD/ADHD (2nd Edition).* New York: Jossey Bass.

Rief, S. (1998). *The ADD/ADHD checklist.* Paramus, NJ: Prentice Hall.

Rhode, G., Jenson, W.R., & Reavis, H.K. (1992). The tough kid book: Practical classroom management strategies. Longmont, CO: Sopris West.

Shapiro, E. S., & Kratochwill, T. R. (2000). *Conducting school-based assessments of child and adolescent behavior.* New York: Guilford Press.

Sheridan, S.M (1995). *The tough kid social skills book.* Longmont, CO: Sopris West.

Sirotowitz, S., Davis, L. & Parker, H. (2004). *Study strategies for early school success: Seven steps to improve your learning.* Plantation, FL: Specialty Press, Inc.

Solden, S. (2002). *Journeys through ADDulthood.* New York: Walker & Company.

Teeter, P.A. (1998). *Interventions for ADHD: Treatment in developmental context.* New York: Guilford Press.

Zentall, S. S., & Goldstein, S. (1999). *Seven steps to homework success: A family guide for solving common homework problems.* Plantation, FL: Specialty Press, Inc.

Thompson, J.G. (1998). *Discipline survival kit for the secondary teacher.* New York: Jossey Bass.

Wilens, T. E. (2004). *Straight talk about psychiatric medications for kids.* New York: Guilford Press.

Video and Audio Programs

Barkley, R. A. (1992). *ADHD—What do we know?*

New York: The Guilford Press.

Barkley, R. A. (1992). *ADHD—What can we do?* New York: The Guilford Press.

Brooks, R. (1997). *Look what you've done! Learning disabilities and self-esteem: stories of hope and resilience.* Washington, D.C.: WETA

Lavoie, R. (1990). *How difficult can this be? The F.A.T. city workshop.* Washington, DC: WETA.

Levy, R. ,& Smith, K. (2004). *I've had it with you.* Dallas, Tx: Effective Behavior Solutions.

Robin, A. L., & Weiss, S. K. (1997). *Managing oppositional youth. Effective, practical strategies for managing the behavior of hard to manage kids and teens!* Plantation, FL: Specialty Press, Inc.

Online Resources

Attention Deficit Disorder Association
www.add.org
Articles and resources about ADHD in Adults

ADD Consults
www.addconsults.com
Books, articles, and information about ADHD

ADD WareHouse
www.addwarehouse.com
Books, videos, and assessment products on ADHD and related disorders.

ADDitude Magazine
www.additudemag.com
Articles about ADHD

Children and Adults with Attention-Deficit/ Hyperactivity Disorder
www.chadd.org
Articles and resources about ADHD across the lifespan

Sam Goldstein, Ph.D.
www.samgoldstein.com

Articles and resources about childhood and adult conditions

Learning Disabilities Association of America
www.ldanatl.org
Articles and resources about learning disabilities across the lifespan

MyADHD.com
www.myadhd.com
Articles and resources about ADHD including assessment tools, tracking tools, and treatment tools.

Resources for Books, Videos, Training, and Assessment Products

A.D.D. WareHouse
300 N. W. 70th Ave., Suite 102
Plantation, Florida 33317
(800) 233-9273 • (954) 792-8100
www.addwarehouse.com

American Guidance Service
4201 Woodland Road
Circle Pines, MN 55014
(800) 328-2560
www.agsnet.com

Boys Town Press
14100 Crawford Street
Boys Town, NE 68010
(800) 282-6657
www.ffbh.boystown.org

Educational Resource Specialists
P.O. Box 19207
San Diego, CA 92159
(800) 682-3528

Franklin Electronic Publishers Inc.
One Franklin Plaza
Burlington, NJ 08016
(800) 525-9673

Free Spirit Publishing
400 First Ave. North, Suite 616
Minneapolis, MN 55401

(800) 735-7323
www.freespirit.com

Gordon Systems, Inc.
P.O. Box 746
DeWitt, N.Y. 13214-746
(315) 446-4849

Guilford Publications
72 Spring St.
New York, New York, 10012
(800) 365-7006
www.guilford.com

Hawthorne Educational Services
800 Gray Oak Drive
Columbia, MO 65201
(800) 542-1673

MHS
908 Niagara Falls Blvd.
North Tonawanda, NY 14120
(800) 456-3003
www.mhs.com

Neurology, Learning and Behavior Center
230 500 East, Suite 100
Salt Lake City, UT 84102
(801) 532-1484

PCI Educational Publishing
12029 Warfield
San Antonio, TX 78216
(800) 594-4263
www.pcicatalog.com

Prentice Hall/Center for Applied Research in Education
200 Old Tappan Road
Old Tappan, NJ 07675
(800) 922-0579

Slosson Educational Publications
P.O. Box 280
East Aurora, NY 14052
(888) 756-7766
www.slosson.com

Sopris West
P.O. Box 1809
Longmont, CO 80502-1809
(800) 547-6747
www.sopriswest.com

Western Psychological Services
Creative Therapy Store
12031 Wilshire Blvd.
Los Angeles, CA 90025
(800) 648-8857

Support Groups and Associations

American Occupational Therapy Association
4720 Montgomery Lane
Bethesda, MD 20814
(301) 652-2682
www.aota.org

American Speech-Language-Hearing Association
10801 Rockville Pike
Rockville, MD 20852
(800) 638-8255
www.asha.org

Association on Higher Education and Disability
(AHEAD)
P.O. Box 540666
Waltham, MA 02454
(781) 788-0003

Attention Deficit Disorders Association (ADDA)
P.O. Box 543
Pottstown, PA 19464
Phone: 484-945-2101
www.adda.org

Children and Adults with Attention Deficit Hyperactivity Disorder (CHADD)
8181 Professional Drive, Suite 202
Lanham, MD 20706
(800) 233-4050
www.chadd.org

Council for Exceptional Children
1110 North Glebe Road, Suite 300,
Arlington, VA 22201
(703) 620-3660
www.cec.sped.org

Learning Disabilities Association of America
(LDAA)
4156 Library Road
Pittsburgh, PA 15234
(412) 341-1515
www.ldanatl.org

National Initiative for Children's Healthcare Quality
(NICHQ)
20 University Road, 7th Floor
Cambridge, MA 02138 USA
866.787.0832
www.nichq.org

Index